William Wilkins

Australasia

A descriptive and pictorial Account of the Australian and New Zealand Colonies,

Tasmania, and the adjacent Lands

William Wilkins

Australasia

A descriptive and pictorial Account of the Australian and New Zealand Colonies, Tasmania, and the adjacent Lands

ISBN/EAN: 9783337153977

Printed in Europe, USA, Canada, Australia, Japan

Cover: Foto ©ninafisch / pixelio.de

More available books at **www.hansebooks.com**

AUSTRALASIA:

A

DESCRIPTIVE AND PICTORIAL ACCOUNT

OF THE

AUSTRALIAN AND NEW ZEALAND COLONIES,
TASMANIA, AND THE ADJACENT LANDS.

By W. WILKINS,

Late Under-Secretary for Public Instruction in New South Wales;
author of "Geography of New South Wales."

LONDON:
BLACKIE & SON, 49 & 50 OLD BAILEY, E.C.
GLASGOW, EDINBURGH, AND DUBLIN.
1888.

PREFACE.

The future of Australia is, in some measure, bound up with that of the countries which lie around its northern and eastern shores, not merely from the fact of their proximity, but also from the commercial intercourse which must of necessity take place, and from the political relations which, sooner or later, must be established between them. It is therefore a matter of great importance to the youth of Australia that they should not only be well acquainted with their own land, but that they should, in addition, possess the fullest information obtainable respecting those countries which are sufficiently near to become, in time, either useful allies or dangerous enemies. To the young people of the mother country, such information may be not less useful, as conveying to them correct views regarding a portion of her colonial empire which even yet is but imperfectly known.

Such have been the chief considerations of the writer in compiling these pages. It is not intended that the volume should be viewed as an ordinary text-book of the geography of Australasia. In fact, so much knowledge of the elements of Australasian geography is pre-supposed, as could be acquired by the attentive study of the maps of the different countries described. It is rather designed for use as a reading-book for advanced classes, and as such will require to be supplemented by explanations from the teacher. While technical terms have been introduced but sparely, they have not been altogether dispensed with; and these, as well as other expressions may not be understood in the absence of the comments usually given by good teachers during reading lessons.

It is hoped that an attentive perusal of this volume may give to the youth of the Australasian colonies just notions of the country of their birth and of its future destiny. When, at no remote period, the Pacific becomes to the modern what the Mediterranean was to the ancient world, the highway of communication between the great empires situated on its shores, the federated Australasian States may take no inconsiderable part in spreading peace and good-will among the nations, while in their firmly cemented union they will be too powerful to dread the hostility of the mightiest foe.

NOVEMBER, 1887.

CONTENTS.

CHAPTER I.

DEFINITION AND GENERAL DESCRIPTION OF AUSTRALASIA, . . 13

1. Australasia; meaning of the term. 2. General definition. 3. Mode of ascertaining the component parts of Australasia. 4. Exclusion of certain islands. 5. Extent of Australasia. 6. An imaginary voyage in Australasian seas. 7. The Indian Ocean. 8. Animal life therein. 9. The Great Southern Ocean and its inhabitants. 10. The Pacific Ocean, its islands and its denizens. 11. The Coral Sea; coral polypes; Barrier Reef. 12. The seas and islands around Papua or New Guinea. 13. Points of resemblance in the countries composing Australasia. 14. Summary.

CHAPTER II.

PHYSICAL FEATURES AND CLIMATE OF AUSTRALIA, ... 22

1. Name. 2. Position. 3. Australia, a continent. 4. The coast-line. 5. Surface; Mountains. 6. Table-lands. 7. Plains. 8. Remainder of Australia; Deserts. 9. Drainage; Rivers. 10. Lakes. 11. Climate.

CHAPTER III.

NATURAL PRODUCTIONS AND ABORIGINAL INHABITANTS OF AUSTRALIA, ... 32

1. Mineral Productions. 2. Vegetable. 3. Brushes. 4. Woodlands. 5. Scrubs. 6. Special Plants. 7. Animal life; its general character. 8. Mammalia. 9. Marsupials. 10. Echidna and Platypus. 11. Fossil Marsupials. 12. Birds. 13. Reptiles. 14. Fishes. 15. Other Marine Animals. 16. Insects. 17. The Aborigines. 18. General Remarks.

CHAPTER IV.

THE COLONY OF NEW SOUTH WALES, ... 57

1. Boundaries and extent. 2. Coast-line and Harbours. 3. Surface. 4. Mountains. 5. Table-lands. 6. Plains. 7. Drainage. 8. Rivers of eastern slope. 9. Rivers of western slope. 10. Lakes. 11. Climate. 12. Soil. 13. Internal communication; Roads. 14. Railways and Telegraphs. 15. Navigable Rivers. 16. Population. 17. Industrial Occupations; Agriculture and Pasturage. 18. Mining. 19. Manufactures. 20. Commerce. 21. Government. 22. Religion and Education. 23. Territorial Divisions. 24. Growth of Towns. 25. Sydney. 26. Other Towns.

CHAPTER V.

THE COLONY OF QUEENSLAND, ... 100

1. Boundaries and extent: coast-line. 2. Surface. 3. Drainage; Rivers and Lakes. 4. Climate. 5. Soil. 6. Population. 7. Internal Communication. 8. Industrial Occupations—Mining. 9. Agriculture, Pasturage, and other industries: Commerce. 10. Government. 11. Religion. 12. Education. 13. Divisions—Districts. 14. Towns. 15. Brisbane. 16. Other towns.

CHAPTER VI.

THE COLONY OF VICTORIA, ... 118

1. Boundaries and extent. 2. Coast-line and Harbours. 3. Surface. 4. Mountains. 5. Table-lands. 6. Plains. 7. Drainage. 8. Rivers of northern slope. 9. Rivers of southern slope. 10. Lakes. 11. Climate. 12. Soil. 13. Internal communication. 14. Navigable Rivers. 15. Roads, Railways and Telegraphs. 16. Population. 17. Industrial Occupations; Pasturage, Agriculture, and Mining. 18. Manufactures. 19. Commerce. 20. Government. 21. Religion and Education. 22. Territorial Divisions. 23. Melbourne. 24. Other Towns.

CHAPTER VII.

THE COLONY OF TASMANIA, ... 146

1. Extent and Coast-line. 2. Surface. 3. Drainage—Rivers. 4. Climate. 5. Vegetable and Animal Life. 6. Soil. 7. Population. 8. Roads and Railways. 9. Occupations. 10. Government. 11. Divisions. 12. Towns.

CHAPTER VIII.

THE COLONY OF SOUTH AUSTRALIA, ... 157

1. Boundaries and extent. 2. Coast-line and Harbours. 3. Surface. 4. Drainage. 5. Rivers. 6. Lakes. 7. Climate. 8. Soil. 9. Internal Communication. 10. Population. 11. Industrial Occupations—Pasturage, Agriculture, and Mining. 12. Manufactures and Commerce. 13. Government. 14. Religion and Education. 15. Territorial Divisions. 16. Adelaide. 17. Other Towns.

CHAPTER IX.

THE COLONY OF WEST AUSTRALIA, ... 169

1. Extent and Coast-line. 2. Surface. 3. Drainage. 4. Climate. 5. Soil. 6. Population. 7. Internal Communication. 8. Industrial Occupations. 9. Government. 10. Divisions. 11. Towns.

CHAPTER X.

NEW ZEALAND.—Physical Features and Natural Productions, ... 178

    1. Position. 2. Name and Extent. 3. Form and Outline. 4. Indentations of North Island. 5. Indentations of South Island. 6. Surface. *North Island:* 7. Mountains. 8. Drainage. 9. The Hot Lakes. *South Island:* 10. Mountains. 11. Plains. 12. Drainage. 13. Lakes. 14. Climate of New Zealand. 15. Mineral Productions. 16. Vegetable Productions. 17. Indigenous Animals. 18. The Maoris. 19. Stewart Island. 20. The Chatham Islands. 21. The Auckland Islands. 22. Smaller islands and groups.

CHAPTER XI.

NEW ZEALAND as a Colony, ... 198

    1. Discovery and Settlement. 2. Industrial Occupations. 3. Internal Communication. 4. Constitution and Government. 5. Religion. 6. Education. 7. Political Divisions. 8. *Auckland District:* General Description. 9. Auckland. 10. Other Towns. 11. *Hawke's Bay District:* General Description. 12. Towns. 13. *Taranaki District:* General Description. 14. Towns. 15. *Wellington District:* General Description. 16. Towns. 17. *Nelson District:* General Description. 18. Towns. 19. *Marlborough District:* General Description. 20. Towns. 21. *Canterbury District:* General Description. 22. Towns. 23. *Westland District:* General Description. 24. Towns. 25. *Otago District:* General Description. 26. Towns. 27. *Southland District:* General Description. 28. Towns.

CHAPTER XII.

The Colony of FIJI, ... 224

    1. Position. 2. Extent and Coast-line. 3. Surface and Drainage. 4. Climate. 5. Natural Productions. 6. Population. 7. Internal Communication. 8. Industrial Occupations. 9. Government. 10. Towns.

CHAPTER XIII.

NEW CALEDONIA and its Dependencies, ... 232

    1. Position and Extent. 2. Surface. 3. Productions. 4. Climate. 5. Population. 6. Internal Communication. 7. Industrial Occupations. 8. Government. 9. Noumea. 10. The Loyalty Islands. 11. The New Hebrides.

CHAPTER XIV.

PAPUA or NEW GUINEA, ... 238

    1. Name. 2. Position and Extent. 3. Coast-line. 4. Surface. 5. Drainage. 6. Climate. 7. Natural Productions. 8. Population. 9. Industrial Occupations. 10. Territorial Divisions.

CHAPTER XV.

THE SOLOMON ISLANDS, NEW BRITAIN, AND NEW IRELAND, ... 247

1. Position and Extent. 2. Surface. 3. Climate. 4. Natural Productions. 5. Population. 6. Settlement.

CHAPTER XVI.

THE PAPUAN ISLANDS, ... 250

1. Waigiou. 2. Booro. 3. Ceram. 4. Kei and Aroo Islands. 5. Timor Laut. 6. Timor. 7. Flores. 8. Sandalwood Island.

ILLUSTRATIONS.

	Page
Tree Fern Scene in a Forest— Victoria, ... *Frontispiece*,	34
Albatross,	16
Frigate-bird,	18
Emu,	20
Falls in Dividing Range,	26
A Woodland,	35
A Scrub,	37
Wombat,	39
Kangaroo,	41
Duck-bill,	42
Lyre-bird,	44
Australian Aboriginals,	51
Map of New South Wales,	58
Coast Scenery,	59
A River View,	65
Road over Blue Mountains—Victoria Pass,	72
A Railway Cutting,	73
Gold-miners' Bark-hut,	76
Town-hall, Sydney,	82
Zigzag Railway over Blue Mountains,	86
A Coast River,	94
Map of Queensland,	101
Coast Scenery, Townsville,	102
Aboriginal of Northern Queensland,	105
Near Gladstone,	115
Map of Victoria,	119
Coast Scenery, Cape Schanck,	120
A River View,	123
Scene on the Murray River,	126
In a Gipps Land Bush,	133
Houses of Parliament, Melbourne,	135
Taradale—a Mining Township,	139
The Huon River,	148

	Page
Mount Wellington,	154
Map of South Australia,	158
A Mountain Pass,	159
Map of Western Australia,	170
Caswell Sound,	181
Mount Cook,	186
Moko Lake,	188
The Pink Terraces,	204
The White Terraces,	205
A Lake View,	219
In Milford Sound,	222
A Coast View,	225
Natives of Tonga and Fiji,	228
Native Hut,	234
Natives of Papua,	243
Natives of New Britain,	248

AUSTRALASIA.

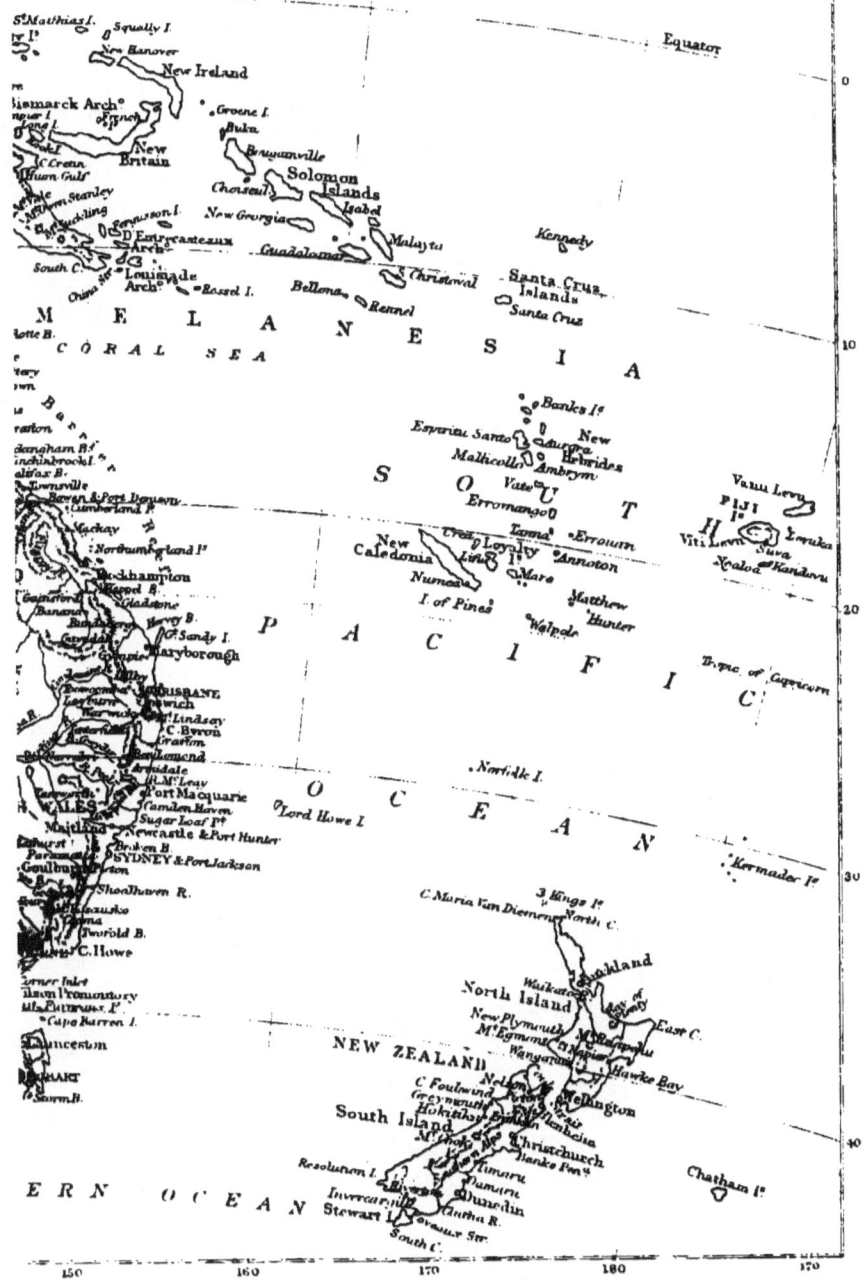

AUSTRALASIA.

CHAPTER I.

DEFINITION AND GENERAL DESCRIPTION OF AUSTRALASIA.

1. Australasia; meaning of the term. 2. General definition. 3. Mode of ascertaining the component parts of Australasia. 4. Exclusion of certain islands. 5. Extent of Australasia. 6. An imaginary voyage in Australasian seas. 7. The Indian Ocean. 8. Animal life therein. 9. The Great Southern Ocean and its inhabitants. 10. The Pacific Ocean, its islands and its denizens. 11. The Coral Sea; coral polypes; Barrier Reef. 12. The seas and islands around Papua or New Guinea. 13. Points of resemblance in the countries composing Australasia. 14. Summary.

1. Taken in a literal sense, the term **Australasia** signifies Southern Asia, but in this sense it is not used, being applied, somewhat vaguely, to the large islands and groups of smaller islands lying to the south and south-east of Asia. No definite understanding, however, has yet been arrived at as to how many of these islands shall be included under the designation of Australasia.

2. If all the islands so situated are not to be considered as belonging to Australasia, it becomes necessary to determine which shall be excluded; and, to this end, some principle of selection must be adopted. From its size and position, the great island of **Australia** is now generally regarded as forming the central mass of Australasia, and its principal component part. If to it are added such of the neighbouring islands as have some natural relation to it, either from near proximity or from similarity in natural productions or inhabitants, the two portions together may be taken as forming Australasia.

3. In order to settle with some degree of exactness what islands shall be so joined to Australia some central point must be fixed upon, from which to reckon how far the term Australasia shall be held to extend. **Cape Byron**, the most easterly point of Australia, is the most suitable for this purpose, being about equally distant from its northern extremity on the one

hand, and from the southern point of Tasmania on the other. Measuring also from east to west, Cape Byron occupies a middle position between the most westerly point of Australia and the Fiji Islands in the Pacific Ocean on the east. Let it now be supposed that a line is drawn from Cape Byron to **Steep Point**, in the extreme west of Australia, and that with this line for a radius, a circle is described with the cape as the centre. Such a circle, speaking generally, will comprehend all the islands that are in any way related to, or connected with Australia, and that, with the latter, are to be included in Australasia.

4. Tracing the circle carefully on the map, a few islands will be found within it, though near the edge, which have no relation to Australia, and which must therefore be excluded from our definition of Australasia. For example, a circle drawn as we have supposed would extend a few degrees to the northward of the equator, and consequently would include some islands lying in north latitude. But all the countries we shall treat of as belonging to Australasia are situated south of the equator. Again, there are on the north-west of New Guinea some islands which in all essential respects resemble the Malay Archipelago rather than Australia, and which on that account cannot be regarded as portions of Australasia.

5. Keeping out of view the portion of the circle which extends beyond the equator, the space within it occupies more than fifty degrees of latitude and nearly eighty degrees of longitude. From the Torrid it stretches far into the South Temperate Zone, and comprises some of the largest island masses in the world, as well as tiny islets which, in comparison, are but mere specks on the ocean. It embraces the island of **Flores** on the north-west, **New Guinea** in the north-east, **Fiji** and **New Zealand** to the eastward, and **Tasmania** on the south. Within these limits is contained, Australia being included, such an area of land as entitles Australasia to rank next to Europe as one of the great divisions of the globe.

6. While the foregoing description will indicate generally the extent of Australasia and its component parts, a more detailed enumeration of the several portions it contains is necessary to an exact knowledge of the subject. Instead of merely naming

the islands, however, it will be both more instructive and more interesting to visit them, in imagination, and observe where they are, and how related to each other. Such a general survey can best be obtained by means of an imaginary voyage, in the course of which all the principal countries are described, and their positions noted.

7. Let us assume then that our voyage is commenced at a point near **North-west Cape** in Australia. Turning the ship's head to the south, we have, on the left, the western shores of the great island-continent; on the right, the **Indian Ocean**. This great body of water bounds Australia on the west, and stretches away to the opposite coast of Africa, distant about five thousand miles. In its northern portion the periodical winds called *monsoons* blow with great regularity, their direction during one half the year being from the south-west, and during the other half from the north-east. Although the monsoons do not prevail on the Australian coast, their influence is felt in some degree, especially at the periods when they change their direction, heavy storms invariably occurring at this time.

8. In sailing southward in this ocean, the mariner may chance to observe a "school" of *cachalot* or sperm whales. These huge animals frequent the warmer waters of the globe, and may sometimes be seen in the Indian Ocean, occasionally raising their enormous heads out of the water to the height of thirty feet, but more frequently floating quietly on the surface with a portion of their bodies exposed to view. Should the vessel stand in near the shore, it may happen that numbers of sharks will be seen, for various species of these voracious creatures abound upon all the Australian coasts, and one of the principal indentations on the western side has been named **Shark Bay**.

9. Sailing with diminished speed on account of the opposition of the Antarctic Drift Current, which sets northward parallel to the western shore of Australia, our ship will at length arrive at the 35th degree of south latitude, where its direction is changed to the eastward. After rounding **Cape Leeuwin** and the peninsula which forms the south-western corner of Australia, we enter the **Great Southern Ocean** which extends from the Australian continent to the Antarctic Circle,

a distance of thirty degrees, or more than two thousand miles. On the left lies the monotonous shore of the **Great Australian Bight,** which stretches east and west for about eleven hundred miles; while on the right is that broad belt of ocean which girdles the earth between the 36th and 66th degrees of south latitude, and is unbroken by any great mass of land except the southern extremity of America. Here the winds blow strongly and with little variation from the westward, raising the waters into a long regular swell, the waves being of great height and immense size. These great swelling billows, which have caused the latitudes where they prevail to be named by seamen "the rolling forties," present a sublime spectacle to the voyager. At times the Aurora Australis may be observed illumining the southern sky, the precursor of heavier gales and more boisterous seas. Whales of several kinds find here a retreat and pasture-ground more secure than most other parts of the wide ocean, and sea-birds range at will over the turbulent waters in quest of food. From the diminutive petrel, which, though apparently so frail as to be in danger of destruction from the shock of the overwhelming waves, is nevertheless always active in a gale, to the great wandering albatross, which

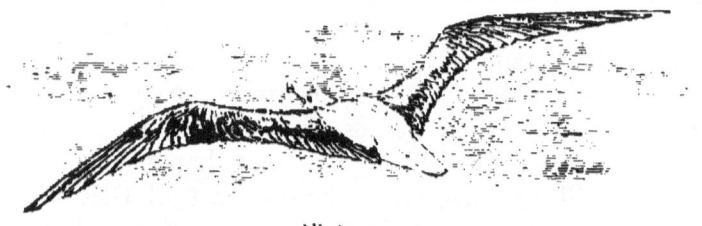

Albatross.

sometimes measures twelve feet in expanse of wing, there is in this region a series of birds varying in size and plumage, but all belonging to the extensive family of the gulls. It is an interesting sight to witness the flight of the albatross as it appears to float through the air on its long pinions, at one moment skimming along the surface of the water to pick up its food, and then, without visible effort, rising to a considerable height and perhaps flying in immense circles round a ship in rapid motion. In remarkable contrast to this great denizen of the air and water, is the penguin, which passes its

(311)

life, for the most part, on and under the waves. Its wings are so short as to be wholly useless for flying, but they are of great assistance to the bird when swimming or diving. Occasionally penguins are met with hundreds of miles from land, and their hoarse quack may sometimes be heard in the darkness of night alongside the ship, startling the voyager by the suddenness with which it breaks the prevailing silence. It seems not a little curious that creatures so different in structure and habits should find a home and be supplied with sustenance by the waters of the same ocean.

10. Leaving the island of **Tasmania** to the northward, we next sail in a south-easterly direction. Away to the southward lies **Macquarie Island**, just upon the edge of our imaginary circle; and as we approach the group known collectively as **New Zealand**, several small isolated pieces of land have to be passed, among which the **Auckland Islands** are the most worthy of note. Coasting along the eastern shores of New Zealand, several small islands will be passed on our right hand. Of these, **Antipodes Island** is the most remarkable, being, as its name implies, nearly at the opposite point of the earth to London. The **Chatham Islands** are next passed; and, sailing northward until we arrive at the **North Cape** of New Zealand, we then incline slightly to the westward, leaving the **Kermadec** group on our right, until we reach **New Caledonia** and its neighbouring islands. In pursuing this course we shall perhaps sail within sight of **Norfolk Island**; but as we must continue our voyage without pausing at any place, we again change our direction to the north-east until we reach the **Fiji** group. In such a voyage a portion of the vast **Pacific Ocean** would be traversed. The wind would no longer be observed to blow for weeks from the same point of the compass, nor would the waters be seen to rise in long and regular undulations. Instead of the albatross and the penguin we may now observe the frigate-bird, whose powerful wings, measuring ten feet across, carry it through the air for days together without resting. Or the more elegant tropic-bird, rose coloured, with two long red feathers projecting from its tail, may attract attention by its powers of flight. At times the voyager is an involuntary but interested spectator of a conflict between a

sperm-whale and its furious enemy the grampus; if, indeed, that can be properly styled a conflict in which the huge but helpless creature vainly endeavours to escape from the ravenous attacks of its assailant. Occasionally a turtle may be seen sleeping or resting on the surface of the water. Seals are not uncommon visitants to the various islands, though their

Frigate-bird.

usual abode is far away to the south. In the shallower waters fishes of grotesque forms and brilliant colours abound, and venomous serpents are also found among the inhabitants of the sea. Sharks, whose hunger no amount of food is capable of satisfying, will follow a ship for days, and watch about the breakers on the coast for victims to their appetites.

11. Having sailed round the beautiful Fijian group, we next steer to the westward, threading our way among the **New Hebrides**, which extend in an irregular line through six degrees of latitude. The **Santa Cruz Islands** then lie on our right hand, and we enter that portion of the Pacific termed the **Coral Sea**, on account of its being so largely peopled by the wonderful little creatures popularly called coral "insects," but more correctly styled "polypes." Though their bodies are of a jelly-like matter, they can extract from the sea a hard substance composed chiefly of lime, and with it build up their habitations, which are often so massed together as in time to form not only rocks, but also vast reefs and whole islands. A "coral" island is but little elevated above the sea-level, for the animal ceases to work when it has reached high-water mark. Perhaps the most astonishing example of the work of these creatures is the **Great Barrier Reef**, which extends along the eastern coast of Australia for about a thousand miles,

with only a few breaks or openings through it. On this reef Cook's vessel, the *Endeavour*, grounded, and was much injured by the sharp and jagged points of the coral rock; and since his day many ships have been wrecked in the attempt to cross from one side to the other. On the whole, the reef runs parallel with the coast, but the interval between them varies in breadth from twenty to seventy miles. Some species of coral show various beautiful forms, and others are equally prized for their striking colours. The latter are small and fragile, in some cases resembling plants in their appearance, and in others bearing a fancied likeness to various articles, such as fans and pens, and therefore highly esteemed as curiosities. Coral reefs and islands are not confined to the Coral Sea, but abound throughout a large portion of the Western Pacific within and near the tropics.

12. If we continue our voyage northward along the Great Barrier Reef, we shall in time reach **Torres Strait**; but turning from **Cape York** somewhat to the eastward we enter the **Gulf of Papua**, which is inclosed on two sides by portions of **New Guinea**. In this part of the sea we may perhaps witness the work of the pearl-fishers, or those other equally adventurous divers who gather *bêche-de-mer*. The substance known in commerce by this French title, and also called *trepang*, consists of the dried bodies of marine animals commonly termed "sea-slugs" and "sea-cucumbers," from their shapes and general appearance. These curious creatures inhabit the shallow waters of the ocean in warm latitudes, and resemble soft leathery bags of various shapes and sizes. When properly prepared and dried the trepang is exported to China, where it brings a high price, and is used as an ingredient in rich soups. After coasting along the shore of New Guinea we again turn eastward, and descry the **Solomon Islands**, inhabited by a fierce race of people addicted to cannibalism; and then make **New Britain**, **New Ireland** and the **Admiralty Islands** are next passed, and again approaching the coast of New Guinea we sail in a north-westerly direction until we reach the groups of islands situated about its northern extremity. Threading **Dampier's Strait** we pass **Waigiou** and some smaller islands on the right, **Batanta** and **Salwatty** on the left. **Mysole, Booro,** the large island of

Ceram, and spice-producing **Amboyna**, all belonging to the Moluccas, are sighted in succession, and in the same **Banda Sea** we notice, besides smaller groups, the **Kei** and **Aroo** Islands. Turning westward from the last we pass **Timor Laut**, the **Serwatty Islands, Timor, Ombay, Flores**, and **Sandalwood Island**, together with some connecting groups, and having sailed through the **Timor Sea** and regained the Indian Ocean we return to the point from which we originally started.

13. Having completed our circuit, we are able to understand of what parts Australasia consists, and we now proceed to mention the points in which these several parts resemble each other. In the first place, the vegetation of Australasia differs remarkably from that of neighbouring countries such as Java and Borneo, and in some parts is strikingly peculiar. As regards animals a similar remark may be made, for all the large mammalian animals so abundant in islands lying very near are entirely absent from Australasia. For example, the tigers, elephants, tapirs, rhinoceroses, bears, and monkeys found in Java, Sumatra, and Borneo are wholly wanting. It is further to be noted that the native inhabitants of Australasia are, generally speaking, not of the same race as those of the islands just mentioned, although in the countries lying near there is a considerable mixture. On the other hand, the greatest part of Australasia has a large number of plants peculiar to itself, the eucalyptus or gum-tree being a prominent example. Still more peculiar is the animal world, which, to a large extent, consists of marsupials, or animals with a pouch for their young ones. The presence of large birds of the ostrich type, such as the emu, cassowary, mooruk, and recently extinct moa of New Zealand, is another characteristic of Australasia. As regards inhabitants, the Malays who inhabit the countries lying to the north, and

Emu.

the Polynesians on the east, are only found in the Australasian islands as intruding conquerors. A striking example of this is to be witnessed in New Zealand, where the Maoris, a Polynesian race, subdued, and probably killed and devoured, the original inhabitants, who are thought to have been of Papuan extraction. The earliest native races were the Papuan in the north and east, and the Australian occupying the great inland continent. These will hereafter be described in detail; it will suffice in this place to remark that they are nowhere to be found outside of the limits we have assigned to Australasia.

14. Summing up the foregoing statements, it may be said that Australasia consists of the island-continent, Australia, and of a chain of islands partially encircling it on the north and east. All these several countries possess, in varying degrees, the following characteristics in common:—

(1) Absence of such mammalia, birds, and reptiles, as abound in the nearest countries to the northward.

(2) Absence of the races of men inhabiting the same regions.

(3) Presence of marsupials and other animals, including birds, which are distinctive of Australia.

(4) Presence of peculiar races of men, which are wholly confined to Australasia.

Each of these points will be fully illustrated in treating upon the individual portions of Australasia.

CHAPTER II.

PHYSICAL FEATURES AND CLIMATE OF AUSTRALIA.

1. Name. 2. Position. 3. Australia a continent. 4. The coast-line. 5. Surface: Mountains. 6. Table-lands. 7. Plains. 8. Remainder of Australia; Deserts. 9. Drainage; Rivers. 10. Lakes. 11. Climate.

1. By the early Dutch navigators, who visited the northern and western coasts of the great island-continent, this country was called **New Holland,** either because of its fancied resemblance to the low-lying shores of their own country, or from a patriotic desire to honour their fatherland. This name it continued to bear for about two hundred years, until Flinders, one of the most noted English explorers, styled it **Australia,** by which designation it is now universally known. As the word signifies "Southern Land," the title suits very well.

2. Lying wholly in the southern hemisphere, its most northerly projection approaches within ten degrees of the equator, and about one-third of its entire area is situated between that line and the tropic of Capricorn. On the other hand, its southern extremity, which may be considered to be **South-east Cape** in Tasmania, stretches as far to the south as the parallel of 43° 40'. Between these two points the country extends about 2400 miles in a straight line, occupying the cooler portion of the **torrid zone** (a sub-tropical region) and the warmer portion of the **south temperate zone.** In this respect Australia is highly favoured, for these are not only some of the most productive parts of the world, but also the pleasantest as the habitation of man. Being situated to the eastward of Greenwich, the place through which the first meridian is assumed to pass, Australia is said to be in "east longitude." A good notion of the effect of difference of longitude may be formed by noting the difference of time between two places at a distance from each other in the direction of east and west. For example, the difference in longitude between Cape Byron and Steep Point is about forty degrees and a half, and consequently the difference in time is nearly two hours and three-quarters. Children in Western Australia are, there-

fore, just beginning school in the morning when those who live on the east coast are on their way home to dinner. Compared with Greenwich, the difference in time is still more striking. For the eastern portion of Australia that difference is about ten hours, so that at the time when the Australian colonists are sitting down to breakfast the inhabitants of the west of England and France are preparing to retire to rest. If we suppose a railway to be constructed across Australia, between the two points before mentioned, and the trains to travel thereon at the rate of twenty miles an hour, without any stoppage, day or night, the journey would not be completed in less than four entire days. In round numbers, the extent of the earth's surface occupied by Australia is 3,000,000 square miles.

3. People are sometimes apt to dispute whether Australia should be termed an **island** or a **continent**. Being entirely surrounded by water, it is necessarily an island. But although America, north and south, is, for the same reason, an island, it is never so styled, but is invariably spoken of as a continent. On the same grounds the term "continent" is equally applicable to Australia. It so far exceeds other islands in size as to stand quite alone in this respect. It is, for example, eleven times the size of Borneo and fifteen times the size of Madagascar. Moreover, it differs from most islands in physical conformation quite as strikingly as in point of size. In general, islands have a chain of mountains or other masses of elevated land running through their central portions in the direction of their greatest length. This rule does not, however, apply to Australia, where the elevated land lies around the edges and not in the centre. Again, in islands the climate is generally equable, as nearness to the sea has the effect of preventing either extreme heat or extreme cold, while in the continents great variations in temperature and moisture are usually experienced. In this respect the Australian climate partakes of the continental rather than of the insular character, being alternately subject to excessive heat and considerable cold, and to droughts and floods. Further, in islands, due regard being had to difference of elevation above the sea-level, the natural productions are spread with some degree of uniformity over the surface, the plants and animals found in one portion being usually obtainable in

others. But in Australia most of the plants and animals have a restricted *habitat* or area where they are met with, as it would be manifestly impossible for any one species to flourish equally throughout the vast territory with its variety of physical and climatic conditions. On all these grounds, therefore—size, conformation of surface, climate, and distribution of plants and animals—Australia is entitled to be regarded as a continent.

4. It is remarkable that none of the continents which extend into the southern hemisphere possess any considerable projections or indentations. South of the equator there is no inlet that, in point of size, can be compared with the Mediterranean or Baltic, no broken coast like that of Norway, and no peninsulas like Jutland, Scandinavia, or the Spanish Peninsula. Though specially descriptive of Africa and South America, this observation is in some measure applicable to Australia. In the first-mentioned continent the coast appears to present an unbroken line throughout its whole extent; while in Australia there are but two considerable openings: on the north the **Gulf of Carpentaria**, and in the south **Spencer's Gulf** and its branch the **Gulf of St. Vincent**. Less conspicuous inlets are **Van Diemen's** and **Cambridge Gulfs** on the northern coast; **King Sound, Exmouth Gulf,** and **Shark Bay** on the west; **Port Philip Bay** and **Western Port** on the south; and **Harvey, Halifax,** and **Princess Charlotte Bays** on the east coast, which possesses no large openings that penetrate far inland. Minor indentations will be noticed in treating of the separate colonies. As regards projections, the most worthy of notice is **Cape York Peninsula**, which terminates at **Cape York**, the most northerly point in Australia. This must not be confounded with York Peninsula, a much smaller projection in the south. Westward of the Gulf of Carpentaria is the peninsula once known as **Arnhem's Land**. These are the only considerable portions of land that are, in any great degree, inclosed by the water, though there are some of smaller extent, such as **Coburg Peninsula** on the north coast; **North-west Cape** and **Steep Point** on the west; and the **Eyria Peninsula** on the south.

5. As regards its **surface**, Australia may be compared to a dish of irregular shape, being depressed towards the centre and raised along the edges. It must not be overlooked, however,

that notwithstanding the efforts of explorers who hazarded their lives in the examination of the western interior, our knowledge of that portion of the continent is still too limited to warrant any positive statements respecting it, except such as are of a general character. The elevated portions of land consist of mountains and table-lands, both of which, so far as is yet known, are more pronounced features of the east than of the west side of the continent. From Cape York on the north to Wilson's Promontory on the south, a chain of elevations runs, with scarcely a break of any importance in its entire length, and is continued on the south side of Bass' Strait into Tasmania. The **Great Dividing Range**, as this chain is called, is situated at an average distance of thirty miles from the sea, though in some places it recedes as much as sixty miles. This range forms the watershed between the rivers flowing into the Pacific and those which, running westward, join the great system of inland drainage which gathers the waters of the eastern half of the continent and delivers them into the Southern Ocean. In its northern portion the chain is of but moderate elevation, but in tracing its course southward summits are occasionally met with that exceed 5000 feet in height, though the average would probably be about 3000 feet. Lateral spurs branch off from the main chain at various points, both to the east and to the west, and individual peaks in some of these offsets attain a greater elevation than those before mentioned. Between the 36th and 37th parallels the chain seems to be gathered into a great mountain knot, in which are numerous peaks rising above 6000 feet in height, and including **Mount Kosciusko**, the culminating point, with perhaps one exception, of the Australian continent. Its elevation, 7308 feet, is somewhat below the snow-line, which for this latitude is about 8000 feet. From this great knot the main chain takes a westerly direction until, in the vicinity of the Gulf of St. Vincent, it ceases to form the distinctive watershed, while farther west it wholly disappears. In most parts of its course this Dividing Range is composed of masses of granite and trap, with rounded or pointed summits; but in that portion called the **Blue Mountains**, in New South Wales, the prevailing rock is sandstone, which is arranged in horizontal layers of immense thickness, but broken up in every direction by vast chasms and ravines, with precipitous sides.

6. On each side of the Dividing Range lie **table-lands** of considerable, but not uniform elevation, and of varying breadth.

Falls in Dividing Range.

The average height, however, may be estimated at 2500 feet, and the breadth about 100 miles. On the eastern side the descent to the coast is rapid, and in many places so steep as formerly to have been deemed impassable; but on the west the decline is gradual and gentle, the land sinking by imperceptible gradations to the level of the interior. Throughout the whole length of the table-land there are scenes of remarkable interest where it descends to the coast district. Mountain and valley, ravine and waterfall, combine to form pictures that awe the spectator by their grandeur or charm him by their picturesque beauty. The surface of the table-land is of an undulating character, and in no part does it consist of such large areas of level country as are found in other portions of the continent.

7. Westward from the table-land, vast level **plains** extend for many hundreds of miles, occasionally crossed by ranges of low hills, but possessing no elevations requiring special remark. These plains consist to a large extent of a deep black soil of the richest description, and in wet seasons are covered with luxuriant vegetation. Sandy or clayey tracts are interspersed among the more fertile portions, and are sometimes covered with dense scrubs of various kinds, consisting either of coniferous plants commonly called pines, or thorny acacias. Both these are useless for pastoral purposes; but in those parts where the "salt-bush" is the prevailing vegetable growth, even though grass may be entirely absent, sheep are found to thrive. Want of water is the great drawback to the productiveness of the Great Plains, which in ordinary seasons maintain millions of sheep, cattle, and horses. During prolonged droughts, however, when no rain at all, or a very small quantity, falls in the course of many successive months, the grass and herbage are dried up by the fierce rays of the sun and crumble into dust, and at such times vast numbers of animals perish from hunger and thirst. In one such year, and in one colony, six millions of sheep, it is said, were lost from this cause, besides cattle and horses. Even the wild marsupials suffered in the same way. Occupying many hundred thousand square miles these plains constitute the most important geographical feature of Eastern Australia, and give a special character to the colonies of New South Wales, Queensland, and South Australia.

8. So far as is yet known, the physical features of the remainder of the continent are less regular and less distinctly marked. Still, it may be said, in general terms, that at a short distance from the coast the land is comparatively elevated in the form of table-lands, across which, in some parts, mountain

ranges extend. In Western Australia these table-lands possess greater breadth than those on the east; and they have, moreover, a character peculiarly their own. While in the eastern table-lands are to be found some of the most productive portions of the whole continent, in the western, as revealed to us by explorers, a large proportion consists of **deserts** and **scrubs**. Both classes of country described by these terms have one characteristic in common—the absence or great scarcity of water. In other respects they differ considerably, the deserts being destitute of vegetation, or clothed only with a coarse spiny grass that cuts like knives, and affords no sustenance to cattle or horses, while the scrubs are composed of a dense growth of shrubs and low trees, often impenetrable until the traveller has cleared a track with his axe. The hardy pioneers who have ventured into this inhospitable region have suffered the greatest privations and hardships, and have incurred the risk of dying the most terrible of deaths. Want of food and of water, the burning heat, the toil of cutting their way foot by foot through the scrubs, the wounds inflicted by thorny shrubs or the dreaded *spinifex* grass, and the loss of the means of transport through the death of horses from hunger and thirst, are all trials of fortitude and endurance of a kind not experienced in the exploration of any other country in the world. Greater demands may be made upon a traveller's courage in fight when he is brought into conflict with savage men or ferocious beasts in the interior of Africa; but the Australian explorer is denied the sustaining power of resistance; he can but endure, knowing that no effort on his part can improve his condition. The northern coast is, in many parts, low and swampy. It is known, however, that mountains exist at some distance from the sea. The western half of the south coast lying along the Great Australian Bight is low and sandy, the adjoining country being barren and of low elevation.

9. In general terms, the **drainage system** may be said to consist of but two slopes—one towards the sea, the other towards the interior. From the proximity of the principal mountain chains to the sea, the rivers flowing seaward from them are comparatively short; and, owing to the irregular rainfall, their volume is inconsiderable, except in time of flood, when they

not only fill their channels but overflow the adjacent country. Among these rivers may be enumerated as the more important on the east coast, commencing from the north, the **Burdekin, Fitzroy, Clarence, Hunter, Hawkesbury,** and **Shoalhaven,** all of which derive their importance from the fact that the upper and more considerable portions of their courses are parallel to the dividing chain and to the coast. Entering the sea on the south are the **Margalong** or **Snowy River, Hopkins, Glenelg,** and **Murray;** on the west, the **Blackwood, Swan, Murchison, Gascoyne, Ashburton, Fortesque,** and **De Grey;** and on the north, the **Fitzroy, Victoria, Liverpool,** and **Flinders.** Of all these the Murray is the only river that attains the dimensions of what may be termed a continental river, and it belongs properly to the system of inland drainage. This system drains the country west of the great dividing chain from the sources of the Thompson about lat. 22° south to the head-waters of the Loddon in about 37° 30′ S., and westward as far as the 133d meridian E. In all this vast territory there are but two main channels by which surplus waters are collected and carried off, the Murray with its large and important tributaries and the **Barcoo.** The former, which has a basin probably exceeding 450,000 square miles, falls into Lake Alexandrina on the south coast, and thence into the sea. Its greatest tributary is the **Darling** (which indeed may be looked upon as the main stream), and next to it is the **Murrumbidgee,** with its tributary the **Lachlan.** The Barcoo, called **Cooper's Creek** in its lower course, empties into Lake Eyre, after draining a large extent of country. It is entirely an inland stream. Throughout the remainder of the continent the rivers draining inland are for the most part small and intermittent in their supply of water, and form no connected system. They rise in some elevated tract, run for a short distance, and then terminate in some lake, often salt, or lose themselves in swamps, but sometimes entirely disappear in desolate sandy wastes. After heavy rain, however, their shallow beds become surcharged with water, and they overflow their ill-defined banks, and submerge the low-lying land along their courses. Almost all the rivers are subject to great irregularities as regards volume.

10. Irrespective of the lagoons lying along the coast, and at

irregular periods communicating with the sea, there are numerous lakes scattered over the continent, in a few cases containing fresh water, but more generally salt. None are conspicuous for their size, as in numerous instances they occupy the craters of extinct volcanoes, and receive the drainage of very limited areas. The largest freshwater lake yet discovered on the continent is **Lake George**, which is situated about seventy miles from the east coast, in latitude $35°$ south, and which has an area of about forty square miles. Of the salt lakes the most important are **Torrens, Eyre**, and **Gairdner**, at the head of Spencer's Gulf, and **Amadeus**, near the centre of the continent, between the parallels of $23°$ and $25°$ s.

11. The **climate** of Australia, while necessarily varying, as regards temperature, with the latitude and elevation above sea-level, has one general characteristic—it is warm and dry. On the whole, it is in the highest degree conducive to health, though there are certain localities, such as the low mangrove-fringed northern coasts, where fevers are prevalent, especially in the warm season. In point of temperature, the climate is generally cooler in summer and warmer in winter than that of countries situated at like distances from the equator in the northern hemisphere. Occasionally during the prevalence of hot winds the heat becomes very great; but these visitations are infrequent and affect but slightly the average temperature of the year. In the more elevated districts ice and snow are common in the winter. The temperature in the interior plains is sometimes oppressive, the thermometer occasionally registering $120°$; but, owing to the dry state of the atmosphere, this degree of heat has less of a prejudicial effect upon the human frame than might be expected. Although the climate is generally speaking dry, rain falls abundantly, as a rule, on the coast districts, and on the mountains and table-lands. In the interior the supply is less bountiful. While it lasts the fall is generally heavy, especially on the coast; but most parts of the continent yet known are liable to rains so copious as to occasion floods, from the inability of the ordinary channels to carry off the water as rapidly as it is deposited. On such occasions large areas of land lie for some time under water, and present the appearance of lakes and even of inland seas. Fortunately for the inhabi-

tants of the settled districts these calamitous visitations are of rare occurrence. Equally infrequent are the periods of excessive dryness, when less than the usual quantity of rain falls, and vegetation becomes parched and withered in consequence. Moreover, it must be borne in mind that droughts and floods do not affect the whole continent at once, but are confined to comparatively limited areas, the remaining portions being in their usual condition. Within the tropic the climate resembles that of other intertropical regions, having but two seasons, the wet and the dry. In the other portions of the continent the four seasons prevailing in temperate zones are distinctly marked.

CHAPTER III.

NATURAL PRODUCTIONS AND ABORIGINAL INHABITANTS OF AUSTRALIA.

1. Mineral Productions. 2. Vegetable. 3. Brushes. 4. Woodlands. 5. Scrubs. 6. Special Plants. 7. Animal life: its general character. 8. Mammalia. 9. Marsupials. 10. Echidna and Platypus. 11. Fossil Marsupials. 12. Birds. 13. Reptiles. 14. Fishes. 15. Other Marine Animals. 16. Insects. 17. The Aborigines. 18. General Remarks.

1. Australia, as a whole, is remarkable for the variety and profusion of its natural productions. In each of the three kingdoms of nature there is an abundance of products useful to, or prized by man, and much that is attractive by reason either of beauty or rarity. Among **minerals** already known to exist in Australia may be reckoned, besides various sorts of stone used in building, such as granite, limestone, marble, and sandstone, many kinds of precious stones, including the garnet, ruby, topaz, sapphire, and even the diamond. Of a humbler class, but higher commercial value, is coal, large deposits of which have been found throughout the eastern portion of the continent. Metals also abound, gold, silver, iron, copper, tin, lead, quicksilver, and antimony being the most valuable. All of these have been worked to a greater or less extent, though much remains to be accomplished both in the discovery of other deposits and in the mode of preparing them for the market.

2. Equally abundant and even more varied are the products of the **vegetable kingdom**. It must be remarked at the outset, however, that the almost total absence of food-producing plants from such an immense region is a matter of astonishment. Besides the *nardoo*, a plant allied to the ferns, the spore-cases of which supply a poorly nutritious article of food, the roots of certain plants of the orchid tribe, locally called "yams," and the seeds of the *bunya-bunya* pine, there is hardly a vegetable growth to be found in the continent that yields suitable sustenance for human beings in any quantity; and although this dearth is, in a measure, compensated for by the superabundance of animal life, it is not the less remarkable that Australia pro-

duces no indigenous root like the potato, no grain equal to the poorest of the cereals, and no fruit comparable even to the gooseberry in nutritive power. The vegetation of Australia is peculiar both in its nature and in its appearance. Comparatively few species of plants native to Australia are found in any other quarter of the globe. In the north are to be found plants belonging to classes which abound in the tropical regions of India and the Malayan islands; and in the south certain natural orders are common, which are also abundant in South Africa. With these and some other trifling exceptions, the plants of Australia may be said to be so peculiar to it as not to be found elsewhere. Moreover, while retaining to the fullest degree the Australian characteristics, the plants of West Australia differ widely from those of the eastern portion of the continent. To give a fairly accurate notion of the indigenous plants, it will be best to treat of them according to the nature of the localities in which they grow, whether *brushes, woodlands,* or *scrubs.*

3. **Brushes** are situated, for the most part, on the seaward side of the Dividing Ranges, in the alluvial soil on the banks of rivers, or in the equally rich soil to be found in mountain valleys and ravines, especially where the mountains are formed of volcanic rock. In these brushes, which resemble largely the jungles of tropical countries, the vegetation is dense and luxuriant; and while the plants are almost without exception evergreens, the foliage is varied in tint and disposition, and therefore free from the monotony which is so depressing a feature in the general aspect of Australian vegetable forms. Conspicuous by their height and enormous stems, certain kinds of Eucalyptus, known as "gum-trees," tower above the general level, and are usually destitute of branches until near the top, and even there the foliage is thinner and less in quantity than the magnitude of the tree would lead an observer to expect. Rivalling the gums in height and thickness are large-leaved figs, which, however, possess crowns that spread wide their thick and abundant foliage. These two species usually form the uppermost layer of the brush forest as seen from above, and they not infrequently rise above the general level, and give the spectator the idea of a forest above the forest. Less lofty than these, though

still of considerable height, come the mass of the brush-trees, including, it may be, nearly a hundred species, among which must be mentioned the palms and the nettles, the latter often rising fifty feet from the ground, and being garnished with large light-green leaves which sting dangerously. Lower still are the tree ferns, which rarely exceed twenty feet in height, though occasionally they are found ten feet higher. All these trees are bound and matted together with the pliable stems of climbing plants, and on the branches may sometimes be found rare and beautiful orchids. Below the ground is covered with decaying leaves and branches which help to fertilize the soil and retain moisture, which is further kept from evaporating by the dense mantle of foliage overhead. Among the brush-trees remarkable for beauty of appearance as well as commercial value, the Cedar (*Cedrela*) takes the first place. The wood of this noble tree closely resembles that of the mahogany, to which, in fact, it is botanically related. The so-called "Chestnut," which is a plant really belonging to the same order as the bean, is found in the brushes of the northern coast, and is a tree of beautiful appearance. Nearly all the brush-trees are believed to be of great value, inasmuch as their wood is useful to the carpenter, joiner, cabinet-maker, coach-builder, cooper, &c.

4. **Woodlands** are open tracts of land, usually clothed with grass, in which grow large trees with little undergrowth. The soil in the woodlands is not generally of high quality; and where it is richest, the timber is smaller and often unsound at the heart. It is in such tracts that the various species of Eucalyptus are most abundant. It sometimes happens that mile after mile is occupied by one kind of gum-tree, and where the variety is greater, the only difference perceptible to the non-scientific spectator is in the colour and texture of the bark, which in some species is rough and persistent, and in others smooth and shed every year. The presence of these trees consequently gives the country an aspect of extreme monotony, and has caused it to be disparagingly termed "the land of the dreary eucalyptus." These plants vary in dimensions from the *Mallee*, ten or twelve feet high, and no thicker than a wand, to the gigantic *Blue Gum*, two hundred feet in height and six feet in diameter. Some specimens of gums, indeed, have been

known to attain the extraordinary height of more than four hundred feet, and, therefore, to be the largest known trees in the world. Though not so large as some of the other gums, the first place is perhaps due to the Iron Bark, in virtue of its hardness, toughness, and strength, qualities which render it of the highest service to man. Next to the gums, the acacias are

A Woodland.

the most conspicuous. Of the three hundred or more species of this tribe and its allies known to be indigenous to Australia, a few may be considered as trees, though the greater number are shrubby in their habit, and some are of very humble growth. One species, called the *Myall*, is of a graceful drooping habit, and its foliage is of a light green colour, giving it the appearance of a small willow. Its wood, which is used for many purposes, is noted for its odour of violets. Some species of Acacia are of economic value; others, of a thorny character, form the detested *Mulga* scrub. In moist or swampy situations, the place of the eucalyptus is taken by various species of trees known to the colonists under the name of Tea-trees—some of which have a peculiar papery bark, and all furnish a hard durable timber, almost imperishable in the ground. Although belonging to the same natural order as the gum, the tea-trees have very different leaves, which resemble those of the pine in shape, though not in arrangement. After the gums no trees are more characteristic of Australia than the Casuarinas, absurdly called "oaks" in the colonies. One species, which is commonly termed the "Forest Oak," grows among gums and acacias in the woodlands, and another, the "Swamp Oak," grows in the beds of rivers and in smaller water-courses, which may often be traced for miles by the belt of dark green, pine-looking trees of this kind. These trees are remarkable as belonging to a class of which few representatives now exist in the world, but which abounded in the forests of former ages, as evidenced by the remains frequently obtained in coal.

5. By **Scrubs** we are to understand tracts of land, usually with poor, dry soil, thickly covered with shrubs and bushes. In some cases scrubs are composed almost exclusively of plants belonging to one family, and even to one species. Of this kind are the *Mallee* scrubs, in which the plant is a dwarf species of eucalyptus, and which occupy an immense area on the lower course of the Murray River; and the *Mulga* scrubs, to which a dense growth of thorny acacias give their name and character. But, more generally, the vegetation of the scrubs is of a varied description, comprising a large number of shrubby plants belonging to different orders. Occasionally trees of large size, gums and tea-trees, for examples, are to be met with in such scrubs. One of the most characteristic plants to be found in the scrubs is the Banksia, of which there are upwards of forty species ranging from one foot to twenty-five feet in height. A West Australian species grows to the height of fifty feet. They are commonly known as "Honeysuckles," and their flowers as "bottle brushes" from their resemblance to those articles. Usually they grow in a crooked, irregular manner;

and while far from being graceful in appearance, their timber is valuable for making knees for boats and ships. In the scrubs now described the plants are, for the most part, thorny and prickly; they grow so closely together as to render passage through them difficult, and sometimes impossible without the aid of an axe: and they often exhibit the most beautiful of the

A Scrub.

indigenous wild-flowers. The obstacles they present to the work of the explorer have already been adverted to. Another plant characteristic of, but not wholly confined to the scrubs, is the so-called "Grass-tree," which has a thick round stem, from the top of which springs a tuft of long, pointed, and sharp-edged leaves. Out of this tuft grows a long, straight, round stalk, from three to five feet in length, and having about a foot of the upper portion densely covered with small flowers. A useful gum or resin exudes from these plants, especially when wounded. The Zamia, a plant which appears as half palm and half fern, is also found in the poor soil of the scrubs.

6. Besides the plants already mentioned there are numerous others which occur in no special localities, but are distributed promiscuously, as it were, in different places. Among these may be mentioned the Moreton Bay Pine, which flourishes in the northern coast district, and furnishes useful timber. The Cypress Pine is equally useful, but is found only in the interior, where, in some places, it spreads with great rapidity in the poorer sandy soils and forms dense "pine scrubs." The Bottle-tree of Northern Queensland is a remarkable plant, the middle portion of the stem being expanded into the resemblance of a gigantic gourd. Flowering plants may be counted by thousands, the most conspicuous, perhaps, being the Waratah with its large crimson flower. Equally remarkable is the Gigantic Lily, which, rising to a height of ten or twelve feet, bears at its top an immense dark-red flower. Ferns are abundant, some of insignificant size, others, as the "Staghorn Fern" and the "Bird's Nest Fern," two or three feet across. Orchids of different kinds are also numerous, some growing upon trees, and some in the ground, and many producing flowers remarkable for their beauty or their singularity.

7. Although Australian vegetation is of the peculiar character before described, the **animal life** is still more remarkable. With some trifling exceptions none of the Australian animals are found in other countries, and none of the animals common in countries at no great distance find representatives in Australia. Australia is pre-eminently the land of Marsupials, or pouch-bearing animals— animals that carry about their young ones in a pouch. With the exception of the native dog and some mice and rats all the quadrupeds of Australia are marsupial. One pouched animal is found in North America, one in the Malay Archipelago, and several closely allied to those of Australia in Papua; but beyond this, the marsupials are confined to this continent. Moreover, the same state of things must have existed in former ages, for the fossil remains of quadrupeds which have been discovered in Australia are almost all of the marsupial order, though some are of enormous size, indicating that the creatures they belonged to equalled the

rhinoceros and hippopotamus in bulk. It would seem as if, for countless ages, Australia had been so isolated from the rest of the world, that no interchange of plants and animals could take place.

8. The sole representative in Australia of the carnivorous order, the lions, tigers, wolves, and bears of other countries, is a kind of dog, called by the colonists the "Dingo," which is usually of a yellowish colour, though the marking and colouring is by no means uniform. Whether it is truly indigenous or introduced by man is a question still open to discussion. Bats, both of the fruit-eating and insectivorous classes, are abundant, about twenty-four species being known. The former are of large size, and are locally designated "flying foxes." They do much mischief in orchards, devouring and spoiling large quantities of fruit. At times they assemble in vast multitudes in some secluded spot in the forest, hanging by day from the branches of the trees and sallying out at night in quest of food. It is customary, when the bats have established one of these "camps" in any neighbourhood, for the settlers to collect and destroy as many as they have time and opportunity for shooting. Rats, mice, and water-rats are also numerous. They all resemble the ordinary rats and mice that infest houses and barns, though the water-rats, as the name implies, frequent streams and ponds.

9. Nearly all the remaining land quadrupeds of Australia belong to the order **Marsupials**, or pouched animals. The marsupials are arranged in groups according to the character of their teeth and the nature of their food, though on this point there is room for discussion.

Wombat.

In the first group, the *root-eaters*, come the Wombats, of which four species are known, all inhabiting the eastern half of Australia and Tasmania. These animals live in burrows, coming out to feed by night. Their habits are consequently but little understood. A wombat of ordinary size weighs about a hundred pounds, and its flesh is very palatable.

In the second group, the *fruit-eaters*, are comprehended several genera which, though shown by their teeth to be connected with each other, differ considerably in external appearance. One of the most peculiar of these is the Koala, locally named the Native Bear, which has but small similarity to the other members of the family. Unlike any other known quadruped, the toes of its fore-feet are so disposed that the two inner can act like a thumb against the three outer, an arrangement which proves of great assistance in climbing the trees in which it lives, and in enabling it to retain a firm hold of the branches. The koala is tailless, and its appearance resembles in some degree that of a bear. After leaving the pouch, the young is carried upon the mother's back. Of the Phalangists, commonly called Opossums, it may suffice to remark that they are perhaps the commonest of the marsupials, being found in all parts of the continent. Formerly these animals formed the staple food of the aborigines. Allied to these are the Petaurists, known in the colonies as Flying Opossums, which have membranes stretching between the arms and legs. When taking their flying leaps from tree to tree, or from branch to branch, these membranes are expanded and help to support the animal, which, it is scarcely necessary to observe, is incapable of true flight. Others of these flying phalangers are smaller, and receive from the colonists such names as Flying Squirrel and Flying Mouse.

The third family of marsupials are styled *grass-eaters*, and include the Kangaroos, Wallabies, and Pademelons, with some smaller kinds. Their general appearance and structure are well known. Their short fore-legs, long muscular tails, and large hind-limbs terminating in formidable claws, and, above all, the pouches in which their young are carried and nourished while in the immature state, are characteristics by which the whole tribe may be recognized, notwithstanding the difference in size and colour among the various species. In general, the prevailing colour is gray, shading off in some species to black, though two species are of a yellowish red. In size they vary from the

Great Kangaroo, which sometimes weighs two hundred pounds, to the Hare Kangaroo, which seldom exceeds ten pounds. The larger number of species are found in the eastern half of Australia.

Insect-eaters form the next class, and include the Bandicoots, the largest species of which is about the size of a rabbit, and others not larger than a rat.

To the last division, the *flesh-eaters*, are assigned some of the fiercest and most destructive of the wild animals of Australia. Two of these are, at the present time, confined to Tasmania, where they not only prey upon domestic animals, but are even dangerous to man.

Kangaroo.

First in destructiveness is the so-called Tasmanian "Devil," a ferocious and bloodthirsty creature, killing, as it would seem, for the mere love of slaughter. There are also two species of "Tigers," which are thus named from being striped, though their general form more nearly resembles that of the dog. On this account they have been also called Tasmanian "Wolves." On the continent the largest predatory animals are the Dasyures—Native Cats as they are absurdly termed by the colonists. These little creatures, which are either black or yellow with white spots, are generally about the size of a half-grown kitten, though specimens have been seen equal in dimensions to a full-grown cat. They do much mischief among poultry, and, like their relatives, the "devils," kill without any intention of eating. Besides numerous species of pouched "rats" and "mice," so called, there belongs to this division an animal, locally termed the "Ant-eater," which preys principally upon ants and their eggs.

10. Belonging to a small but very remarkable order are two

animals which are confined exclusively to Australasia, and which in some respects resemble birds, notably in producing their young from eggs. These are the **Echidna** and the **Platypus** or Ornithorhynchus. The former, which is variously known as the "hedgehog" and the "porcupine ant-eater," is covered with sharp spines that form an effectual protection against such foes as the dingo, and are not altogether unavailing even against man himself. Its food consists of ants and their eggs, to obtain which it makes use of its long, round, slimy tongue, which it protrudes from its long beak-like snout. Its powerful claws enable it to penetrate ant-hills and to burrow in the ground with great rapidity. Extraordinary as its structure is, it is a true mammal, suckling its young in a peculiar fashion. One species inhabits Australia, and another Tasmania. Equally remarkable is the Ornithorhynchus, called "duck-bill" and "water-mole" by the colonists. The head of this creature terminates in two horny mandibles resembling the bill of a duck, its feet are webbed, and the males have spurs on their hind-legs. It frequents streams and ponds, and forms its dwelling by burrowing deeply into the banks. To some extent it is sought after for the sake of its thick, warm, dark-brown fur, but otherwise it is not much noticed by the colonists.

Duck-bill.

11. The discovery of **fossil** bones of marsupials and of scarcely any others has been mentioned above. Remains of a dog, of rats and mice, and of a species of sloth, have been discovered; but, for the most part, the fossils are those of marsupials of a similar kind with those now existing, but distinguished by their enormous size. A kangaroo ten feet high when erect is wonderful enough, but becomes insignificant in comparison with an allied animal, the Diprotodon, nearly as large as an elephant, of which remains belonging to several species have been exhumed. Fragments of other huge crea-

tures, a wombat as large as a tapir, and animals resembling in some points both the wombat and the kangaroo, and equalling the rhinoceros in size, have also been discovered. All these appear to have been herbivorous; but another large extinct animal is thought to have been carnivorous. If such were the case, its size, which must have been that of a lion, would have rendered it a most formidable enemy to even the enormous beasts before mentioned. Besides these creatures remarkable for their dimensions, there were numerous species, now extinct, of kangaroos, wallabies, and others.

12. While the mammals of Australia are thus peculiar, its **birds** are not less characteristic. Altogether it is estimated that Australia, so far as it is yet known, possesses more than six hundred distinct species. In regard to distribution, it would appear that birds most abound in the north, where about four hundred and fifty species have been observed, and to diminish in number as we proceed southward, until in Tasmania little more than a hundred and sixty species are met with. It would be impossible to describe in detail so numerous a class of animals, and mention will therefore be made of those only which may be considered to be specially Australian. By this it is not to be understood that there is any correspondence between the mammals and the birds in this continent as regards their restricted habitat; for, as a rule, the same orders of birds as are indigenous here may also be found in other parts of the world, a statement obviously inapplicable to the quadrupeds. There are, nevertheless, certain kinds which, owing to some peculiarity in structure, colour, or habits, may be deemed peculiarly Australian.

Among these the *Emu* may be noticed first, as from its size, the absence of apparent wings, and the unusual texture of its feathers, it differs greatly from ordinary birds. Formerly abundant in all parts of the country, it is now only to be found in the most sparsely peopled districts, having been hunted down and destroyed, often from the mere instinct of destructiveness. In height the emu reaches six, and even eight feet; its wings are mere rudiments concealed by its long plumage; and its feet, adapted for running, have three toes. Its food is principally vegetable. Harmless and timid it seeks for safety by its speed in running, but when brought to bay, a kick from its powerful leg is dangerous, and strong enough to break a bone. The emu may be domesticated, and breeds in captivity.

Equally remarkable, though smaller, is the *Menura*, the "lyre-bird" or "lyre-tail" of the colonists, and so termed because the two outer tail-feathers are curved into the shape of an ancient lyre, while the intermediate feathers, stiff and wiry, represent the strings. Up to the present time naturalists have not agreed as to its position in the arrangement of birds, some classing it among gallinaceous birds, such as the pheasant and common fowl, and others among the perchers with thrushes and wrens. With the former it agrees in its habit of scratching the ground when searching for food, but with the latter in the form of the bill and in its musical powers. Its own notes are not particularly melodious, but it imitates with great fidelity the song of other birds, and any but a close observer would thereby be led to believe in the near presence of birds that were not at the time within hearing. On this account it is often called the mocking-bird, but the common name for it is the "native" or "brush" pheasant. The latter epithet it obtains from the fact that it haunts "brushes" and ravines in mountain sides, where the dense vegetation conceals it from view.

Lyre-bird.

Still more peculiarly Australian are the "mound-building" birds, of which there are three species. They are thus spoken of from their habit of scraping together large mounds of dead leaves and decaying vegetation, in which they make deep holes and deposit their eggs. The heat caused by the fermentation of this mass hatches the eggs, and the young escape, not in the helpless condition usual at such an age, but able to procure their own food and dispense with the assistance of their parents. These birds are generally known as "brush-turkeys."

Less remarkable for the strangeness of their habits, but worthy of notice for their numbers, variety, and beauty of plumage, are the parrot tribe, represented by more than sixty species, from the great Black Cockatoo to the diminutive Grass Parakeet. Some of the parrots subsist upon honey, which they are enabled to collect from the flowers with their brush-like tongues. Doves and pigeons are also abundant, and in many cases are remarkable for their plumage, especially the fruit-pigeon of the northern districts.

There are several kingfishers, clothed like their congeners in other parts of the world in bright colours, though one species, somewhat grotesque in form and droll in its habits, does not frequent the water, but derives its subsistence exclusively from the land. This is the laughing Kooka-burra, or gigantic kingfisher, which utters a loud and continuous cry resembling a burst of idiotic laughter, combined with the braying of an ass. From this circumstance it has obtained the local name of the Laughing Jackass; while, from the regularity with which its call is sounded at day-dawn and dusk of evening, it has acquired the more complimentary title of the "settlers' clock." Its food consists principally of the smaller reptiles, and it is serviceable in keeping down the number of snakes.

Among rapacious birds the Australian Eagle takes a conspicuous place. It commits great havoc among lambs, but is not averse to carrion. No vulture has yet been observed in any part of the continent, but hawks of various species are numerous; and owls are common, one of them having a note like the word "cuckoo." The Black Swan is a noble bird, capable of domestication; the Pelican of equal size is often seen in flocks; and wild ducks are abundant. One species makes its nest in the hollow of a tree. Of the smaller kinds of birds the numbers are very great, and include honey-eaters, finches, robins, swallows, wrens, and crows. Some of these have a pretty song; and the piping-crow, popularly called the magpie, also has a melodious note. Many are brilliantly coloured; the robins have red breasts. The coasts are frequented by hosts of sea-birds. On the southern coasts the albatross may often be seen. There are also gulls of various kinds, divers, and penguins.

13. Including those which inhabit the Australian seas, the **reptile** class numbers about two hundred and fifty species, which vary in size from the crocodile, thirty feet long, to the diminutive frog of an inch, and which differ in their qualities from the edible turtle to the deadly serpent. Fresh-water tortoises, of which seven species are now known to exist, are found in streams and pools in all parts of the country, and are numerous. On the coast four species of turtle have been observed, some of large size, and including the green turtle, so dear to epicures; the hawk-bill, which yields "tortoise" shell; and the leathery turtle, from which oil is obtained.

Lizards are still more abundant, and most of them are peculiar to Australia. Pre-eminent among them for size and voracity are the crocodiles, of which two kinds are known to inhabit the northern territory. One grows to the length of thirty feet, and is destructive to domestic animals and dangerous to man; the other is smaller. The next tribe, the monitors, is known under the name of "lace-lizards" and "iguanas." Some of these have been seen eight feet in length, and their flesh is reputed to be extremely palatable. Some of the lizards closely resemble snakes, for which, at a hurried glance, they are often mistaken. Certain species, locally termed "stump-tails," are covered with large rough scales, and bear the appearance of having the ends of their tails chopped off. Nocturnal lizards, the geckos, are common. Their feet being furnished with discs or suckers, they are able to creep up walls, and are not unfrequently found in dwellings, where their unpleasant appearance and supposed power of mischief make them unwelcome visitors. Others deserving of special mention are the water-lizard, which is amphibious and attains a length of three or four feet; the frilled-lizard, which has round its neck a loose skin capable of being erected at pleasure into a stiff frill; and the *moloch*, perhaps the strangest-looking creature of all that inhabit Australia. Its repulsive appearance is mainly due to the strong, sharp spines and scaly protuberances with which it is irregularly covered from head to tail. It is, nevertheless, perfectly harmless and inoffensive. Its movements are sluggish, and it possesses the power of changing colour like the chameleon. It is found in South and Western Australia only. Lizards seem to have abounded in Australia in former ages, for bones of many species have been obtained from the Wellington Caves, and teeth of large crocodiles were found on the Darling Downs. A skeleton, nearly complete, of the lizard named Plesiosaurus was discovered in Northern Queensland.

Of the snake family about sixty species are known to inhabit Australia and Tasmania. Two-thirds of these are venomous, but only five are dangerous to man; none, however, are so deadly as the Indian cobra or the American rattlesnake. To the family of pythons or rock-snakes belong the diamond and carpet snakes, which are common throughout the continent except its most southern portions, and also four other species which are restricted to the warmest districts. These are not venomous, but kill their prey by constriction. The tree snakes, usually long and slender, are also harmless. The most deadly of all are, the brown-banded snake, and another named the broad-scaled snake, which are distributed over the whole continent and Tasmania. The black snake and the brown snake, which are so named from their respective colours, are also, when of large size, highly dangerous. Less deadly, though very venomous, is the death or deaf adder, which approaches in its structure the viper family. It is, compared to other snakes, short and stout, and its movements are sluggish. As a rule all snakes are anxious to avoid mankind; and when a person has been bitten, it would be found on inquiry that he had either trodden upon the snake or driven it into a position from which it could escape only by taking the offensive. This is particularly liable to happen with the death adder, which lies in wait for its prey by roads and paths which, being partially overgrown with grass, conceal the reptile from the view of the passer-by. Snakes are more irritable, however, and more disposed to attack human beings when they first rise from their winter sleep and during the pairing season, which is usually about the month of February. Fifteen species of venomous sea-snakes have been observed in the Australian seas, and occasionally specimens are found on the shores, upon which they are cast during storms. Notwithstanding the danger of being bitten—a danger, it should be remarked, which is extremely small to an observant person—it is questionable whether the benefits conferred by snakes do not outweigh the injuries they inflict. Their office is evidently to keep down the numbers of rats, mice, and small marsupial animals, which, if allowed to multiply without check, would in a few years become a plague.

Frogs constitute the next order of reptiles. About forty species are known to inhabit the parts of Australia which are settled or which have been thoroughly explored. Pools, marshes, and swampy places are the usual habitat of frogs, though they sometimes wander to considerable distances from water. Some of them are prettily marked, but as a rule their colours are dull and, especially in the case of the tree-frogs, changeable. One of the frogs, of a bright green colour, has a deep, strong voice; and as it is fond of climbing up to the rafters of houses, its loud croak is certain to be heard by the inhabitants. It is the largest of all the Australian frogs.

14. The class of **fishes** is well represented in the Australian seas: fresh-water fishes are less plentiful. So great is the number of species that it will be possible to mention those only which are remarkable for some peculiarity of structure or which are of value as food. Among the fresh-water fishes the first place must be assigned to a species of perch, oddly named by the colonists the "Murray cod," having first been observed in that river, though it is found in others. Specimens weighing eighty pounds have been captured. The cod is highly esteemed as an article of food. Eels, sometimes of great size, also inhabit the Australian rivers and fresh-water pools. In the northern rivers a very remarkable fish, the Ceratodus, is found. It belongs to a genus allied to one which flourished in distant ages, but which seemed to have become extinct. This fish, with others belonging to the same class, forms a link between fishes and frogs. Of the multitudes of salt-water fishes those principally used for food are the schnapper, whiting, bream, mullet, and gar-fish. Others deserving of notice are the sharks, of which

about twenty species infest the Australian seas, some individuals attaining a length of twelve feet. One species possesses a saw, its upper jaws or beak being lengthened and armed on each side with teeth.

15. Besides the fishes there are **other marine animals** which may be noticed here. Whales and their congeners, though less common than in former years, are still frequently to be met with near the coast; and seals not only visit the shore but occasionally ascend the rivers, especially in times of flood. Three species have been found on the coasts. That peculiar animal, the dugong, frequents the north-east coasts. Though a warm-blooded mammal, and allied to the whale, it differs from the latter in some important particulars. Its usual length is about twelve feet; its food consists of sea-weeds, and its flesh is said to be very palatable. The dugong is noted for attachment to its young. Of the smaller animals the cray-fish, commonly called the lobster, is considered a choice article of food. Another species of less size inhabits the fresh-water streams, pools, and lagoons. Oysters are abundant, and are of great value; the pearl oyster is equally plentiful in the shallow sea on the north about Cape York, where also the trepang abounds. Shrimps or prawns are found in the estuaries of rivers, and are extensively caught and sent to market.

16. **Insects** and other small creatures, popularly classed with them, exist in great numbers. Spiders of various kinds, some of which excavate dwellings in the ground and close them with trap-doors, are numerous. Others weave strong tough webs that would embarrass even small birds; and the so-called tarantula, a huge hairy creature, which, when full-grown, would cover a saucer, inflicts a serious bite with its venomous fangs. Equally noxious is the centipede, which has been known to attain the length of eighteen inches, and the scorpion which stings viciously with its tail. Compared with other countries in similar latitudes the butterflies cannot be deemed numerous or brilliantly coloured, but some of the moths are of large size. The beetle family is much more abundantly represented; and the species, both large and small, peculiar in form and striking in colour, are remarkable not less for their variety than for the number of the individuals comprised in each. As in other

countries so here members of this family make themselves conspicuous by the ravages they commit among trees. Equally abundant are the grasshoppers, one species of which is at times found in some of the interior plains congregated in such numbers as to remind the observer of the clouds of locusts that ravage certain parts of Asia and Africa. The grasshoppers, however, do not fly; they take flying leaps. They are exceedingly destructive to vegetation when gathered in large swarms. The cicadas, or tree-hoppers, are called locusts in the colonies, although they do not resemble the latter insects either in appearance or habits; they are remarkable chiefly for the noise they make. Bees are indigenous to Australia; they are smaller than the European bee, and the honey they make differs greatly from that produced by the latter. In the warmer districts mosquitoes abound and torment man and beast as is the wont of the tribe; and flies of various kinds are almost as troublesome by day as the mosquitoes at night. Fire-flies may be observed also in the hotter regions, especially in "brushy" spots near the banks of streams. A small beetle also shines with a phosphorescent light. Australian ants are universally distributed. No spot seems to be free of their presence. Some species affect damp localities; but the larger number frequent dry and arid places; some are solitary, but most live in communities. They vary in size from more than an inch to less than a line, and the larger species—"soldiers" and "bull-dogs," as the children term them—are armed with a sting more formidable than that of the wasp or bee. The so-called white ants are also widely distributed. They subsist upon decaying wood, and are very destructive to the timber of houses if they once effect an entrance. Their own dwellings, composed of particles of clay moistened with a liquid secreted by themselves and hardened in drying into a cement, are occasionally eight feet in height. Among the curiosities of insect life may be mentioned the "walking leaf," which so exactly resembles the leaf of a tree that it is difficult to discriminate between them except upon close inspection. Even more deceptive are the "walking sticks," which resemble dry twigs of various sizes broken off from a shrub. Some are twelve inches in length.

17. Turning now to the **native man**, we find the whole

Australian continent inhabited by one race, of which the main features, bodily and mental, are remarkably constant throughout. In the extreme north some infusion of Papuan blood may have taken place; but, if such be the case, the intermixture has produced so slight a result as not to modify the general character of the race in any perceptible degree.

Widely differing accounts have been given by writers as

Australian Aboriginals.

to the qualities of the Australian aborigines. By one class they are described as the lowest and most degraded of the human family, neither well-made nor robust in body, and with mental capacity but little above that of the more intelligent brutes; while by others they are credited with bodily and intellectual powers of a high order. Neither of these representations is altogether correct. In some respects the intelligence of the native man is high, especially in matters which appeal to the perceptive powers; but in all that concerns thought or abstract ideas he is woefully deficient. It would be unfair, however, to judge of the character of the race from the remnants of the tribes that are to be found in the settled districts, where they are corrupted by intercourse with the white man, weakened by diseases he has introduced, and degraded by intemperance.

When the country was first discovered the people were undoubtedly a much finer race than their descendants. Allowing for such differences as would, among any people, result from variation in the quantity and quality of food, and the influences of climate, the same description will apply to the aborigines in all parts of the continent. In stature the men were at least equal to the average of Europeans, and some tribes exceeded that limit. Their colour was a sooty brown, differing widely from the jet black of the African negro, and individuals were not unfrequently met with of a dark chocolate. These variations in hue are probably analogous to the differences of complexion among the white races, and do not indicate any essential distinction between such individuals and the race generally. With regard to muscular development they were robust, though formed more for activity than great strength or endurance, had deep chests, and were well proportioned except that their lower limbs were thin and the legs well-nigh destitute of calf. The head was large, with a broad, projecting forehead, from beneath which their bright dark eyes looked out with a steady but piercing and fearless gaze. The nose was in general broad, especially at the nostrils; the mouth wide and garnished with strong, white teeth. Their carriage was upright, their gait easy and graceful, and their demeanour bold and unembarrassed.

It is more difficult to describe their mental qualities. Their sight was keen; they were good marksmen, and able to secure their quarry when hunting with weapons which would be useless to a white man. They could track a man or other animal by indications which to a civilized European would be simply non-existent; and in short, in all matters requiring the exercise of the perceptive powers, they were surpassed by no people upon the face of the earth. In the higher qualities of judgment and reasoning, however, they appeared to be mere children. These contradictions are forcibly exemplified in their languages, which, though possessing the same structure throughout, totally differed in their several vocabularies, so that adjoining tribes were mutually unintelligible. These languages abound in expressions for denoting physical actions, and even minute variations in such actions, and for naming physical objects; but in none of them have words been discovered expressive of such notions as we understand by the words "God," "right," "love," or "five." As with other savages, the better qualities of their moral nature were displayed only to members of their own tribe; with all others their usual condition was one of war and violence. They seem to have respected the rights of property, of which their wives formed the most important part; but their power of self-restraint being small, even their low standard of right was not always regarded. Towards male children parental affection was, in general, strongly manifested; but the women were treated with the utmost brutality—by those tribes, at anyrate, that had come into contact with the whites. As regards religion, it is now believed that they had no idea of God or a future state, though they had some superstitious notions by which many of their customs and practices were regulated.

It has been mentioned already that there were no indigenous roots, seeds, or fruits capable of affording sustenance even to moderate numbers of people, and that the aborigines were therefore compelled to live chiefly upon animal food, which was comparatively abundant. But as game naturally became scarce after a time in the neighbourhood of a "camp" of the blacks, they were compelled to shift their quarters frequently. It was, therefore, useless to construct dwellings of a permanent character; and those of a temporary nature consisted of "gunyahs," composed of branches and boughs, and better adapted to afford shade from the sun than shelter from bad weather. Often a single piece of bark stripped from a tree was made to answer this purpose; and in summer time even this slight protection was dispensed with. The climate in general being so genial clothing was deemed superfluous, though in winter, in the colder districts, "cloaks" or mantles of opossum skins were worn. In preparing their food they knew of but one method.

The game was simply thrown upon the fire for a few minutes, and then devoured half-raw. They had consequently no need for vessels of any kind, and the potter's art was entirely unknown to them. The women made nets or bags for carrying the few articles they valued, while the men made weapons to be employed in their only occupations, hunting and war. Spears were used for both purposes, and the aborigines showed great dexterity in throwing them, having recourse at times to the aid of the "throwing-stick," by which they were enabled to impel their weapons with greater force and velocity. Clubs formed out of solid heavy timber, such as iron-bark, and carefully polished, were used for combat at close quarters. But the most singular of the native weapons was the *boomerang*—a flat curved stick which possessed the curious property of returning to the thrower if hurled through the air in the proper manner. Aboriginal conflicts were seldom of a fatal character, native warriors being so quick of sight and so expert by training that they received the spears of their enemies on their shields, while their skulls were so hard that even terrible blows from the club failed to produce a serious result. Should a wound be inflicted, their simple surgery generally effected a cure even in severe cases. Disease was uncommon, and when it occurred was attributed to the malign action of an evil spirit or of a member of some other tribe.

Their food consisted chiefly of the marsupial animals they were able to capture, the opossum being the commonest article of diet. On the coast and near the rivers fish was largely used. But in point of fact no living creature was too repulsive for their appetites; snakes, lizards, tortoises, frogs—all were welcome; and even insects were not rejected. A large white grub found in certain trees was considered a dainty morsel. Usually there was abundance of food of this kind, and it was eked out in particular localities with seeds and roots —which, however, afforded but little nourishment. In one district in Queensland, where the bunya-bunya pine abounded, the aborigines assembled periodically to feast upon the seeds produced in its cones; and so important was the harvest considered that various tribes congregated at the spot to secure their shares of the provision thus supplied.

No reliable estimate can be formed of the number of aboriginals even in the districts that are known. It is certain, however, that the number is rapidly diminishing, and that the race will at no distant period become extinct. A little reflection will show that the native Australians, debarred from communication with the rest of mankind, possessing no cultivable plant, and supplied with no domestic animals fit for human food, could only subsist as a race of rude hunters, and that all the circumstances which assist a nation to advance in civilization were absent in their case.

By some writers the Australian aborigines have been accused of cannibalism, but the charge has not been supported by sufficient evidence. The practice was certainly not general, and in this respect they were superior to the inhabitants of neighbouring countries more advanced in civilization. If an occasional case of cannibalism occurred it would, if thoroughly inquired into, probably be found to originate in famine, when the black man would lose self-restraint, as even Europeans have been known to do in similar circumstances.[1]

18. Such is the brief description of Australia. All the facts in the physical history of the country tend to prove that during many ages it was completely isolated from the rest of the globe, forming, as it were, a little world of itself. Notwithstanding the variety and abundance of its natural products, it was strangely deficient in the food-plants and animals common in other parts of the world, by the help of which other races of men have raised themselves in the scale of civilization. Its luxuriant pastures sustained no herds of cattle: its grassy uplands fed no flocks of wool-bearing sheep; and its fertile tracts no grain that was worthy of culture; and were it otherwise, there was no horse to draw the plough. Moreover, the race in possession of the land were incapable, under the circumstances in which they were placed, of making any effectual effort for their own improvement, and of turning to profitable account the natural advantages by which they were surrounded. The country waited, as it were, for the appearance of civilized

---

[1] We have spoken of the Australians in the past tense, since in the settled parts they are no longer found living in their natural state; of those living in the less known parts the description will still in the main hold good.

man upon its shores, with the plants and animals, as well as the implements, by means of which its vast resources might be developed. Less than a hundred years ago the desired arrival of a higher race took place. What the results of the entrance of that race into the country have been thus far it will be the aim of the succeeding pages to describe.

CHAPTER IV.

THE COLONY OF NEW SOUTH WALES.

1. Boundaries and extent. 2. Coast-line and Harbours. 3. Surface. 4. Mountains. 5. Table-lands. 6. Plains. 7. Drainage. 8. Rivers of eastern slope. 9. Rivers of western slope. 10. Lakes. 11. Climate. 12. Soil. 13. Internal communication; Roads. 14. Railways and Telegraphs. 15. Navigable Rivers. 16. Population. 17. Industrial Occupations; Agriculture and Pasturage. 18. Mining. 19. Manufactures. 20. Commerce. 21. Government. 22. Religion and Education. 23. Territorial Divisions. 24. Growth of Towns. 25. Sydney. 26. Other Towns.

1. Originally, **New South Wales** comprehended the whole of that part of the Australian continent which stretches from the Pacific Ocean on the east to the 129th meridian of east longitude on the west, and from the Timor Sea and Indian Ocean on the north to the Great Southern Ocean on the south. In 1834, however, the colony of South Australia was established, its boundaries being then fixed at the 141st meridian on the east and the 132d on the west. When, in 1850, the Port Philip district was constituted a separate colony, under the name of Victoria, a further severance of territory took place, and New South Wales lost the whole of its southern coast-line. A still further reduction in its area was effected on the separation of Queensland in 1859. At present, therefore, the **boundaries** of New South Wales are—*East*, the Pacific Ocean; *west*, South Australia, the 141st meridian being the line of demarcation; *north*, the 29th parallel of south latitude, the Dumaresq River, and Macpherson's Range, which separate it from Queensland; and *south*, the River Murray, and a straight line 110 miles in length from the head-waters of that stream to Cape Howe, by which the colony is divided from Victoria. In form this colony resembles an irregular four-sided figure, of which the extreme length is 900 miles and the greatest breadth 850 miles, while the average length and breadth are each 500 miles. Its area in round numbers is 325,000 square miles.

2. No large **indentations** and no conspicuous projections mark the coast-line of the colony. There are, however, numerous bays and inlets of no great size, the largest of which is **Jervis Bay**, in latitude 35° S. In fact, the whole of the coast

may be said to consist of a succession of bold and rocky headlands, with bays between them, margined with sandy beaches.

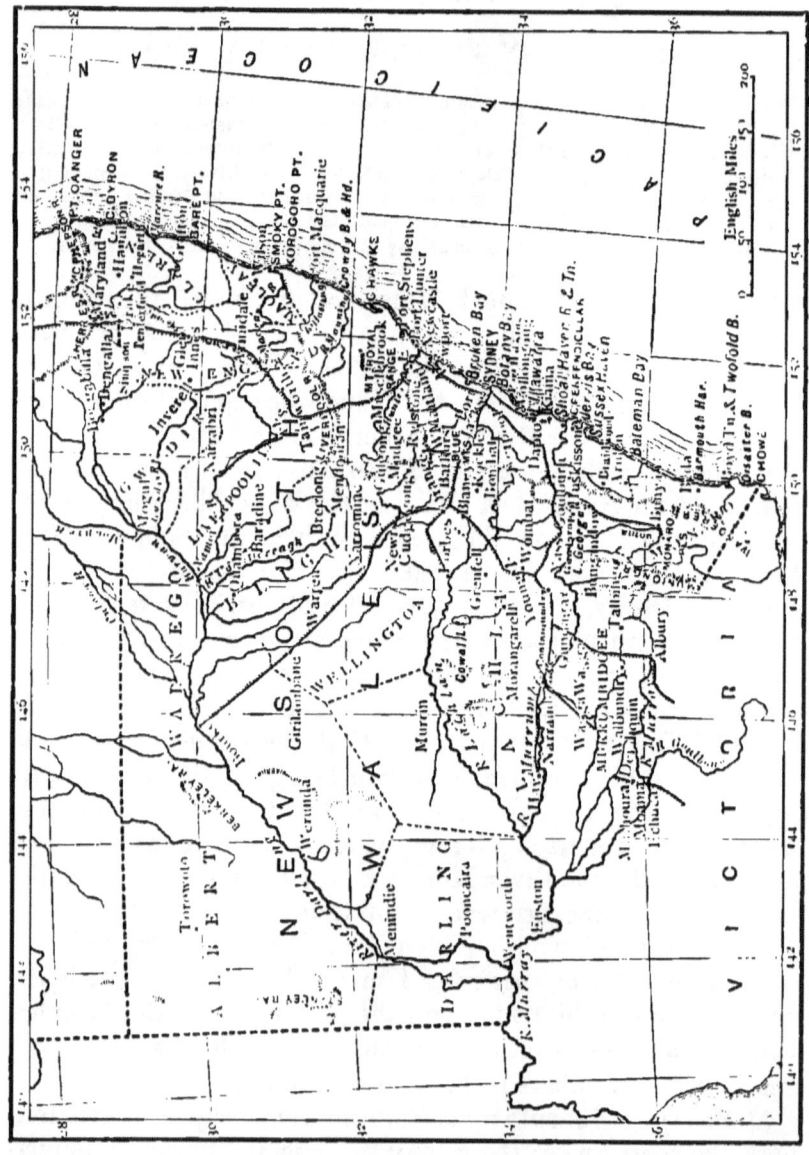

Cape Byron is remarkable as the most easterly point of the continent, **St. George's Head** for its prominence, **Green Cape**

for a similar reason, and **Cape Howe** as the southern extremity of the colony. Few natural harbours exist on the coast, and, with the exception of **Port Jackson**, all are so inclosed with mountainous or unproductive country, as to be practically of little value. Such for example are Port Stephens, Broken Bay, and Twofold Bay, harbours that could hardly be surpassed for the convenience of shipping, but difficult of access from the landward side for the transport of produce from the richer districts.

Coast Scenery.

On the other hand the estuaries of some of the rivers, though for the most part obstructed by sand-bars, and sometimes difficult and even dangerous to enter, form convenient outlets for the products of rich and extensive districts. The most important of these are the estuaries of the Clarence, M'Leay, Hunter, Manning, and Shoalhaven. **Sydney Harbour** or Port Jackson is not only the finest in Australia, but is surpassed by few in the whole world. **Botany Bay** is a name associated with the beginning of the colonial history.

3. As regards **surface** New South Wales, as might be expected in a country of such wide extent, is greatly diversified.

Rugged mountains and fertile valleys, gentle slopes and steep acclivities, elevated table-lands and low-lying plains, distinguish various portions of its area; and while some of these features are on so large a scale as to convey to the beholder the impression of monotony, yet, on the other hand, the elements of the picturesque in scenery are generally abundant. This is especially the case with the eastern portion of the country, the western being characterized by little variety. It is usual to consider the surface of New South Wales as formed of three distinct portions—the Coast District, the Table-lands, surmounted by the loftiest mountains of the colony, and the Plains. The two latter will be separately described; the former, a narrow strip lying along the coast, consists of undulating and generally fertile country crossed at intervals by mountain ridges, between which are river valleys of greater or less extent.

4. The **mountains** of New South Wales belong chiefly to the **Dividing Chain** of eastern Australia, which traverses the whole of New South Wales from north to south, and sends off its lateral branches to the east and west. From the sea to the foot of this chain is a space of about twenty miles on an average; but the distance from the shore to the actual division of the waters may be estimated at forty miles, though in one portion it reaches one hundred miles. Different portions of the chain are distinctly named. The most northern is the **New England Range**, with **Ben Lomond** 5000 feet high as its culminating point. Next follows the **Liverpool Range,** running east and west, which rises in **Oxley's Peak** to the height of 4500 feet. These two portions consist mainly of granite and trappean rocks; but in the **Blue Mountains**, which come next in order, the eastern slope is composed of sandstone lying in horizontal strata, but rent and cleft into vast chasms and narrow ravines, shut in with perpendicular walls of rock of great height. In the limestone rocks, lying on the western edge of this range, extensive caverns have been discovered, which, as objects of public interest, are cared for by the government. Passing over some parts of the chain which are of lower elevation, we next note the **Gourock Range** (35° to 36° S. lat.), a wild and confused mountain tract of great elevation, which, in Mount Jin-

dulian, reaches the height of 4300 feet. That portion of the chain which, south of the 36th parallel, turns in a north-west direction, is named the **Manero Range**, and in many points exceeds 4000 feet in altitude. The last and highest portion of the chain is called the **Muniong Range**, such being the aboriginal name for the highest peak, which, however, is more generally known as **Mount Kosciusko**. The height of this mountain is 7308 feet, that being Dr. Clarke's measurement of the peak he ascended; but since the date of his visit it has been affirmed that another peak is still higher. Although below the line of perpetual snow, which in this latitude is about 8000 feet, snow and ice may be found all the year round in hollows of the mountain sheltered from the sun.

Offsets from the main chain are numerous, and some of them important. For example, the most northern, which runs easterly to the Pacific at Point Danger, and is known as **Macpherson's Range**, forms the boundary in this part between New South Wales and Queensland. Its highest summit, **Mount Lindsay**, attains an elevation of 5700 feet. Omitting some smaller spurs, the **Mount Royal Range** (lat. 32°) and the **Hunter Range** (lat. 33°) may next be noticed. Together with the Dividing Chain they inclose the valley of the Hunter River. From the west side of the chain branch out the **Nandewar** and **Warrambungle Ranges**, which are nearly parallel, and bound, the former on the north and the latter on the south, the broad expanse of the Liverpool Plains. The **Macquarie Range**, originating in lat. 34°, runs in a similar direction, and includes the peaks called the Canobolas, said to be 4600 feet in height. Between the main chain and the sea, in certain portions, there are secondary ranges which, while inferior in elevation to the principal chain, contain peaks of great elevation. The northern of these Coast Ranges, as they are called, culminates in **Mount Seaview** (about 31° 30′ S.), which attains an elevation of 6000 feet. In the southern Coast Range are **Mount Budawang**, 3800 feet, and **Coolungabbera**, 3712 feet in height. Near the western limit of the colony lie several ranges apparently forming portions of a mountain system, and known as the **Barrier Ranges** and the **Grey Range**. These are believed to rise to the height of 3000 feet. Besides the mountains already mentioned there are many others which cannot be connected with any distinct range.

5. From the Coast District the country rises abruptly to the height of between two and three thousand feet, spreading out into broad **table-lands,** and extending for some distance to the westward of the Dividing Chain, where, by a gradual descent, they sink down into the level plains of the interior. On the seaward side, and especially where flanked by the Coast Ranges, the descent is steep and often precipitous; and in the earliest period of settlement, the barrier interposed by the perpendicular rocks which form the eastern edge of the table-land prevented the colonists from penetrating to the interior for a quarter of a century. The average height of the table-land may be estimated at 2500 feet, though some portions exceed 3000 feet in elevation. The surface is generally undulating, covered to a large extent by the kind of forest before described as woodland, but in parts consisting of grassy downs lightly timbered or altogether bare of trees and shrubs. These open downs are commonly called "plains" by the colonists, who, in the naming of geographical features, are frequently unmindful of the precise meanings of the terms they employ. Where the correct term has been applied it is sometimes displaced by a popular but inexact designation, as in the case of the Brisbane *Downs*, which occupy the southern portion of the table-land, but are now universally known as the Manero *Plains*. The valley of the Hunter River divides the table-land into two parts—the northern, which extends into Queensland; and the southern, which is continued in Victoria. With the exception of the Liverpool Range, the Dividing Chain traverses the whole of the two table-lands, and its spurs help to vary the somewhat monotonous aspect of this elevated portion of the country. In places igneous rocks appear on the surface, and decomposing have formed very fertile soil well fitted for agricultural purposes; but in general these districts are better adapted for pasturage. Excepting coal, useful minerals are abundant, and the gold obtained in the country has been found on the table-lands and on the slopes of the Dividing Chain.

6. From the foot of the table-land on the west the country may be described as a dead level as far as the Barrier Ranges

on the extreme west, but dotted here and there with granite hills and with ranges of low elevation. The general fall of the land in these plains is towards the south-west, but so slight is the slope that the beds of some of the rivers deviate from an absolute level by less than six inches per mile on the average. One consequence of this flatness is, that after long-continued heavy rain the channels of the rivers are insufficient to carry off the water, which consequently inundates the neighbouring country for considerable distances, and converts it, for the time being, into a vast but shallow lake. Immense tracts in these plains are composed of rich black earth of great fertility. In fact the accounts sometimes given of its productiveness border upon the marvellous. Grass and herbage, it is said, attain a height of ten or twelve feet, and their nutritive qualities are so great that cattle feeding upon them fatten in a very short time. Interspersed among the tracts of black soil are sandy ridges, sometimes covered with "pine" or "mulga" scrub, but often producing the valuable shrub known as "salt-bush," of which both cattle and sheep are extremely fond. These plains are pre-eminently the pastoral region of the colony, and support many millions of sheep and cattle, besides horses. Their only drawback is the scarcity of water, the rainfall being but twenty inches per annum, much of which is absorbed by the thirsty ground, and no inconsiderable portion is also lost by evaporation. Of late years, however, much has been done to remove this disadvantage by the construction of dams and by sinking wells; and many blocks of land, formerly regarded as practically useless, are now converted into valuable holdings for pastoral purposes. There are some tracts, however, especially in the extreme western portion of the colony, which are so arid and consist of such sterile soil that they may be considered as little better than deserts.

7. From the Dividing Chain the land slopes, generally speaking, to the eastward and westward, and the **rivers** run in the corresponding directions. There are some notable exceptions to this general statement, however. On the east of the Dividing Chain some of the principal river-valleys lie between that watershed and the Coast Ranges, and the rivers which drain them run in a direction parallel to that of the mountains

for portions of their courses. It thus happens that rivers, the sources of which are barely thirty miles from the sea in a straight line, have courses hundreds of miles in length. West of the Dividing Chain the ultimate slope of the land is to the south-west. The courses of all the principal streams are at first northerly, then north-west, and finally south-west. They consequently describe large curves, which, while adding largely to their length, enable them to water a greater extent of country than would be possible with courses more direct. In the extreme south of the table-land the drainage is toward Bass Strait and the Southern Ocean, in consequence of the Dividing Chain in that portion of its length taking a direction from south-east to north-west. In one small district of the southern table-land the streams empty themselves into Lake George, the only distinct example of inland drainage in the country. The fall on the east side of the Dividing Chain being rapid, the rivers in the upper parts of their courses flow swiftly. Lower, where the influence of the tides is felt, the current is slow; and the body of water poured into the sea being in ordinary seasons inconsiderable, the opposition of the tide results in the deposition of great quantities of sand, which forming bars greatly impedes navigation. In like manner the fall on the west of the Dividing Chain is at first rapid, but as the rivers reach the plains their currents become sluggish and frequently cease altogether.

8. Omitting the smaller streams, the principal rivers draining the coast district have certain characteristics in common. They rise in the Dividing Chain or on the table-land, flow rapidly down the declivity, and in the lower portion of their courses are filled with salt-water, and rise and fall with the tide. Their valleys in this part of their courses are wide and flat, and composed of rich alluvial soil. Commencing on the north, the first river of importance is the **Richmond**, which flows through a very fertile district, but is obstructed by a sand-bank at its mouth. Farther south is the **Clarence**, a fine stream, 240 miles in length, which drains a considerable portion of the northern table-land, as well as a large area of the coast district. A large proportion of the land in its lower basin consists of excellent soil, and notwithstanding the bar at its mouth,

the river is navigable for about 50 miles by sea-going steamers. The **M'Leay** resembles the Clarence in many respects, but is shorter, and drains a less extensive basin of 4800 square miles. The Hastings and Manning are still smaller, though the latter is navigable for small vessels. One of the most important rivers of New South Wales, and even of Australia, is the

A River View.

Hunter, 300 miles in length, and draining an area of about 8000 square miles. It has numerous important tributaries, is a tidal river in the lower part of its course, and navigable by sea-going steamers to a distance of 35 miles from its mouth. About 50 miles south of the estuary of the Hunter River is Broken Bay, forming the mouth of the **Hawkesbury**, which, rising in the Cullarin Range, about lat. 35° S., flows northward for nearly 300 miles, and then makes a sudden bend to the east. Tributaries flow into it from all directions, and the area drained by it is not less than 8000 square miles. At its mouth is an extensive bay which forms an excellent harbour; vessels of moderate size may be taken as far as Windsor, 140 miles from the sea. Like the Hawkesbury, the **Shoalhaven** flows first northward, and then bends suddenly to the eastward, entering the sea a little to the northward of Jervis Bay. It drains about 3300 square miles, and is navigable for a short distance only. The Clyde, though short and draining little more than 450 miles of country, is important from the fact that it is navigable for some distance and has a good harbour near its mouth. Passing the Moruya, the Tuross, the Bega, and other smaller streams, we reach the **Towamba**, which flows into Twofold Bay, a splendid harbour capable of berthing a whole fleet of ships. The **Snowy River** in the extreme south rises in the Muniong Range, and after a circuitous course of 240 miles through mountainous country, enters the colony of Victoria.

9. It may be said that the whole of the western slope is drained by the river **Darling** and its affluents. Most of these have their sources in the Great Dividing Chain of New South Wales, but the main stream itself rises farther north in Queensland, and will again be noticed in the account of that colony. Under the name of the **Barwan** it enters New South Wales at the 29th parallel of south latitude, and about 149° E. longitude. In its course towards the south-west it receives in succession the Macintyre, Gwydir, Namoi, Castlereagh, and Macquarie, from the eastward; and is joined by the Culgoa and its connected streams from the westward. The next of its feeders are the Bogan on the left bank and the Warrego on the right. From the junction of the latter it receives no tributary on either bank, until joined by the **Murray** a little south of the 34th parallel and near the 142d meridian. Here its volume is increased by the collected waters of another series of important streams which drain the southern portion of the western slope, which empty themselves into the Murray, and of which the **Lachlan** and **Murrumbidgee** are the most important. From the point of junction with the Murray the stream continues to bear this name; though, having regard to its length and the area of its basin, the river, from a geographical point of view, must be considered to be the Darling. From its most distant sources to the sea the course of the Darling is 3200 miles in

length, and that portion of it which lies within the territory of New South Wales is at least 1850 miles long. Its navigable length in favourable seasons is 2345 miles. Excluding the area drained by the Murray and its affluents, the basin of the Darling extends over about 300,000 square miles. It is on these grounds entitled to rank as one of the great rivers of the world. Even with the limited rainfall on the plains and western slope, the volume of the Darling ought to be much greater than it is; for if the river carried to the sea but a trifling proportion of the water deposited in its basin, the existing channel would be far too small. In point of fact, however, the Darling sometimes ceases to flow entirely, and it becomes but a succession of pools. This comparatively insignificant volume in proportion to the area drained and the rainfall therein, arises mainly from the soakage which takes place in the porous soil of the plains; and the water, instead of being carried off to the sea, is stored in an underground reservoir, which only needs to be tapped to yield an abundant supply.

West of the Darling the tributaries can be considered such in name only, for, excepting during the highest floods, their waters never reach the main stream. The immense block of country lying between the Bogan, Darling, and Lachlan is wholly destitute of running streams, and was long regarded as worthless, or fitted for occasional occupation only during the most favourable seasons. By the construction of dams, however, and by sinking wells, even this territory has now been rendered useful for pastoral purposes.

The eastern tributaries of the Darling in New South Wales are naturally arranged in four groups. The first of these includes the **Macintyre**, and **Gwydir**, which drain the district bounded north and south by the Herries and Nandewar Ranges respectively, embracing a portion of the table-land and a large stretch of plain country. Next comes the **Namoi**, draining with its tributaries another portion of the table-land, and in its lower course the Liverpool Plains. On the north the basin of this river is closed in by the Nandewar Range, and on the south by the Liverpool Range. This range also forms the northern boundary and watershed of the area drained by the third group, the **Castlereagh, Macquarie**, and **Bogan**.

The southern watershed of this basin is formed, not by a mountain range, but by land which, though of comparatively low elevation, is nevertheless higher than the plains to the north and south. This raised tract throws the waters of its southern slope into the Lachlan, and so bounds on the north the area drained by the fourth group of rivers, the Lachlan, Murrumbidgee, and Murray. The two latter have their sources in the most elevated land of the continent, and being filled by the rains and snows which fall upon the mountains, their volume is larger and the stream of a more lasting description than that of other rivers.

10. For the extent of its territory, the **lakes** of New South Wales are neither numerous nor important. A number of salt-water lakes or lagoons are to be found along the coast. A group of these lies a little to the north of the 32d parallel, and includes **Lake Innes, Queen's Lake,** and **Watson Taylor's Lake,** the entrance being known as Camden Haven. Another group, including **Wallis Lake** and the **Myall Lakes,** lies a little south of the same parallel. Between the mouth of the Hunter River and Broken Bay is **Lake Macquarie,** which may be grouped with the **Tuggerah Lake** still further south. Lake **Illawarra** lies between 34° and 35° S. lat., and some smaller lagoons occur a little to the southward of the 35th parallel. Most of these lagoons abound in fish and wild-fowl, and in a few cases the passages connecting them with the sea are navigable. Inland lakes containing fresh water are even fewer in number. The most important is **Lake George** on the south table-land, in lat. 35° S. This lake is twenty miles in length by seven in width, and receives the waters of a small area of inland drainage having no outlet. **Lake Bathurst,** in the same neighbourhood, is of the same character, but smaller. There are upon the table-lands several small lakes, but they do not need special mention. On the plains, near some of the larger rivers, especially the Lachlan and Darling, lakes are formed in wet seasons by the overflow from the augmented streams, but they are shallow, and their waters are rapidly absorbed or evaporated.

11. While the **climate** of New South Wales may be described generally as warm and dry, it differs considerably in various

parts in accordance with the differences of latitude and elevation. Taking the coast district first, it may be stated that the mean temperature of Sydney, which is about midway between the northern and the southern limits of the colony, is 62·6°, while Grafton in the north, and Eden in the south, have a mean temperature of 68° and 60° respectively. Of course, the temperature during the summer months is higher, and on a few extraordinary occasions may rise as high as 106° in the shade, but such instances are extremely rare. On the other hand, during the winter months, the temperature sometimes falls to 40°. As regards humidity, the average rainfall at Sydney is fifty inches annually; at Eden it is forty-five, and at the Tweed River seventy inches. While this must be considered an abundant supply, it must also be noted that the rainfall is unevenly distributed throughout the year, one half of the average yearly amount having been known to fall in a single month. Strange to say, in the corresponding month of another year the whole amount of rain that fell was less than one-tenth of an inch. From the former of these two facts the inference is plain that the rainfall is at times exceedingly heavy, in fact tropical in its character; and from the steepness of the slope of the watershed, floods are liable to occur at such periods. Most of the rains in this district are brought up by winds from the southward and eastward, which largely prevail in summer. During that season the sea-breeze, blowing between north-east and south-east, is felt daily, and helps to modify the temperature otherwise to be expected. Occasionally the sea-breeze is interrupted by a hot wind from the north-west, which raises the temperature, and from its exceeding dryness greatly injures vegetation. Generally this is followed by a cold breeze from the southward, to be in its turn succeeded by the sea-breeze. The prevailing wind in winter is westerly, and much rain is sometimes found to fall while the wind is between west and south. Off the coast the winds are usually moderate, though at intervals violent storms, of the nature of cyclones, occur, in most cases about the time of the equinoxes.

On the table-lands the temperature is lower, ranging according to latitude from 57° to 52° as the mean of the whole year; and the rainfall averages about thirty inches. Westerly winds are the most common, and in winter produce the sensation of great cold; but, except during the night, the thermometer rarely falls below the freezing-point. Snow is not uncommon, and under favourable circumstances may remain a day or two upon the ground, though it more frequently melts in a few hours. Higher temperature, drier atmosphere, and less wind are the characteristics of the climate of the plains. Here the thermometer not unfrequently registers 110° in the shade during the summer months, but the mean maximum temperature at that period may be estimated at 96°. On the other hand, during the winter the average of greatest cold is about 37°, and the mean temperature for the whole year is 64°. The average rainfall may be estimated at twenty inches, though in exceptionally dry years this amount is reduced to ten inches. The prevailing winds are westerly, but they usually blow with little force.

One of the most remarkable characteristics of the climate of New South Wales, as it is, indeed, of Australia generally, is the abundance of sunshine. The "gray days" so frequent in northern countries are almost unknown here; clouds seldom obscure the sky except when they bring rain; and when that has ceased to fall, the clouds disappear and the sun shines forth with undimmed brilliancy. There can be no question as to the healthiness of the climate of this colony. Where not prevented by injudicious habits of life, neglect of ordinary sanitary precautions, or unwholesome practices, the influence of the climate is highly favourable to mental and bodily vigour and conducive to long life. Nor is it less suitable to domestic animals. Horses, cattle, and sheep thrive and multiply, and appear to be exempt from the epidemics which in Europe sometimes carry off thousands in a few weeks.

12. In a country of such wide extent it is to be expected that soils of varying qualities are to be met with in different districts; and while much of an inferior character may be found, as on the Blue Mountains, yet, speaking generally, the worst will be found to afford pasture for sheep, and is therefore not altogether useless. In fact, in many parts the mountains are grassed to their very summits. For a large proportion of the

whole area of the colony the soil may be described as suitable for pasturage, but not fitted for agricultural purposes. On the banks of the rivers and smaller streams deposits of rich alluvial soil are to be found, frequently of great depth, and of extraordinary fertility. This is especially the case with the coast rivers, where the extent of the alluvial soil is largest, and where it is replenished by the occasional floods which leave after them a fresh deposit by which the ground is again fertilized, as the Egyptian delta is by the overflow of the Nile. Portions of the coast district and of the table-lands also contain rich soil, produced by the decomposition of trap, basalt, and other volcanic rocks, and suited for the cultivation of grain. The soil of the plains consists of alternate patches of light sandy soil, which at times becomes little better than pure sand, and of a rich black loam of a fertility, when well supplied with moisture, which is almost incredible. Up to the present the want of a sufficient supply of water has checked any systematic attempt at cultivation on these "black soil" plains, which are now used only for pastoral purposes. In their natural state the alluvial soils of the coast district are covered with dense vegetation, which forms what we have formerly described as "brushes," and which requires to be "cleared" before the land is available for cultivation. The black soil plains, on the other hand, are usually destitute of trees, or dotted with clusters of the elegant myall and a few others.

13. One of the most necessary tasks in a new country is the establishment of the **means of communication** between one settlement and another. At first the **roads** of the colony were simple tracks; and so long as the weather was dry, and the traffic light, these fully answered the purpose. But as population increased, and produce had to be brought to market, the need for properly-formed roads became urgent. After the country west of the Blue Mountains had been opened up by explorers, and settlement therein had commenced, the construction of a road across that formidable barrier became a question of great moment with the colonists, and the engineering skill and resources available at the time were taxed to the uttermost to carry out the work. Common roads, more than 30,000 miles in length, have now been constructed in various

directions, but chiefly in three main lines, running north, west, and south from Sydney. From these minor roads branch off in all directions, covering the whole country with a network of highways. In forming these roads hills have been cut through and swamps filled up; in some instances the necessary materials have been brought from long distances, and bridges

Road over Blue Mountains—Victoria Pass.

have been constructed across rivers and creeks. The amount of labour and money expended upon these necessary adjuncts of civilization has been enormous, but the benefits that have accrued have been commensurate with the outlay.

14. Equally great have been the advantages arising from the construction of **railways**, of which about 1800 miles have been completed and opened for traffic. Like the common roads the railroads have been formed on three main lines, each with its branches. The Great Southern Railway connects Sydney with Albury, and, by means of the junction with the Victorian railway system, with Melbourne. It has several

branches. The Great Western Railway connects Sydney with Bourke on the Darling River, and has also several branches. These two great lines will in a short time be connected with the Great Northern Railway, which commences at Newcastle, and runs northward to Queensland, so that travellers will be able to perform the whole journey from Melbourne to Brisbane

A Railway Cutting.

by rail. A large scheme of additional railway extensions has been sanctioned by the legislature, and when carried out will cover the more thickly peopled part of the country with a network of railways that will render internal communication easy and facilitate the interchange of products of different districts. From the description before given of the conformation of the country it will readily be inferred that the construction of roads, whether railroads or common roads, over the mountains and up the eastern fall of the table-land, was a work of great difficulty and expense. Communication by means of the electric telegraph has been extensively established, few places of any note being unsupplied with telegraph stations. The total length of telegraph lines is about 15,000 miles. Telegraphic communication is also maintained with all the Australian colonies, as well as with Europe, Asia, and America. Telephonic communication is largely made use of in Sydney and its vicinity.

15. Communication between the different **ports** of the colony is maintained by steamers and sailing vessels, and most of the coast rivers are navigable for some distance from their mouths. Much of the internal commerce of the colony is carried on by this means. Some of the inland **rivers** are also navigable in favourable seasons. The Murray, for example, is navigable for small steamers and barges for a distance of 1700 miles from its mouth. Its tributary, the Murrumbidgee, is also navigable in the same way for 500 miles of its course. Regarded as the principal stream of which the Murray is an affluent, the Darling is navigable from its mouth in Lake Alexandrina to Walgett, a distance of more than 2300 miles. Although of great importance to the trade of New South Wales and Victoria, this system of water communication is too uncertain to compare with that of some other countries, such as the United States of America, in extent or regularity.

16. Scanty for the size of the country, even when first discovered, the aboriginal **population** has so greatly diminished since settlement commenced that the survivors may be reckoned by hundreds; and it may safely be predicted that, within a short period, the race will become extinct. Excepting these and a small proportion of Chinese, the population of the colony, which may be estimated at 1,000,000, is either European or of European descent. Probably every country of Europe is represented to a greater or less extent; but the great body of the people are of British origin, being either immigrants from the United Kingdom or their descendants. A few have come direct from America, chiefly from the British colonies, but are of the same stock as the majority of the colonists. In old countries females are found to preponderate over the male inhabitants; but the reverse is the case in New South Wales, where males are more numerous than females.

17. **Agriculture**, with its connected occupations, forms the

most important industry of the colony. **Pasturage** supports a large number of people, especially on the western slopes of the table-lands where the finest wool is produced, and on the great interior plains. As evidencing the extent to which pastoral pursuits are carried it may be mentioned that the average number of horses in the colony is about 350,000; of cattle, 3,000,000; and of sheep, 25,000,000. The annual value of the products derived from them is estimated at £7,000,000. Tillage, in which is to be included dairying and the rearing of pigs, also employs a large number of people, especially in the coast district where the principal grain cultivated is maize, other staple crops being sugar-cane and lucerne, which is made into hay. On the table-lands wheat is the crop most largely grown, and next to that oats, of which hay is made. In both districts dairying is carried on to a large extent, milk being sent to supply the metropolis, and butter and cheese being made for the same purpose, and for sale in the other towns. Bacon is produced in great quantity, though not sufficient for consumption within the colony. Fruit-growing is becoming of greater importance every year. Oranges, grapes, and peaches in the warmer parts of the coast district, and apples and other fruits of temperate climates in the colder portions, and on the table-lands, are the principal objects of cultivation. This industry is capable of almost indefinite expansion, soil and climate in ordinary years being eminently favourable to the production of fruit.

18. **Mining** is another important industry. The existence of **gold** in Australia was originally discovered in New South Wales, and for many years gold-mining was followed by a larger number of persons than any other pursuit. Though now giving occupation to a much smaller number, it is still one of the recognized industries of the colony, and there is some probability that it will hereafter be largely revived. The gold-fields or "diggings" are situated on the slopes of the Great Dividing Chain, or on the adjacent table-lands, the greater number being situated to the westward of the chain. Within the last few years **silver-mining** has become an industry of some importance. This metal was known to exist, and had been partially worked, at various points in the main range many years ago, but not in a thorough or systematic manner. A rich deposit has since been

discovered on the western slope of the Blue Mountains, a short distance from Bathurst, where mining operations are now carried on. But a far more extensive "silver"-field has recently been opened up in the distant Barrier Ranges, near the western boundary of the country, where mining for this metal gives employment to a large number of people, and a new town, named **Silverton**, has in consequence sprung into existence. The silver district is fifty miles long and about half as wide. Although

Gold-miners' Bark-hut.

iron abounds in many parts of the country, mining for that metal appears to fail. Some works formerly established for the reduction of the ore have been abandoned, although the quality of the material is excellent. There can be little doubt, however, that in time it will become a most important industry. Mining for **copper** has been more successful. Deposits of copper ore of various kinds and qualities exist in various parts of the table-lands, and have been worked at different times: but the principal copper-producing district at present is that between the Lachlan, Bogan, and Darling, where the mines of

Cobar and Nymagee have attained considerable celebrity. Another of the metals which afford occupation for miners is **tin**, which is abundant on the northern table-land, and has been profitably worked there for some years. Lead, mercury, and antimony are known to exist in different parts of the country, the last in great quantity. By far the most important of all the mining industries, however, is that connected with the production of **coal**. Nearly the whole of the coast district is a vast coalfield, which extends into and in some points beyond the Great Dividing Chain. The principal seat of the coal industry is in the valley of the Hunter River, at the mouth of which is the coal-shipping town Newcastle; but the Blue Mountains, and the district south of Sydney named Illawarra, and situated between the 34th and 35th parallels, also supply large quantities of this mineral. Hitherto coal-mining in New South Wales has not been attended with such serious accidents as in the mother country. Kerosene shale is found in some of the coalfields, especially in the Blue Mountains, and furnishes employment to a large number of persons both in mining and in the manufacture of the oil yielded by that material. The quarrying of slate and of marble have been begun, and there are numerous other minerals of a useful description which some day will increase the number and extent of the mining industries of the colony.

19. New South Wales has not yet attained to the distinction of being a **manufacturing** country; nor, while its natural products continue to be so abundant, and its population so sparse, is it likely to become the rival of such nations as Great Britain or America. Nevertheless, although there is no great staple manufacture for export, there are many classes of minor manufactures which have become regular and important industries within the colony. For example, the manufacture of flour, malt, biscuits, and maizena from Australian grain, gives employment to large numbers of persons, as does also the preparation of preserved meats. Wine-making and brewing are also carried on to an extent that is yearly increasing. Tanning and the working up of the leather so made into boots and shoes and saddlery; spinning and weaving wool into the cloth called tweed and forming it into garments; and the manufacture of shirts

and similar articles are all extensively carried on, the various products being used for home consumption chiefly. In the building trades, stone-cutting, brick and tile making, pottery, timber getting and sawing, iron-founding, and the construction of furniture—all employ large numbers of workmen. In fact, in all the manufactures usually styled domestic, the country is fast learning to supply itself, and the various forms of manufacturing activity are too numerous to be mentioned in detail. As being of more than average importance, shipbuilding, engineering, coach factories, and smelting works are worthy of special note. Manufactures of soap, candles, sugar, tobacco, and salt are also flourishing.

20. The **commerce** of New South Wales is extensive and varied. Timber from British Columbia; lacquered ware from Japan; tea and silk from China; rice and coffee from India and the Malay Islands; sugar from Mauritius; tobacco, kerosene, hardware, and "notions" from the United States; and manufactured goods of all kinds from the United Kingdom, are among the commodities which the foreign commerce brings to the colony. Its intercolonial trade is not less active. Copra and bananas from Fiji; sugar from Queensland; potatoes from New Zealand; fruit and hops from Tasmania; flour and manufactured goods from Victoria; and wheat and flour from South Australia, are among the characteristic imports supplied by these colonies. Allowing for fluctuations in value, it may be estimated that the total external commerce of New South Wales averages £27,000,000 annually. Of this amount a little more than one half is the value of imports. About five-ninths of the whole is the proportionate value of the foreign commerce, the remainder being absorbed in the intercolonial trade principally with Australian colonies. Except for purposes of revenue, no taxes are levied upon imports or exports, and the policy of the colony in this respect is that of free-trade in opposition to that of protection.

21. New South Wales has a system of full **self-government** on the lines of the British constitution. Its legislature consists of two houses; the upper, styled the Legislative Council, consisting of an indefinite number of members appointed by the governor; and the lower, called the Legislative Assembly,

composed of about a hundred and twenty members elected by the people. These two bodies are empowered to make, in conjunction, any laws they may see fit, provided they are not calculated to affect injuriously the imperial interests. All measures passed by the legislature must receive the queen's assent, which is usually signified through the governor, but in certain cases is given by the queen herself through her responsible advisers. The executive consists of the governor, who is the principal and ultimate authority for all the acts of government, and a certain number of ministers chosen from members of the legislature, but chiefly from the assembly. One of these is called the premier, and he is regarded as first in rank of the ministers, and as being specially the governor's principal adviser. The various duties of the government are carried on at a great cost. The funds necessary for this purpose, having been granted by the legislature, are raised by taxation principally upon goods imported into the colony, by the sale and lease of public lands, and by various other means of less importance. In this way about seven millions sterling are obtained yearly, and the average expenditure is about equal to the revenue. A large amount of money has, however, been borrowed for the purpose of constructing railways, and constitutes the public debt.

22. In harmony with the freedom of its constitution there are other points in which members of the community are placed on a footing of equality, as, for example, **religion** and **education**. There is no state church supported by public funds, but the members of all religious bodies enjoy equal rights and privileges. As regards numbers, the members of the Church of England preponderate; next in order come Roman Catholics, Presbyterians, and Wesleyans, with less numerous denominations. Each of these bodies is organized in accordance with its own established rules, and divides the colony into dioceses, presbyteries, or districts. Great progress has been made of late years in the erection of churches, and in the general organization of religious work. Education is to a large extent a matter of state concern, and is provided in a university with three affiliated colleges, a grammar-school in Sydney, high schools in Sydney and some important country towns, and primary schools spread all over

the country. The state system of education is undenominational, and in this respect is based upon the National System established in Ireland some fifty years ago. By the great majority of parents education is highly prized and eagerly sought for on behalf of their children; but the compulsory provisions of the school law have still occasionally to be enforced.

23. While New South Wales is, for various purposes, portioned off into different districts, the only permanent **territorial division** is that into **counties,** of which there are a hundred and forty-four, and **parishes.** For administrative or governmental purposes, however, this division has no significance, being useful only in connection with the survey and description of land. With a view to the effective working of the police arrangements, the colony is divided into seventy-one police districts, the boundaries of which, however, are liable to alteration. The like objection applies to the seventy-two electoral districts, those portions of the territory which each return one or more members to the Legislative Assembly. Besides these, there are land, registration, school, and other districts, each serving some useful purpose, but not providing for any general local administration, or implying any power of local self-government or spontaneous local organisation for public objects. Perhaps the most important territorial division at present in force is that instituted by the Land Act of 1884, by which the whole colony is partitioned into three areas corresponding in some degree with its natural features. These are termed the Eastern, Central, and Western Divisions, the conditions upon which land may be acquired, either as freehold or leasehold, differing in each. These divisions are also liable to alteration.

24. As in other newly settled countries, the **growth of towns** and cities is usually slow, though it occasionally happens that a city springs into existence, as it were, at a bound; and although it may not boast of handsome, or even substantial buildings, it will contain the most important constituent of a city, a large population. Generally, however, the process of growth is of the following kind. A "bush" inn is established in some spot where some traffic passes, travellers require ac-

commodation, and there are settlers sufficiently near to ensure local custom. In a short time the same considerations induce a blacksmith to settle down near at hand, and the attractions held out by these two having had the effect of drawing people to the locality, a store is opened. This increase of conveniences forms a great inducement for other people to take up their residence in the vicinity, and a post-office is soon required for the augmented population. When this has been secured, the town is regarded as being established; for the future it has only to grow. Other tradesmen follow; a second store is set up; another public house is opened; and the town assumes the appearance of a long straggling street with numerous gaps between the houses and a total disregard of style in the buildings. If, by any fortunate circumstance, the traffic through the town is materially increased, by so much does the town prosper through the extension of trade and addition to population. If there be also some local product, as timber, grain, or cattle; or, should a manufactory be established, such as a flour-mill or a tannery, the growth of the town is rapid. But should the local product be a mineral—gold, silver, tin, or coal—the town "improves" at even a quicker rate, and stores, hotels, and workshops multiply as fast as the necessary buildings can be erected. All towns, however, are not thus fortunate. Some linger for many years in the earliest stage, and never advance beyond it, while others stop short in the march of improvement after having made considerable progress. But whatever their ultimate fate may be, stagnation or development, all have a family likeness; and, except for some accident of position, well-nigh the same terms may be used in describing each. We shall here notice those only that are really of most importance.

25. **Sydney,** the oldest settlement in Australia, and the capital of New South Wales, is situated on the shores of Port Jackson, that magnificent harbour, which, if equalled, is certainly not surpassed by any other in the world. Owing to the numerous bays and coves formed by this inlet the city seems built upon a number of peninsulas, and the amount of water frontage thus available for business or pleasure constitutes one of the great advantages of its position. Occupy-

ing an undulating surface of about two square miles, the city proper has about 150 miles of streets, all properly formed and lighted with gas. Though not so wide as in more modern

Town-hall, Sydney.

towns, the streets are well laid out, those of greatest importance running north and south, with others at intervals crossing them from east to west. In the municipalities which surround the city the direction and width of the streets have been determined by the contour of the surface, or by accidental circumstances. Many handsome and stately buildings, both public and private, adorn the city and some of the suburbs. Among the former may be mentioned the public offices, the museum, the general post-office, and the town-hall. Banks, insurance offices, and some of the mercantile establishments are among the most conspicuous of the ornamental private buildings; and, besides many beautiful churches belonging to the various religious bodies, the Anglican and the Roman Catholic cathedrals are fine specimens of ecclesiastical architecture. The university, affiliated colleges, and Prince Alfred Hospital are outside the city boundary, and, being all upon the same block of land, they form a distinctive feature in the locality where they are situated, besides supplying some ornamentation to four adjoining suburban municipalities. In the enumeration of buildings which give a character to the city the grammar-school and the public primary schools ought not to be omitted, many of the latter being distinguished for their architectural taste and skill. Six public parks, and a botanic garden remarkable for its exquisite beauty, supply the means of healthful outdoor recreation, and add to the general salubrity of the city. Water is obtained from an extensive reserve adjoining the city; a further temporary supply is brought from the Nepean River, near Penrith; but eventually the principal service will be furnished from the upper Nepean, the works for which are in an advanced state. Not only the city but all the surrounding municipalities are lighted with gas, and in addition the electric light is used in a few places. Too much space would be required to describe in detail all the other appliances of civilized life which have been introduced into Sydney in order to promote the health, safety, and comfort of its inhabitants. It must suffice, therefore, to state that, for its size, Sydney is as well supplied in this respect as most cities of the civilized world. The population of the city and suburbs is 250,000.

Besides the ordinary handicrafts numerous works of a manufacturing kind are carried on in Sydney and its neighbourhood. Among the more important of these are engineering and joinery works, in which steam is the motive power; shipbuilding; clothing and boot factories, including a cloth-weaving establishment; coach factories; tanneries; breweries; and tobacco manufactories. All these have an importance beyond what attaches to establishments which aim merely at supplying the local market, some of the goods they produce being exported. The manufacture of soap and candles, of glass-ware, and of pottery is also carried on to a considerable extent, and other industries are continually springing up or developing into greater importance.

It is in relation to commerce, however, that Sydney takes the highest rank. It is the great emporium of the colony, being the only port into which goods are imported, and from which they are exported to countries outside the limits of Australasia, with the exception of Newcastle, to which reference will be made hereafter. Of the thirteen millions of pounds sterling, which is the estimated value of goods annually exported, probably nine-tenths leave the colony by the port of Sydney; and a larger proportion of the imports, which average fourteen millions of money, are received through the same channel. Regular communication with the ports of the colony situated south of Sydney is maintained by a line of coasting steamers which carry produce to the metropolis, and convey manufactured goods in return. The ports on the north are similarly connected with the capital by several lines of steamers, which effect the same purposes for these portions of the colony. Besides these, sailing vessels are constantly engaged in the same traffic. There are, moreover, three lines of large and powerful steamships by means of which the intercolonial trade is carried on between Sydney and Melbourne and Sydney and Brisbane, independently of sailing vessels and steamers running casually. Another line connects Sydney with the New Zealand ports; and Fiji on the one hand, and Tasmania on the other, also possess the like means of communication with New South Wales. The principal ports of China, together with Singapore, are regularly visited by the steam vessels of another line, and there is also a service between Sydney and San Francisco. With the mother country communication is kept up by means of two lines of steamships, which include some of the largest and best appointed vessels afloat; and a third line, under French auspices, also serves to render such communication more regular and frequent. The greater part of the trade of Sydney is carried on with London, and besides the means of transport already mentioned there are many large sailing vessels constantly employed in voyaging between the two ports. The inland trade is not less considerable. All the main lines of railway from the interior converge upon Sydney, and bring produce of various kinds for shipment or for consumption in the metropolis. Wool from the great plains about and beyond the Darling; copper from Cobar and neighbouring mines; gold from the various fields scattered throughout the colony; silver from the Barrier Ranges; coal from the Blue Mountains; tallow and hides from all the pastoral districts—all reach Sydney by rail. The result of this concentration of traffic is that Sydney is remarkable as a centre of commercial activity. As the seat of government, the head-quarters of the several administrative departments, and the site of the principal courts of law, Sydney is also characterized by activities of another kind, but all tending to make it a busy and thriving city.

26. Fourteen miles to the westward of Sydney, on one of the numerous arms of Port Jackson, is **Parramatta**, the second town in Australia in respect of age. The surrounding country has a picturesque appearance and is admirably adapted for fruit-growing. Its orchards, vineyards, and orangeries have an Australian reputation, and furnish employment to a large number of people. The adjoining municipal borough of **Granville** may be said to form one large town with Parramatta. Here the main line of railway from Sydney diverges to the south and west; and as the traffic of the whole of the southern half of the colony must pass through the station, the scene is at all times a busy one. Besides the tweed factories in Parramatta several large industries are located at Granville, and the two places form a thriving and important town. Numerous government institutions have been established at Parramatta, including a jail, hospital, lunatic asylum, and two orphanages. An extensive park affords the means of outdoor recreation. The population of the two places is probably not less than 12,000.

Penrith, on the Nepean River, which is here crossed by a railway bridge of iron, derives its chief importance from the fact that trains stop for adjustment before commencing the ascent of the Blue Mountains. This ascent, which is very steep, is accomplished by means of a zigzag, the railway being cut through rocks in places, and in others carried over gullies by viaducts. Employment is found for a large number of

Zigzag Railway over Blue Mountains.

persons in connection with the railway works, but the district generally is agricultural, maize being the chief product. The railway bridge over the river is on the tubular principle, and is one of the finest in the colony.

Following the railway across the Blue Mountains, at a distance of 145 miles from Sydney, the city of **Bathurst** is reached. Situated on the Macquarie River, on the edge of extensive open plains and in view of the Dividing Chain, Bathurst occupies a position that is both healthful and picturesque. Its elevation, 2300 feet above the sea-level, renders the climate comparatively cool and enjoyable in summer, though in winter frosts are of common occurrence, and occasionally snow falls in great quantities. Being the centre of an extensive district well adapted both for agriculture and pasturage, while it also abounds in the precious metals and in valuable minerals, the city is in a highly prosperous condition. Gold, silver, and copper are found and worked within the district; roofing slate is also abundant. The chief agricultural products are wheat and maize; and sheep number some hundreds of thousands. The city is well laid out with broad streets and is lighted with gas. Most of the ordinary domestic manufactures are carried on in Bathurst, and afford employment to a considerable proportion of its population of 8000.

Wellington, at the junction of the Bell River with the Macquarie, is also a station on the Great Western Railway. The country in the immediate neighbourhood is well suited for farming and grazing—a fact which led to the formation of a settlement here in the early days of the colony. In the neighbourhood are several gold-fields, which, however, are little worked at present. Wellington is celebrated for the caves which exist in the limestone rocks composing much of the district. Fossil bones of marsupial animals abound in these caves, and, in connection with similar remains found in other localities, prove that ages ago Australia was tenanted by animals of the same class as now form its indigenous fauna. The population is about 2000.

Following the course of the Great Western Railway, at a distance of 278 miles from Sydney, **Dubbo** will be reached. This town is situated on the Macquarie River, near its junction with the Talbragar, and is the business centre of an extensive pastoral district. Some amount of agriculture is carried on in the neighbourhood, as well as the usual industries of a manufacturing kind. Gold exists in the district, though mining is followed to but a slight extent. The vine has been successfully cultivated near the town. The present population is estimated at 3500.

From Dubbo the western line of railway continues to **Bourke**, on the Darling River. The immense level plains which surround this town are devoted to pastoral purposes, but at no great distance copper-mining is carried on to a large extent. Its connection with Sydney by rail and with South Australia and Victoria by the Darling River, which in the season is navigable for the whole of its course downwards, renders Bourke a town of great importance in a business point of view, and its future promises to be highly prosperous. Its population amounts to 1200.

In this district are **Cobar** and **Nymagee**—two townships which owe their existence to the copper-mining operations which have been successfully carried on at each town, and which have placed them at the head of copper-producing localities in New South Wales.

Returning along the western railway, between Wellington and Bathurst we arrive at **Orange**, 192 miles from Sydney. This town is situated at an altitude of nearly 3000 feet above the sea, and in consequence enjoys a very bracing climate, snow and ice being common in the winter. It is the centre of one of the finest wheat-producing districts in the colony, and the grinding of wheat and export of flour are among the principal industries of the town. In the neighbourhood are several gold-fields, and at one of these, **Ophir**, gold-digging was first begun in the colony. Copper also abounds in the district, though copper-mining is but languidly carried on at present. Additional importance attaches to Orange by reason of its being the point from which a railway line branches off towards the west, passing through Molong and terminating at Forbes on the Lachlan. At present the population numbers about 3000.

On this branch line the first place of any consequence is **Molong**—a flourishing town supported by a fine agricultural district which produces large quantities of wheat and maize. Copper abounds in the district, though little worked, and coal is known to exist. The population is estimated at 800.

Parkes, a mining locality on the Billabong gold-field, was at one time noted for the large population which was attracted by the productiveness of the mines. It has, however, declined in population, which now numbers about 1900.

Forbes, on the Lachlan River, will for the present be the terminus of the branch railway line from Orange. Gold has been obtained here in large quantities; and though this industry has greatly decayed, the town has established itself as the business centre of an immense area of country lying between the Lachlan and the Darling. In this district pastoral pursuits are carried on to a large extent, about a million and a half of sheep and sixty thousand cattle being depastured therein. Tillage, for which the rich soil in the vicinity of the river is well adapted, also flourishes, wheat being largely grown. The present population is 2000.

Between Orange and Bathurst is the town of **Blayney,** 2800 feet above sea-level. It is surrounded by an agricultural and pastoral district, but has acquired greater importance from the fact that from this point a branch commences from the western line to connect with the southern at Murrumburrah. Mining for gold and copper has been carried on to a considerable extent in the neighbourhood. The population is estimated at 1000.

Cowra, on the Lachlan River, which is here crossed by a wooden bridge of superior construction, is a place of some importance, the land in the immediate neighbourhood being taken up for agricultural purposes, and that at a greater distance being devoted to pasturage. Its importance will be increased when the branch line from Blayney reaches this point, as it will then be placed in direct communication with the metropolis, and ultimately with Melbourne. The present population is estimated at 700.

From **Wallerawang** another branch from the western line runs to Mudgee, a distance of eighty-five miles. Independently of this circumstance Wallerawang is a place of some prospective importance from the abundance of coal and iron found in the neighbourhood, the former being somewhat extensively worked. It is estimated that the population of the township is 2500.

Mudgee, the terminus of the branch line just mentioned, is situated on the Cudgegong River, in the midst of a district abounding in mineral wealth, and at the same time fitted for pastoral and agricultural pursuits. Besides gold, which is found at many points in the neighbourhood, coal and iron are known to exist. The wool from this district has long been celebrated as among the finest produced in Australia; while, from the fertile alluvial soils lining the river banks, large crops of wheat and maize are gathered. Considerable activity is shown in manufactures of the domestic kind, and much business is transacted with the extensive pastoral area lying to the westward. The population is probably not less than 2500.

Another branch from the western line commences at Blacktown and extends to **Windsor** and **Richmond**—two towns on the Hawkesbury River, both being among the earliest settlements in the colony. The surrounding district is agricultural, for which purpose it is eminently fitted by reason of the abundance of alluvial soil of the most productive character. In fact this part of the country was regarded as the granary of the colony in its infant days, and supplied most of the grain consumed by the first settlers. The whole district is liable to floods, which, though they generally enrich the soil by depositing on the surface a layer of fresh alluvium, sometimes prove destructive to crops and stock, and even to human life. On the opposite side of the Hawkesbury the district is known as the Kurrajong, which comprises the first portion of the eastern slope of the Blue Mountains, and attains an elevation of nearly 2000 feet. It is noted for the salubrity of its climate and general productiveness. The population of Windsor is estimated at 2000, and of Richmond at 1300.

Proceeding next along the Great Southern Railway from Granville, at a distance of 22 miles from Sydney, is **Liverpool**, which was founded very early in the history of the colony. The district is mainly agricultural and pastoral, but there are several factories within the limits of the town. One of these is a paper-mill; others are wool-washing and fellmongering establishments and a tannery. A benevolent asylum for destitute old men also exists in the town, and is supported by the government. The population of the town is at present supposed to reach 2500.

Campbelltown, 12 miles distant along the line, is another of the old settlements, and formerly was a flourishing town. After a long period of stagnation its prosperity has now begun to revive. Agriculture is the principal occupation of the district. A tram-line connects this place with **Camden**, eight miles distant, which also was founded in the early days. The surrounding district contains much arable land of excellent quality; the grape is cultivated to a considerable extent, and large quantities of hay are produced. The rearing of horses, cattle, and sheep also occupy many of the residents.

Mittagong, 77 miles from Sydney and 2000 feet above sea-level, is a thriving town. The neighbourhood is much frequented on account of its bracing air; but the principal support of the town is derived from the mineral resources of the neighbourhood, among which may be mentioned iron, coal, and kerosene shale.

Berrima, about six miles distant by road from Mittagong, contains one of the largest penal establishments in the colony. It is situated in a fine agricultural district, which is also rich in minerals, especially coal.

At a distance of 134 miles from Sydney by rail is **Goulburn**, the chief town of an extensive and prosperous district, and a place of great trade. The town is well laid out with broad streets, which are ornamented with many fine buildings, public and private. The surrounding district contains all the elements of wealth, mineral, pastoral, and agricultural. Gold, copper, marble, slate, and lime are at present the principal mineral products; sheep, cattle, and horses are reared in large numbers; and wheat, maize, oats, and barley are largely cultivated. In the town and its immediate vicinity, milling, tanning, and brewing are the leading industries, in addition to boot-making, for which there are two factories. The present population is about 7000.

Though situated some little distance from the railway, **Tass**, 187 miles from Sydney, may be considered the next important town on the line. The surrounding district is chiefly pastoral and agricultural, though mining is carried on to some extent. The population is estimated at 2000.

Wagga Wagga, 309 miles from Sydney by rail, is an important town, situated on the river Murrumbidgee. Being the centre of an immense pastoral district, the chief product is wool, but agriculture is also carried on to some extent. The Southern Railway crosses the river here by a splendid iron bridge. The population of the town may be estimated at 5000.

The Great Southern Railway terminates at **Albury**, 386 miles from Sydney. This town stands on the right bank of the

Murray, and in addition to its importance as a border city, it is the centre of a rich agricultural district, in which some mining for gold is also carried on. Tobacco and grapes are raised in large quantities, and other farm produce to a smaller extent. Farther from the town, the country is chiefly occupied for pastoral purposes. In favourable seasons the Murray is navigable as far as Albury. The population is about 6000.

Several branch lines have been formed from the Great Southern Railway. From Harden, a small station, 228 miles from Sydney, a branch has been constructed to **Young**. This town is situated in a pastoral and agricultural district, but was formerly much more populous, having been the centre of the once famed Burrangong Gold-field. The population now numbers about 2000.

Grenfell, in the adjoining district, resembles Young in its history and present circumstances. Originating in a "rush" to a new gold-field, it was for some years a great mining centre, but now depends for its prosperity upon pastoral and agricultural pursuits. The population is estimated at 1700.

At Junee Junction, 287 miles from Sydney, the South-Western Railway branches off, and extends to **Narrandera**, 60 miles distant. This town, 347 miles from Sydney, is situated on the right bank of the Murrumbidgee River. During the last few years the population of the town and neighbourhood has largely increased and now exceeds 1200. The surrounding district is of a pastoral character, but some agriculture is also carried on.

From Narrandera a branch of the South-western line crosses the river and runs in a southerly direction to **Jerilderie**, which is the capital of a fine pastoral district, with a population of about 500.

The South-western Railway is continued from Narrandera to **Hay**, a town on the Murrumbidgee, 454 miles from Sydney. Hay is a place of great importance, the district of which it is the centre being extensive and almost exclusively pastoral. The town is well laid out, and approached from the opposite side of the river by an iron bridge. The population exceeds 2000.

A third branch of the Great Southern Railway commences at Goulburn, and is intended to connect that town with Cooma.

At present it is completed to Bungendore, a small town, 177 miles from Sydney.

Queanbeyan, which will be the next station on this line, is the centre of an important district, which contains good agricultural as well as pastoral land, and is also rich in minerals, gold, silver, copper, lead, and iron. The population of the town is estimated at 1000.

Cooma, the proposed terminus of this branch line, is situated in a fine pastoral district forming part of the so-called Maneroo Plains. Agriculture is also carried on to some extent. Being about 2600 above the level of the sea the climate is cool and bracing. The population is about 1200.

From **Cootamundra**, a thriving town, 253 miles from Sydney by rail, a branch line has been constructed to **Gundagai** on the Murrumbidgee River. Cootamundra is the outlet of a large pastoral and agricultural district and also of the Temora Gold Field. Its population exceeds 1000.

Gundagai, including settlements on both banks of the river, has also a population of about 1000. The neighbouring district is rich in minerals, among which asbestos is specially worthy of note. Agriculture and pasturage are also carried on with much success.

Tumut, in the same district, is famed for its production of wheat, maize, and tobacco. It is a flourishing town with a population of about 900.

Proceeding now to the Great Northern Railway, we commence at **Newcastle**, the southern terminus of the line. Newcastle derives its importance not only from this circumstance, but also from the fact that, being situated at the mouth of the Hunter River, it possesses a port which, as regards the extent of its trade, ranks next to Sydney. As the outlet for the pastoral products of a large portion of the northern half of the colony, for the agricultural produce of the Hunter Valley, and for coal obtained in the vicinage, this city gives employment to a large quantity of shipping. Besides what is consumed in the district or sent to Sydney, coal is exported to neighbouring colonies and to ports in Asia and America. Other industries also occupy the inhabitants of this city, among which ship building, copper smelting, fellmongering, brewing and biscuit baking, are of the most consequence. There are also carriage factories, foundries, and engineering establishments. The population of the city and adjoining municipalities is probably about 15,000.

About 18 miles from Newcastle are **East** and **West Maitland**, which may be considered as practically one town, situated upon

A Coast River.

the same side of the Hunter River. From the rich alluvial flats among which the town is built, immense crops are reaped in ordinary seasons, lucerne and maize being the principal; but occasionally floods destroy all the hopes of the farmer. Other products of the district are tobacco, grapes, and oranges; and large quantities of wine are made in the district. Coal is also abundant, and is raised to a considerable extent. In the more distant parts of the district the rearing of stock is successfully carried on, and cattle, sheep, and horses must be included among the general products. Manufacturing industry also receives attention. The population of the town may be estimated at about 10,000.

Proceeding onward by rail, at a distance of 49 miles from Newcastle, **Singleton** is reached. This town is situated on the right bank of the Hunter River, on a large alluvial flat which produces wheat, barley, maize, tobacco, and grapes. Cattle, horses, and sheep are also bred in the district, and coal is found at a little distance. The usual domestic manufactures are carried on in the town, the population being estimated at 2500.

The next place of importance is **Musclebrook**, 80 miles from Newcastle. This town is situated in an agricultural and pastoral district, wheat, maize, tobacco, and grapes being the principal crops. Wine is also produced, and horses, cattle, and sheep are raised in considerable numbers. The population numbers about 1500.

Murrurundi, 120 miles from Newcastle, is a thriving town situated at the foot of the Liverpool Range, which in this part attains an elevation of about 3700 feet. The town itself is 1500 feet above sea-level, and possesses a healthy, bracing climate. The district is pastoral and agricultural. The population is supposed to be about 1000.

At a distance of 183 miles from Newcastle, on the banks of the Peel River, stands **Tamworth**, the capital of a large and flourishing district. The chief products of this district are those derived from pastoral pursuits, but agriculture is also largely followed, and gold-mining is carried on at several places for which Tamworth is the business centre. The population is now estimated at 4000.

Armidale, 260 miles from Newcastle, is noted for its bracing climate, which it owes to the fact that it is elevated 3300 feet above the sea. This town is the capital of the famed New England district, so named from its supposed resemblance in climate and cultivated products to Old England. Pasturage, agriculture, and mining are extensively carried on in this district, and there are also some manufactures of the kind before described as domestic. The present population is probably about 2000.

Glen Innes, 324 miles from Newcastle, is the next important town on the Great Northern Railway. It is higher by two hundred feet than Armidale, and like the latter enjoys the healthful climate of the table-land. The district contains much excellent agricultural land, but pastoral pursuits are followed to a large extent. The population is about 1500.

Tenterfield, the last town of the colony on the Great Northern Railway, about 390 miles from Newcastle, is also situated on the table-land, and is the centre of a fine pastoral, agricultural, and mining district. Gold, silver, tin, antimony, and plumbago are obtained in the district, and have been extensively worked. The population at present numbers about 2000.

A branch from the Northern Railway commences at Werris Creek, and under the name of the North-Western Line runs for about a hundred miles through the Liverpool Plains. The first place of note on this line is **Gunnedah**, situated in a fine pastoral district, in which some agriculture is carried on. The population may be estimated at 1500.

Narrabri, the present terminus of the line, is a town of similar character, but with a smaller population, which probably numbers about 1000.

Besides the towns already mentioned which derive increased importance from their position on lines of railway, there are others which are of consequence owing to their situation on the banks of rivers. The following belong to the Coast District.

Lismore, the principal centre of population and trade on the Richmond River, has regular communication with the metropolis by means of steamships which convey the local products, principally timber, maize, and sugar, to market. The district is pastoral and agricultural, and is one of the most prosperous in the colony. The present population is estimated at 1000.

In the Clarence River District, **Grafton** is the principal town. Steamships of considerable tonnage trade regularly between this place and Sydney, the exports consisting of sugar, molasses, tallow, preserved meats, and wool, besides timber, gold, and antimony. The district near the river is mainly agricultural; farther back, pastoral; and in the mountainous parts gold mining is followed to some extent. The population probably exceeds 5000.

The chief town of the Macleay River District is **Kempsey**, which has a population of about 1500. The district is well fitted for agriculture, which is largely followed, but rearing cattle and mining are also important industries.

Southward of Sydney, and at a distance of about 50 miles, is **Wollongong**, the principal town in the beautiful Illawarra district. Dairying and coal-mining are the leading occupations of the residents. The population is probably somewhat under 2000.

In the Shoalhaven District the chief place is **Nowra**, with a population of about 1000. The district is agricultural, having a large extent of alluvial soil.

Further south is a fine agricultural district named after the river which flows through it, the **Moruya**. The chief town bears the same name, and has a population of about 1000. Gold and silver are found in the vicinity, and have been worked.

The southernmost coast town of note is **Bega**, on a river of the same name, near the mouth of which is a port. Regular communication is maintained with the metropolis by means of steamships. The district around the town is agricultural and dairying; but it is also the outlet for a large extent of pastoral country. Maize, maizena manufactured in the district, butter, cheese, bacon, hams, leather, and wattle-bark are exported to Sydney and to the neighbouring colonies. The population numbers about 2000.

There are other towns of sufficient importance to deserve mention. These are for the most part situated either on the table-lands or on the banks of rivers flowing into the interior, and are of consequence as centres of local trade.

Inverell, on the Macintyre River, is situated in a rich and thriving district, which produces wheat, maize, and wine in considerable quantities. Pastoral pursuits are also carried on to a large extent, and the tin-mining industry adds to the resources of the district. About 2000 people reside in the town.

Emmaville, formerly known as Vegetable Creek, is in the same district, but at a greater elevation than Inverell. The surrounding country contains excellent agricultural land, and sheep and cattle farming is extensively carried on; but the chief industry of the town is mining for tin. The population is estimated at 1000.

Another tin-mining township in the same district is **Tingha**, which, at the last census, had a population of 2500.

On the Darling River are **Walgett** and **Brewarrina**, two rising townships which are local centres of trade for immense pastoral regions lying around them and to the westward.

Lower down the Darling is **Wilcannia**, a flourishing town, chiefly supported at present by the pastoral interest, and likely to improve as a central entrepôt of pastoral products. There are also in the vicinity indications of the existence of metals, copper in particular, which may in the future become a great source of wealth. The population is about 1500.

At the junction of the Darling and Murray is **Wentworth**, which occupies an unrivalled position for trade with the adjacent colonies. Although the surrounding district is entirely of a pastoral character, the traffic with towns and stations on the Darling and the Murray all passes through Wentworth, and is growing yearly in extent and value. The population is approximately 1000.

On the Castlereagh River, in the centre of a fine grazing district, is **Coonamble**, a thriving town with a population of about 1000.

Hillston, on the Lachlan, is a thriving town, situated in an extensive pastoral district, in which there is a considerable area of land suitable for agriculture, and also some mineral wealth. The present population is estimated at 500.

Cobar, between the Lachlan and the Darling, is the seat of a great copper-mining industry which gives employment to a large number of people, and creates a considerable amount of traffic. The population is about 2000.

On the table-land between Bathurst and Mudgee is **Hill End**, the seat of a gold-mining industry, and inhabited by about 1000 people.

Braidwood, situated upon the table-land, 150 miles to the south of Sydney, and at an elevation of 3300 feet above the sea, is a centre for several important industries, pastoral, agricultural, and mining. Though its importance has declined of late years on account of the supposed exhaustion of some of the neighbouring gold-fields, it still has a population of more than 1000 persons.

On the southern table-land on an affluent of the Snowy River, is **Bombala**, the centre of an agricultural, pastoral, and mining district. Copper, lead, and gold are found in the vicinity. The population is about 1000.

Adelong, on a tributary of the Murrumbidgee, is a mining township of some importance. The surrounding country abounds in reefs, from which large quantities of gold are obtained. It has about 800 inhabitants.

Tumberumba, on an affluent of the Murray, is also rendered important by its position on a gold-field, though farming is also carried on in the vicinity, and the neighbouring district is pastoral. The population is about 800.

On the right bank of the Murray, at its southernmost angle, is **Moama**, important as a border town, and one of the places at which the river may be crossed into Victoria. Its present population is estimated at 1400.

Connected with it by a railroad, the property of a private company, is **Deniliquin**, on the Edward River. This is the centre of a large and important pastoral district, and carries on an extensive trade in pastoral produce, together with some amount of agriculture. The population is probably about 3000.

Balranald, near the junction of the Murray and Murrumbidgee, is also a pastoral township with a population of about 700.

CHAPTER V.

THE COLONY OF QUEENSLAND.

1. Boundaries and extent: coast-line. 2. Surface. 3. Drainage; Rivers and Lakes. 4. Climate. 5. Soil. 6. Population. 7. Internal Communication. 8. Industrial Occupations—Mining. 9. Agriculture, Pasturage, and other industries: Commerce. 10. Government. 11. Religion. 12. Education. 13. Divisions—Districts. 14. Towns. 15. Brisbane. 16. Other towns.

1. This colony occupies the north-eastern portion of the continent, and lies between the 11th and 29th parallels of south latitude, and the 138th and 154th meridians of east longitude. On two sides, east and north, it is **bounded** by the sea; on the west, the boundary is artificial, being the 138th meridian from the waters of the Gulf of Carpentaria to lat. 26° S., that parallel eastward to the 141st meridian, and that meridian to lat. 29° S. The southern boundary, which separates it from New South Wales, is formed by the 29th parallel, the Macintyre and Dumaresq Rivers, and M'Pherson's Range. The territory included within these boundaries is estimated at 678,000 square miles; its greatest length from north to south is about 1200 miles, and its extreme width about 1000 miles. For every 300 square miles of area the colony has a mile of coast-line, the whole extent of coast being estimated at 2250 miles. The chief irregularity in its shape consists in the long projection known as **Cape York Peninsula**, forming the extreme north-east portion of the continent, and terminating at **Cape York**. Throughout its whole length the eastern coast is fringed with islands, and broken up by projecting points and indentations, while for about 1000 miles it is skirted at some distance by the chain of coral formations known as the Great Barrier Reef. Some of the indentations form excellent harbours. Of these the most considerable are **Moreton Bay, Hervey Bay, Broad Sound, Repulse Bay, Halifax Bay, Trinity Bay,** and **Princess Charlotte Bay.** The principal islands are **Stradbroke, Moreton, Great Sandy, Whitsunday,** and **Hinchinbrooke Islands** on the east coast; **Prince of Wales, Banks,** and **Mulgrave** at the northern extremity; and the **Wellesley Islands** in the Gulf of Carpentaria.

2. In its main features the **surface** of Queensland resembles that of New South Wales; and, like the latter, may be divided into the Coast District, the Table-land, and the Interior Plains.

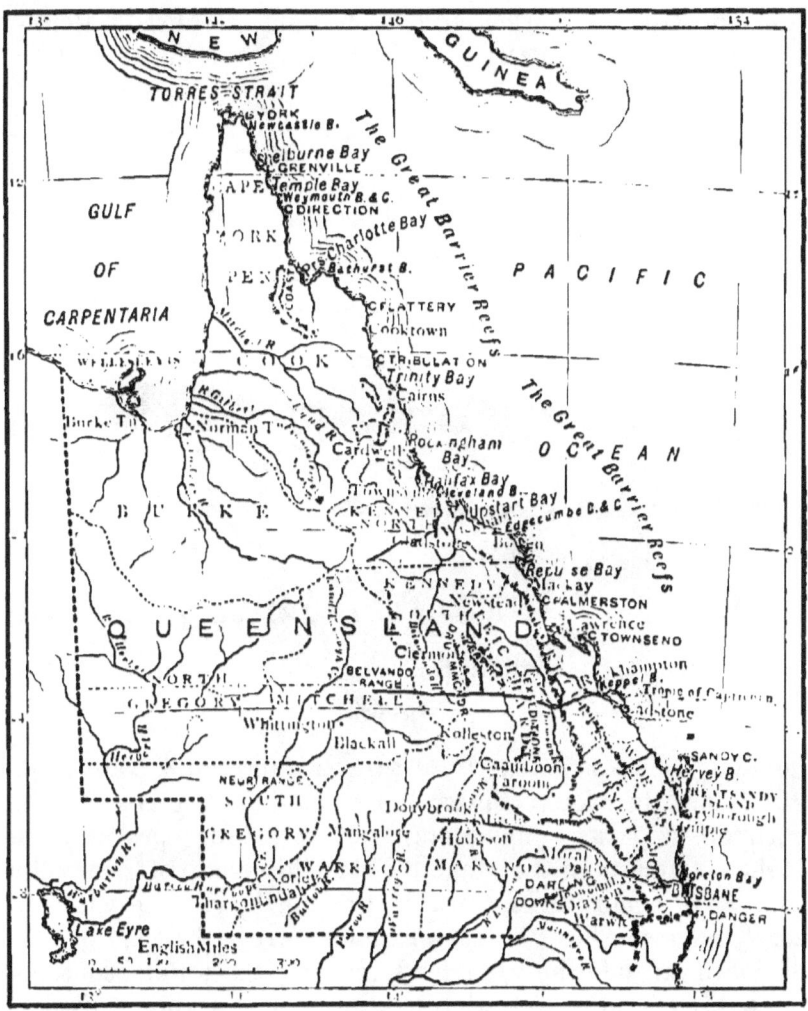

The narrow coast district is bounded on the west by ranges of hills and the slope of the table-land. Westward of this tract is the table-land, extending northward as far as lat. 16°, and sloping gradually towards the interior. Its average elevation is probably less than 2000 feet. Through this table-land the **Great Dividing Chain** is continued from New South Wales northward as far as **Cape Grafton**, and forms the watershed between the rivers flowing into the Pacific and those running into the Gulf of Carpentaria, or forming the head-waters of the **Darling** and **Barcoo.** While the general direction of the

Coast Scenery, Townsville.

Dividing Chain is northerly, it turns westerly at a point about 26° S., and in **Mount Pluto,** 300 miles from the coast, forms with other peaks a mountain knot containing probably the highest summits in the range. From this group of mountains the range again turns towards the north, uniting with the coast range south of the 16th parallel. Near the 21st parallel of south latitude the high land forming the watershed sends off a branch in a westerly direction, which forms a dividing chain between the waters flowing northward into the Gulf of Carpentaria, and those which have a southerly course into Lake Eyre. The culminating point of the whole mountain system is to be found in the **Bellenden-Ker Range,** near Cape Grafton, where one of the peaks attains an altitude estimated at 5158 feet. Various branches are thrown off from the Dividing Chain, chiefly towards the eastward, and these spurs give the country they traverse an undulating character. Nearly the whole of the remainder of the colony is occupied by the great plains, which resemble in their main features those of New South Wales, but probably contain a larger proportion of good land, while they are hotter and, on the whole, dryer, except those portions which lie sufficiently within the tropics to share in the tropical rains. In the south-west, however, there are some of the arid tracts sometimes styled "deserts."

3. Having the sea on two sides, Queensland has three slopes and three drainage areas. In other respects the **river systems** resemble those of New South Wales. In the coast district most of the rivers rising in the coast ranges or on the table-land, and flowing into the Pacific, have short and rapid courses. Some, however, run for considerable distances parallel to the coast either on the table-land or in longitudinal valleys among the coast ranges. Of this class the **Burdekin** is the most conspicuous example. This river has its source at about 18° S., and flows south-easterly, parallel with the general direction of the coast, to a point a little south of 20°, where it is joined by the Belyando, which flows northerly from a point near 24° S. The stream, thus augmented, then turns to the east, and finally to the north-east, finding its way to the sea by two channels. Another river that has a similar course is the **Fitzroy**, which receives the Isaacs from the north and the Dawson from the south, both of these tributaries running parallel with the coast. Of the other rivers the most important are the **Burnett, Brisbane,** and **Mary**. On the northern slope the **Flinders** is the longest and most important stream; the **Mitchell** ranks second; and the Norman, Gilbert, Staaten, and Albert follow in order. All these flow into the Gulf of Carpentaria. Flowing south and west into Lake Eyre in South Australia is the **Barcoo**, which drains an extensive area, and is known in its upper course as the Victoria, a name conferred upon it by its discoverer, Sir Thomas Mitchell. Under the name of **Cooper's Creek** this river will long be memorable in connection with the unhappy fate of the explorers Burke and Wills. The remaining rivers of the interior slope are tributaries of the

Darling. They are the **Paroo** and the **Warrego**, flowing southward the **Maranoa**, which has a south-easterly course, and the **Condamine**, which may be considered the principal source of the Darling. Rising in the dividing chain about sixty miles from the sea, the Condamine flows north-westerly for two hundred and fifty miles, when it curves round to the west and south; and being joined by the Maranoa, runs to the southwest, assuming the name of **Balonne**. Farther south this appellation is exchanged for that of **Culgoa**, under which title it enters New South Wales. The lakes of Queensland are unimportant. It may be remarked, however, that west of the Belyando River, and about 22° S., there is a small basin of inland drainage, in which are situated some salt-water lakes of considerable extent.

4. Owing to the tropical position of a large portion of the country, the **climate of** Queensland cannot be properly described with reference to the colony as a whole. In the northern portion the temperature is high, though it is not felt to be so oppressive as in other countries not farther removed from the equator. Here the seasons are two in number, the wet and the dry. In the former much rain falls, the average for the year ranging between 90 and 100 inches; in the latter the weather is dry, the air pure, and the sky cloudless. In what may be called the temperate zone of the colony the climate approximates to that of New South Wales, but is somewhat warmer. In the coast district outside of the tropic the mean annual temperature is about 70°, the annual rainfall 50 inches, and the prevailing winds easterly and southerly. Except in the hottest summer months, the climate is conducive to health and extremely enjoyable. On the table-land the temperature is lower, and may be estimated at a mean of 62°, and the annual rainfall at 32 inches. Farther west, on the great plains, the temperature rises and the rainfall diminishes, the former being about 80°, and the latter ranging from 20 to 10 inches according to position and distance from the sea. Here the prevailing winds are westerly, but the whole country is free from the hot winds which, in the southern colonies, are so injurious to vegetation and so disagreeable to human beings. Changes of temperature, depending mainly upon alterations in

the direction of the wind, are sometimes rapid, but never so extreme as in Victoria and New South Wales. Altogether the climate may be said to be healthy in a high degree, the principal exception being the tendency to produce fever in low-lying districts in the rainy season.

5. Every variety of **soil**, as might be expected, is to be found within the Queensland borders, from the rich alluvium of the brush lands of the coast to the sandy and stony tracts in the south-west, which may be termed deserts. Besides the alluvial soil, the coast district also possesses much rich land, where the soil is the result of the decomposition of volcanic rocks. Soil of this kind is even more abundant on the tableland, especially in the south. On the plains the soil is similar to that of New South Wales in the like position, extensive tracts of rich black volcanic soil alternating with sandy belts covered with scrub. In the extreme west, however, the more barren soil preponderates; and near the Gulf of Carpentaria it becomes marly in character, producing the well-known "salt-bush" and other salsolaceous plants which furnish food for cattle and sheep. On the whole, it may be said that Queensland contains a large proportion of excellent soil, and not a little that is unsurpassed in fertility.

Aboriginal of Northern Queensland.

6. As yet the **population** of Queensland is small, considered

with reference to its extensive area. Although the great body of the people are of European blood, there is an Asiatic element of some importance. Assuming the present population to be about 321,000, about one person in 65 would be either Chinese or Polynesian. The number of these last, however, is gradually diminishing, as the term expires for which they were engaged to labour in sugar-plantations, and they are returned to their homes in the Pacific Islands. No estimate can be formed of the number of the aborigines, although there is warrant for the belief that it is still considerable, and not less than 20,000. It is worthy of remark, that, notwithstanding the comparative youth of the colony, no mean proportion of the population consists of natives of the country and of other parts of Australia.

7. From the number of excellent harbours on the coast the facilities for **communication** between different parts of the colony by water are very great, and several lines of large and well-appointed steamships trade regularly between the several ports and with the principal maritime cities of the other Australian colonies. Common **roads** are general throughout the territory, and lead from the capital and principal towns on the coast to all the places of any note in the interior. **Railway** construction has been vigorously carried on for some years. Of the lines opened for traffic the principal starts from Brisbane, and runs westward through Dalby for 410 miles, and is to be extended to the Warrego River. A branch from this line at Toowoomba runs to Warwick, and is now continued southward to the border, to connect with the New South Wales railway system at Stanthorpe. Another principal line is that called the Central Line, which commences at Rockhampton and runs in a westerly direction for a distance of 305 miles to a place called Jericho, with a branch from Emerald to Clermont. This line when further continued will divide the colony into two parts, and from that circumstance derives its name. A third principal line, the Northern, commences at Townsville, and is carried in a south-westerly direction for 147 miles to Betts' Creek, and is to be extended to the Flinders River. There are some short branches from this line. Other short lines are those from Maryborough to Gympie, and from

Bundaberg to Mount Perry. Others are projected, and will no doubt be constructed as favourable opportunities occur. Communication by means of the electric telegraph is now practicable with all the principal towns of the colony, with other Australian colonies, Tasmania, and New Zealand, and even with the mother country and the rest of the civilized world.

8. From the richness and variety of its natural resources it might be anticipated that the principal **industries** of the colony would consist in the work necessary for their development. Mining for **gold** continues to occupy a considerable number of people, from the produce of whose labour about a million's worth of the precious metal is exported annually. The auriferous country extends from the Gulf of Carpentaria to near the southern boundary of the colony, not continuously but in detached areas, which constitute the "gold-fields." **Copper-mining** is also largely followed, much of the ore being very rich; but the low price of the metal has to some extent checked this industry. Towards the south, on the table-land adjoining New South Wales, mining for **tin** has been carried on for some years; but a falling off in the production has taken place, the depreciation in value having removed the encouragement to a vigorous prosecution of the work. Although coal-measures are known to exist over a large area, comparatively little has been effected towards the development of coal-mining as one of the great industries of the colony. In the future, however, there can be no doubt this will prove a great source of national wealth. Besides these more important mining operations, a commencement has been made with antimony, bismuth, cinnabar, and manganese. Iron and lead, though known to exist, appear not to have been worked as yet.

9. **Agriculture** is largely carried on, the principal objects of cultivation being wheat, maize, potatoes, sugar-cane, arrowroot, cotton, tobacco, grapes, bananas, pine-apples, and oranges, together with such plants as tea, coffee, vanilla, indigo, and spices. Should the difficulty of procuring suitable labour be overcome, sugar-growing will probably become the most important branch of agricultural industry, the rich soils and climate of the northern rivers being perfectly adapted for the growth of the cane. A very large proportion of the terri-

tory of Queensland is devoted to **pastoral pursuits**, including the rearing of horses, cattle, and sheep. New country is constantly being taken up for these purposes; and, as showing the amount of capital invested in this industry, it may be mentioned that the number of horses in the colony exceeds two hundred and fifty thousand; of cattle, four and a half millions; and of sheep, nine and a half millions. **Timber-getting** forms an important and increasing industry, for which the splendid trees of the colony afford ample scope. In the southern portion of the country the trees are of the same kinds as those found in New South Wales, with the addition of some species of eucalyptus and pine. Further north the brushes and forests contain trees which are akin to those of the Malay Islands, and which are peculiar to the tropical regions. Of these little is yet known as to their commercial value. No staple manufactures have yet been established, those now in existence being such as are necessary to prepare the natural products for the market. Such, for example, are saw-mills and flour-mills; wine, tobacco, arrow-root, and sugar-making; and cotton cleaning, meat-preserving, and "boiling down." In addition to these, the usual domestic manufactures are carried on, such, that is to say, as provide articles for home use and not for export. On the coast the pearl-fishery, the collection of trepang, and the dugong-fishery employ a considerable number of men, and a large amount of capital is invested in these enterprises. **Commerce** also occupies a large number of persons. The home trade consists mainly in the distribution of imports throughout the colony, and the collection at certain centres of goods for export. Intercolonial trade, the interchange, that is, of products and imports between different colonies, is also extremely active, and is carried on principally by steam-ships, though many sailing vessels are also engaged in the business. The foreign trade is limited to the mother country and China, with occasional ventures to or from other countries. Among the imports may be mentioned tea and coffee, manufactured goods of every description, chiefly from London, and American implements, machines, and notions, the value of the whole being about six and a half millions per annum. The principal exports are gold, wool, tallow, hides, sugar, tin, and copper. The total annual value of the exports amounts to more than four and a half millions.

10. Originally a portion of New South Wales, Queensland was constituted an independent colony in 1859, with a separate **government** modelled upon those of the older colonies. The Legislative Council consists of about thirty members, appointed for life by the crown, but with power to elect their own president. The other branch of the legislature, the Assembly, is composed of fifty-five representatives chosen by the people, the franchise being so liberal that practically any person who is of ordinarily careful habits may become an elector. While these two bodies make laws for the colony, subject to the approval of the governor as the Queen's representative, the authority to put them in force is exercised by the governor in conjunction with the executive government. This body, also termed the ministry, consists of members of the legislature, who preside over the different public departments, and are responsible for their proceedings to the Assembly. These departments of the public service differ little from those of the other colonies, except in being fewer in number. Justice is administered by a supreme court, with three judges who are independent of the government, and by the inferior district courts. In effect, the colony is self-governing, the only restriction upon its powers of legislation being the necessary one that requires measures that in any way affect imperial interests to be reserved for the Queen's pleasure respecting them to be ascertained. In other words, such laws, when passed by the local legislature, cannot be put in force until the Queen's advisers in the mother country recommend them for her sanction. To carry on the business of the government the money required is raised by taxation and by the leasing of public lands. The revenue thus obtained is about two millions and three quarters annually, and the expenditure, exclusive of the sums devoted to railway construction, is about the same amount.

11. As regards **religion**—in New South Wales the most perfect religious equality exists. No church receives support from public funds, and no control is exercised by the government in church matters. Every one, therefore, is at liberty to practise his own religious views provided they do not contravene the

equal rights enjoyed by others. Except that a larger number of Mohammedans and Pagans are to be found in Queensland, the various Christian churches are represented by about the same proportions of members as in the older colonies. Each denomination possesses its own organization, and divides the colony into dioceses or districts as is found expedient. It is believed that the ordinances of religion are as fully provided as is possible in a country so sparsely populated in some portions. The Chinese, Kanakas (or Polynesians), and other inferior races are for the most part Pagans, and there are a few Mohammedans.

12. An effective system of public primary **education** has been in operation for many years. It is secular in so far as it excludes direct religious instruction by the state-paid teachers, and it is free, inasmuch as no fee is charged for tuition. Schools are established in all localities where the population is sufficiently numerous, and they are as well attended as could be expected when the circumstances of the country are taken into account, the total number of pupils at the same period being over 52,000. These are instructed by a staff of more than 1100 teachers. Provision has been made for more advanced education by the establishment of grammar-schools in the more populous localities. Seven of these are now in operation. Further encouragement to this grade of education is given in the shape of scholarships to deserving pupils from the state schools, and by exhibitions to universities. These educational institutions are under the authority of the minister of education, who presides over the whole department and controls all its operations.

13. As in other Australian colonies the government of Queensland is mainly carried on from the capital, the system being to a large extent one of centralization. Some progress has, however, been made towards local government and organization by the institution of divisional boards, which have been invested with some of the powers of a municipal corporation, and perform for larger areas many of the functions discharged by borough councils in towns. Besides this division there are several others, such as counties, which are useful in matters relating to the survey of land, and electoral districts, of which

there are forty-three, and which are the areas represented by members of the Assembly. Practically, however, the division of the colony into twelve large districts is that which is most generally recognized and best understood. On the coast, commencing at the south, is the **Moreton District,** which extends westward to the Dividing Chain, and northward to a range of hills named D'Aguilar Range, which forms the watershed between the waters of the Burnett and those of the Brisbane River. This district, therefore, comprises all the country of which Moreton Bay may be considered the natural outlet. It is to a large extent agricultural and timber-producing. It is nearly bisected by the trunk line of railway towards the interior, has been the longest settled, and is the most thickly peopled. Northward of this district is that named **Wide Bay and Burnett,** which stretches northward to a point on the coast lying a little to the north of the 25th parallel, and extends inland to the range which divides the waters of the Burnett and Dawson rivers. It is largely timber-producing and agricultural towards the coast, where sugar growing is an important industry. The famed Gympie gold-field is in this district, and coal has been found near the Mary River. In the western portion, which is mountainous, copper-mining and sheep-farming are the principal pursuits. The **Port Curtis District** comes next in order, extending northward to Broad Sound, and westward to the coast ranges. Pasturage, agriculture, gold and copper mining are the principal industries. Marble is found and quarried in one part of the district, and in favourable seasons meat-preserving is extensively carried on. The **Kennedy District** commences at Cape Palmerston, and extends to Rockingham Bay, stretching inland as far as the Great Dividing Chain. On the coast sugar, cotton, and maize growing are the chief industries, further inland pastoral pursuits. It includes the Charters Towers gold-field, one of the most productive in the colony. The whole district is well watered. The Cape York Peninsula north of Cape Grafton is included in the **Cook District,** which has the sea on all sides except the south. The northern portion from the parallel of 14° S. has but few inhabitants, and is little more than an appendage to Cook District proper. There are in this district important gold-fields, notably those of the Palmer River and Hodgkinson, which have proved to be exceedingly rich. Tin is also found in considerable abundance, and coal-measures are known to exist. There is a large proportion of soil fit for agriculture, and much of the country is taken up for grazing purposes. Along the Gulf of Carpentaria, and westward of the Kennedy District, is the **Burke District,** a vast tract largely utilized for pastoral pursuits, being watered by numerous streams, but containing also a goldfield on the Gilbert River. Gold is also obtained at the Cloncurry River, a tributary of the Flinders, and mining for copper has been carried on for some time in the same neighbourhood. South of this district, and occupying the extreme west of the colony, is the **Gregory District,** which is comparatively little known. The occupied portions are taken up for pastoral purposes. In this district are several areas which, in the present state of our knowledge, are considered as deserts. East of the Gregory District are the **Mitchell** and the **Warrego Districts,** both entirely devoted to pastoral pursuits. East of Mitchell lies the **Leichardt District,** which, in the north-east, reaches nearly as far as the sea-coast at Broad Sound. It is chiefly pastoral, but possesses gold and copper, which have both been worked. The Central Railway passes through this district. South of Leichardt, and east of Warrego, is the **Maranoa District,** consisting of the western slope of the table-land and plains which are occupied for pastoral purposes. The remainder of the colony, comprising the southern portion of the table-land and its western slope, forms the celebrated **Darling Downs District,** which contains perhaps the finest agricultural and pastoral land in Australia. Coal is said to exist in various places, but it has not been worked.

14. What has been said respecting Australian **towns** in the account of New South Wales is equally applicable to those of Queensland. As it will serve no useful purpose merely to enumerate the scores of villages and small towns which, though growing in numbers and wealth, and forming the centres of intelligence and business for surrounding districts, possess no distinctive features, only the more important will be mentioned in the following account of the Queensland topography.

15. In the Moreton District is the capital **Brisbane,** so

named from a former governor of New South Wales, Sir Thomas Brisbane. Its foundation dates from 1825, but it was not till 1859 that it took rank as a colonial capital. It is situated on the banks of a fine stream bearing the same name, over which an iron bridge has been constructed. The city has a good water supply, is adorned with parks and reserves, including a botanical garden, and possesses some handsome public buildings. Brisbane is the principal port of the colony, both for the intercolonial trade and that with the mother country. It is also the terminus of the western and southern railway system, and the natural outlet for the agricultural and pastoral produce of the Darling Downs and other districts to the westward. Besides being the chief business centre of the colony this city is also the seat of government and of the legislature. The population is 51,000.

16. **Ipswich**, on the Bremer River, an affluent of the Brisbane, has communication with the capital by rail and steamer. The vicinity is mainly agricultural, cotton being one of the plants in cultivation; but some woollen manufacture is also carried on, and coal-mines in the neighbourhood are profitably worked. The population is supposed to number 8000.

In the Wide Bay District, **Maryborough** is the chief town. It is situated on the Mary River, and is the shipping port for the produce of the adjacent agricultural district, and of the Gympie gold-field. The growth and manufacture of sugar, timber-getting, soap manufacture, and iron-foundries are the chief sources of industrial employment. The population is about 7000.

Gympie, on an old-established and still flourishing gold-field, has a population of 6000. In the surrounding country many different minerals have been discovered, among them being silver, copper, antimony, cinnabar, bismuth, and nickel. There is also good agricultural land. The town is connected with Maryborough by rail.

Bundaberg, a port near the mouth of the Burnett River, is the centre of a rich mining, pastoral, and agricultural district. Copper is the chief mineral product, and coal abounds in the vicinity though not yet worked. From the pastoral regions on the upper courses of the Burnett and Dawson rivers wool and other produce is brought to Bundaberg for shipment. The principal agricultural industries are maize and sugar growing, for which the fertile alluvial and volcanic soil is well adapted.

Rockhampton, which ranks as the second city of the colony, is situated on the south bank of the Fitzroy River, about forty-five miles from its mouth. As the outlet of the important district of Port Curtis, and the Leichardt District to the westward, Rockhampton is a place of great trade. The products of the surrounding country are gold, copper, and silver, wool, tallow, preserved meats, and maize. From Rockhampton a railway has been constructed which is intended to penetrate into the western interior, and to connect the rich copper-yielding country of Peak Downs with the port of shipment. The population is estimated at 10,000.

Another important town in the Port Curtis District is **Gladstone**, situated on the coast, and possessing a fine harbour. Considerable trade is carried on between this place and New Caledonia, to which island cattle are largely exported.

In the Kennedy District the most important town is **Townsville**, on Cleveland Bay. It is the port to which the produce of a vast territory is sent for shipment. The surrounding country is mostly devoted to pastoral purposes, but there are gold-fields at Charters' Towers, Milchester, and Ravenswood. With the first of these Townsville is connected by rail. The port is an open roadstead, but by the erection of a breakwater it is expected that ships will eventually be able to lie alongside the wharfs. Already the population approaches 4000, and the port ranks as the third in importance in the colony.

Another rising port in this district is **Bowen**, which has an excellent harbour called Port Denison, and is the outlet for a large pastoral district lying to the westward. Coal abounds in the neighbourhood, and there is also good agricultural land.

Cardwell, on Rockingham Bay, is another seaport in the same district, which bids fair to become a place of some consequence, there being excellent land in the neighbourhood. Sugar-growing is carried on to some extent. In the bay large numbers of dugongs are caught, and works have been erected for the extraction of their oil.

Mackay, on the Pioneer River, near the southern boundary

Near Gladstone.

of the district, is the centre of a fine agricultural area which is specially adapted to the cultivation of the sugar-cane, although coffee, tobacco, and other sub-tropical plants also flourish in the same soil. There is also some pastoral country, and there are copper-mines at no great distance.

Cooktown is the chief centre of population in the Cook District. This town is situated on the Endeavour River, famed in connection with the history of Captain Cook. It is supported chiefly by the traffic carried on with the Palmer gold-field, though there is some good pastoral country lying around. The population, including Chinese, of whom there is a large number, is about 8000.

On Trinity Bay is the settlement of **Cairns**, which is the outlet for a gold-mining district. The vicinity produces excellent timber, and there are tin **mines** at a little distance inland.

In the Burke District the settlements have been made in the gold-fields which lie among the upper courses of the Norman and Gilbert Rivers. The most important town, however, is **Normanton**, on the river of that name, and the terminus of the telegraph line from the capital.

Roma, the principal town in the Maranoa District, is the centre of a large pastoral district, with great agricultural capabilities. The vine has been successfully cultivated.

In the Darling Downs District there are several towns of some importance. The principal is **Toowoomba**, with a population of about 5000; **Warwick** and **Dalby** rank next, all three being supported from the contiguous agricultural areas. **Stanthorpe**, farther south, is the chief town in the tin-mining district of Queensland.

Among the smaller towns a considerable proportion bid fair to become places of importance. Some of these are mining townships, in which gold-digging and quartz-crushing are carried on. Such are **Charters Towers, Milchester,** and **Ravenswood**, in the Kennedy District. **Herberton**, in the same district, is the centre of the tin-mining industry, though silver, lead, and copper are also worked in the vicinity. Another mining township is **Hughenden**, in the Burke District, on the Flinders. **Georgetown**, on the Gilbert gold-field, is of the same character. In the Leichardt District **Clermont** is an important mining township, being in the vicinity of the celebrated Peak Downs copper-mines. In the Coast District **Port Douglas**, on Trinity Bay, and **Gayndah**, near Wide Bay, are deserving of mention.

Among the inland towns **Emerald** in the Leichardt District, **Mitchell** and **St. George** in Maranoa, and **Goondivindi** in the Darling Downs, are of some importance; and further west, **Aramac** and **Blackall** in Mitchell, and **Charleville, Cunnamalla**, and **Thargomindah** in Warrego, are local centres for pastoral areas.

CHAPTER VI.

THE COLONY OF VICTORIA.

1. Boundaries and extent. 2. Coast line and Harbours. 3. Surface. 4. Mountains. 5. Table-lands. 6. Plains. 7. Drainage. 8. Rivers of northern slope. 9. Rivers of southern slope. 10. Lakes. 11. Climate. 12. Soil. 13. Internal Communication. 14. Navigable Rivers. 15. Roads, Railways, and Telegraphs. 16. Population. 17. Industrial Occupations; pasturage, agriculture, and mining. 18. Manufactures. 19. Commerce. 20. Government. 21. Religion and Education. 22. Territorial Divisions. 23. Melbourne. 24. Other Towns.

1. Though the most populous of the colonies on the continent of Australia, Victoria is the smallest in extent, having an area of but 88,198 square miles. On the south and east it is **bounded** by the ocean; on the north by New South Wales, from which it is separated by the river Murray and an artificial boundary line running from Cape Howe to the source of the Indi, one of the head-waters of the Murray; and on the west lies South Australia, the dividing line being the 141st meridian of east longitude. Victoria is wholly contained between that meridian on the west and the 150th on the east; and between the 34th parallel of south latitude on the north and the 40th on the south. Cape Howe is the extreme eastern point; the most northerly, a point on the Murray River, near the intersection of the 141st meridian and the 34th parallel; the most southern, Wilson's Promontory. Its greatest length from east to west is 480 miles, and its width, from north to south, 260 miles.

2. The irregular **coast-line**, estimated at 600 miles in length, is marked by several conspicuous projections and indentations, especially to the westward of the 148th meridian. Eastward of that line, however, a long stretch of sandy beach without projections of any size occurs, named, from its supposed extent, the Ninety Mile Beach. Among the more prominent of the projections are **Capes Bridgewater and Nelson** on the west; **Cape Otway, Cape Liptrap,** and **Wilson's Promontory** in the centre; and **Cape Howe** the farthest east. **Portland Bay,** near Cape Nelson, is a considerable inlet, affording good anchorage for ships. The principal indentation on the coast, however, is

the unnamed bay or bight lying between Capes Otway and

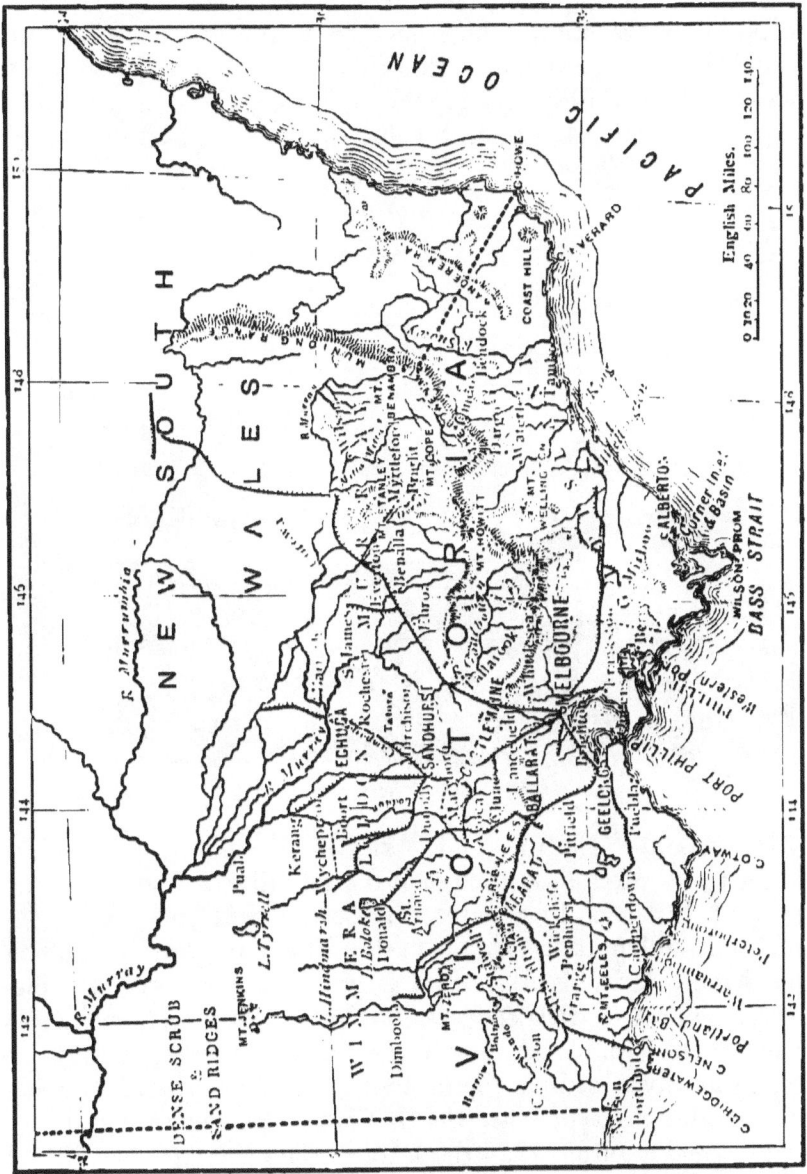

Liptrap, at the head of which, and connected with it by a narrow channel, is **Port Phillip**, an extensive sheet of water, forming the largest and most important harbour in the colony. Eastward of Port Phillip is another inlet from the great bay, named **Port Western**, which has two entrances, formed by an island at its mouth called Phillip Island. On the peninsula between Port Phillip and Port Western are Point Nepean and Cape Schanck. **Anderson's Inlet** lies farther eastward; and

Coast Scenery—Cape Schanck.

between Cape Liptrap and Wilson's Promontory is a bay known as Patterson's, though it bears other names. On the east of Wilson's Promontory is **Corner Inlet**, the last considerable indentation on the coast. There are, however, along the Ninety Mile Beach, several large salt-water **lagoons**, sometimes connected with the sea, but often with their entrances blocked up with sand. In all respects these lakes, as they are called locally, resemble the lagoons already mentioned as existing on the coast of New South Wales, but the former are of much greater extent than the latter. The principal are named Victoria, with an area of 90 square miles; and Wellington, which covers 70 square miles. Numerous islets stud the coast in the neighbourhood of Wilson's Promontory.

3. In many points the **surface of Victoria** resembles that of New South Wales, though the natural features are upon a less extensive scale. There is a coast district, a table-land through which runs a dividing chain, and some interior plains. As these are included in so small a territory they necessarily cause the surface to be more varied. The coast district consists for the most part of undulating country, with an average breadth of about forty miles. The eastern portion is the most level.

4. The great **Dividing Chain** from New South Wales enters Victoria, crossing the boundary line a little to the north of the 37th parallel, and thence runs in a westerly direction until it approaches the 142d meridian east longitude, where it sinks down into low plains. Various ranges branch off from the main chain—some in a northerly direction, others towards the south. The width of the Dividing Chain, including its principal spurs, may be estimated at a hundred miles. The most elevated land is to be found in the north-east, where many of the summits in the Dividing Chain exceed 6000 feet in height, and the culminating point, **Mount Bogong**, attains the altitude of 6508 feet. This portion of the chain is sometimes styled the **Australian Alps**; a more distinctive appellation is the **Warragong Mountains**. Tracing the Dividing Chain westward the elevation will be found to decrease, the average height being about 2500 feet. The westerly prolongation of the chain receives the names of the **Pyrenees** and the **Grampians**. These are the lowest parts of the chain, though there are some lofty summits, and **Mount William**, in the latter, rises to the height of 5600 feet. The lateral branches are not conspicuous for height, but fall gradually down to the Murray Valley on the one side and to the ocean on the other. On the average the height of the whole system may be estimated at 3000 feet. Though no active volcanoes now exist in Victoria, the evidences of volcanic action in past ages are abundant, and craters of extinct volcanoes are numerous, especially in the western parts of the colony.

5. On each side of the Dividing Chain and its continuation stretches a narrow **table-land**, with an undulating surface and an average elevation of less than 2000 feet. As in New South Wales the fall of the table-land towards the sea is rapid; but

on the northern side it declines gradually down to the Murray Valley and the plains. Towards the west its general height is considerably below the average.

6. In the north-west are the most extensive level tracts in the colony. Though limited in extent these **plains** possess the same general character as those adjacent to them in New South Wales. With some good land there is a large area containing soil of an inferior description, and, generally speaking, the supply of water is scanty. Through a large portion there flows no considerable stream, even as that phrase is understood in Australia, and many hundreds of square miles are covered with the detested mallee scrub.

7. The **drainage system** of Victoria is very simple. There are two principal slopes—one to the north into the Murray River, the other to the south into the Great Southern Ocean. The Dividing Chain forms the watershed between the two. There is also a system of inland drainage in the north-west, where certain streams discharge their waters into lakes from which there is no outlet.

8. In general terms it may be said that the whole of the northern slope is included in the basin of the **Murray**. This river, although belonging to New South Wales, may also be considered a Victorian stream, inasmuch as some of its head-waters take their rise in Victoria, and it is also fed by numerous tributaries from the latter colony. Among these the chief are, commencing from the east, the **Mitta Mitta**, the **Ovens**, the **Goulburn** (which is the most important), the **Campaspe**, and the **Loddon**. The first two of these rise in the Warragong Mountains, and are swollen by the rains and by the melting snows of that region. Their supply of water is consequently more constant than is usually the case with Australian rivers. The Goulburn is the longest of the purely Victorian rivers, having a course of about 250 miles. In this northern slope the system of inland drainage may be included, inasmuch as the rivers connected with it take their rise on the north side of the watershed. These are the **Avoca**, which falls into Lake Baal Baal, and the **Wimmera**, which empties itself into Lake Hindmarsh.

9. On the southern slope the longest river is the **Snowy**,

which rises in New South Wales and enters the sea eastward of the Ninety Mile Beach, after a course of 400 miles. Numerous smaller streams, draining the southern side of the watershed, deliver their waters into the coast lakes, the Mitchell being the most important. These flow from north to south; the Latrobe, which has a similar termination, runs easterly into Lake Wellington. The **Yarra** flows westerly, and after a course of 90 miles empties into Port Phillip Bay, which also receives several other streams of less importance. Farther

A River View

west the **Hopkins**, rising in the Pyrenees, enters the sea a short distance east of Portland Bay; and the **Glenelg**, from the Grampians, after a devious course of 200 miles, reaches the coast where it is cut by the 141st meridian.

10. Besides the salt-water lagoons before described, Victoria possesses numerous **lakes** properly so called. Some of these occupy simple depressions in the surface; others, the craters of extinct volcanoes. A few are of considerable size, but generally speaking, they are of small extent. Few of them have any outlet. The largest is Lake **Corangamite**, situated west

of Port Phillip and north of Cape Otway. It has an area of 76 square miles, and its waters are salt. Lake **Bolac**, in the same district, is fresh, and has an area of 10 square miles. The principal lake region, however, lies in the north and north-west, where numerous salt lakes are to be found. Lakes **Hindmarsh** and **Tyrrell** are the largest of these; the former may have an area of about 10 square miles.

11. In its general character the **climate** of Victoria resembles that of the other portions of Australia, which lie in the South Temperate Zone. As regards temperature, the same conditions exist here as elsewhere. Thus the elevated tracts occupying the north-eastern portion of the colony are much colder than any other part, snow and ice being common in winter, and the heat less in summer. Along the coast district, where the modifying influence of proximity to the sea is felt, the average temperature of summer is lower and that of winter higher than among the mountains. On the table-land frosts sometimes occur in winter; but, except in the most elevated portions, the temperature does not greatly differ from that experienced in the coast district. In the plains on the north-west, however, and along the valley of the lower Murray, the heat is usually very great in summer, and in winter the thermometer at night often falls below the freezing-point. In fact, there is little difference between the temperature of these plains and that of the neighbouring portions of New South Wales. The mean temperature of the year is in Melbourne about 56°. In point of humidity the climate may be generally described as dry. It would be impossible, in the absence of sufficient observations, to state exactly the average yearly rainfall for the whole colony. In Melbourne it is said to be 26 inches; among the mountains, 36 inches; and on the plains, about 14 inches. The proportion of wet to fine days is small, and the sky is generally unclouded and bright. The prevailing winds are westerly, and on the coast the south-west wind usually brings rain. Occasionally, the hot winds which cause so much injury to vegetation in New South Wales are felt in Victoria, though in the latter they blow from the north. Though unpleasant while they last, these winds are not deemed unhealthy; and, as they occur but on a few days only in each summer, they

cannot be regarded as altering the general character of the climate in any material degree. On the whole the climate of Victoria must be pronounced one of the most healthy and enjoyable in the world.

12. So large is the proportion of excellent **soil** that one of the names first proposed for Victoria was Australia Felix. In the river valleys the alluvium is deep and rich; but the largest areas of good soil are found where trap, basalt, and other volcanic rocks have been disintegrated. These soils, when sufficiently watered, are productive in the highest degree, and are fitted not only for the growth of wheat and other cereals, but also for the cultivation of tobacco and semi-tropical plants generally. Besides soils of this description, there are others of a lighter character, which, though unfit for cultivation under present circumstances, are nevertheless well adapted for pasturage, and are largely used for that purpose. Some soils, which are too poor to be turned to account in any other way, produce excellent timber. The amount of absolutely useless soil is therefore very small.

13. In common with other Australian colonies, Victoria is little favoured with natural means of **internal communication**, as she possesses few navigable rivers. Her common roads are in general more indebted to nature than to art, being, over a large extent of country, mere tracks through the bush or over the plains. Her railway system, however, is largely and effectively developed, and now comprises 1700 miles of line in actual operation. Telegraphic communication, both within and without the colony, is also provided to a large extent.

14. The **Murray** is the principal navigable river, and forms a highway of trade for the whole of the colony north of the Dividing Chain. The vessels which ply on the Murray are small steamers, which tow after them barges laden with stores on the upward, and with wool and other products on the return trip. Necessarily traffic of this description is limited to the times and seasons when the water in the river is of sufficient depth, and is often stopped in summer and during periods of drought. The **Yarra** is the only other navigable river, and by it vessels of considerable size can be brought up to the business

Scene on the Murray River

portion of Melbourne, and unlade their burden as it were into the warehouses.

15. In the early days of Victorian independence, after the discovery of gold had given rise to an enormous traffic, the common **roads** were merely tracks cleared through the bush, and covered with sand or dust in summer, and with mud in winter. Stone of the proper kind being abundant, however, macadamized roads were formed in many directions. But it was soon perceived that in the long run **railways** would be cheaper and more lasting than even such roads, and railway construction was in consequence vigorously proceeded with by the government, which is now the owner of all the lines in the colony. Melbourne is the centre from which the railway system proceeds, but the lines are already much reticulated; and, as extensions are formed, the whole scheme will become more complicated. The following are the principal lines:— The Eastern line connects Melbourne with Sale in the Gipps Land district, and has a length of 127½ miles. From Melbourne to Wodonga, 187 miles, the connection is made by the North-Eastern line, which, besides several short branches, has an important extension from Mangalore to the Murray river at a point opposite Tocumwall. The Northern line and its branches connect Melbourne with Echuca, also on the Murray, and there are extensions to Kerang and Wycheproof. A loop-line connects this with the North-Western line, which runs south-west to Geelong, and thence north-westerly to Ballarat, where it forks, the right-hand branch proceeding to Donald, and the left-hand to Dimboola. From this branch a line proceeds in a south-westerly direction connecting Portland with Ararat, and ultimately with Melbourne. An extension from this branch runs westerly to Casterton on the Glenelg river. The Western line connects Geelong with Camperdown, 123 miles to the westward. The work of railway extension is still proceeding, and internal communication by this means is rapidly being improved and cheapened. Telegraphic communication keeps pace with railway construction; and, up to the present time, upwards of 4000 miles of line, requiring about 9000 miles of wire, have been opened for service. Few even of the smaller towns are now without this important appliance of civilization.

Communication is also maintained with the mother country, with Tasmania, with New Zealand, and with other parts of the world by means of the telegraph systems of other colonies and submarine cables. Steamships and sailing vessels enable the different ports on the coast to keep up regular communication with the metropolis, as well as with places in other colonies. The postal system is not less perfect, and, as may be gathered from the preceding statements, the means of internal communication in Victoria are in advance of those in any other Australian colony.

16. As the census is taken but once in ten years it is not possible to state with confidence the number of **inhabitants** in the colony; but, judging from the sources of information at present available, it may be estimated at more than a million. On this calculation the increase of population proceeds at the rate of about 30,000 per annum. While representatives of most European, and some Asiatic, nations may be found among the people, the vast majority are from the United Kingdom, or descendants of those who migrated therefrom. Males still preponderate over females, though the inequality in the number of the two sexes is believed to be gradually diminishing. Of the aboriginal natives, but a small remnant, probably not exceeding 700, now remains, and in a few years even they seem likely to disappear.

17. In proportion to size **pasturage** occupies as large a number of the people as in any of the other colonies. Victoria depastures about 10,000,000 sheep, 1,250,000 cattle, and 300,000 horses, besides rearing pigs, of which there are about 250,000. Wool continues to form the most valuable article of export, and the other pastoral products, hides and tallow, are of considerable importance. **Agriculture** is also carried on to a large extent, the crops raised being of many different kinds. Of these the principal are wheat, oats, barley, potatoes, and hay; and the less considerable are barley, peas and beans, hops, and tobacco. Much attention is also paid to the culture of the vine. All the common European fruits are grown, and culinary vegetables are produced in sufficient quantities to furnish a surplus for exportation. Upwards of 2,300,000 acres of land are under tillage, so that Victoria not only provides for her own wants,

but is also able to supply her neighbours. The mining industry, though less flourishing than in former times, still employs large numbers of men, and **minerals** continue to form an important part of the colonial products. Gold is still the most valuable of the metals raised in Victoria, though the total amount obtained yearly is not known. Silver, copper, tin, and iron have been worked, but these branches of mining industry are not carried on with much energy. Lead, zinc, antimony, and bismuth are even less extensively sought for, although they are plentiful. Numerous other metals of the rarer kinds are known to exist, but have not yet been the subjects of systematic mining operations. Coal is less plentiful, but has been worked to some extent. The search for diamonds and other precious stones is an occasional rather than a regular pursuit.

18. Victoria surpasses all the other Australian colonies in the extent and value of her **manufactures**, and a large proportion of her people are engaged in, or dependent upon, such occupations. While many of these are of the kind already described as domestic, some have been designedly established with a view to the production of commodities for export. Among these may be mentioned flour and the various articles prepared from it; meat preserving; tobacco and cigars; wine, beer; paper and such goods as are made of it; leather, boots and shoes, and the different articles for which leather is used; timber and carpenters', joiners', and cabinet-makers' work; pottery and glass ware: woollen cloth and clothing; and rope and twine. These are only the more important manufactures. Besides them there are a large number not individually of much consequence, but forming in the aggregate a means of employment for some thousands of persons.

19. The internal **commerce** of the colony consists chiefly of the interchange of the products of different districts, and the distribution of imported goods on the one hand, and the transmission to the ports of native products and manufactures for export. Of a similar character is the intercolonial trade, which is even more extensive, and which is carried on principally by means of steam-vessels plying to the chief ports in the neighbouring colonies. The foreign commerce with the United Kingdom, America, China, and other countries of less note, is

of great extent and importance. Among the exports those of greatest consequence are wool, gold, coined and in bullion, leather, tallow, boots and shoes, flour and biscuits, which, together with commodities of less value, amount to about £16,000,000. The principal imports consist of cotton, woollen, silk, and linen goods; live stock; boots and shoes; tea and sugar, grain; paper, stationery, and books; metals and hardware; building materials; cordage and bags; glass, earthenware, and porcelain; tobacco and cigars; and spirits, wines, and beer. In this list no mention is made of numerous classes of goods, the values of which as imported range from £10,000 to £100,000. The total value of imports annually is about £19,000,000. It will readily be seen that a commerce so vast in proportion to the limited population must give employment to great numbers of persons, and that the progress or decline of this occupation will always be an index of the prosperity of the colony. Another means of estimating the value of Victorian commerce is furnished by the return of shipping which enters and leaves her ports, and which numbers about 4000 vessels, with an aggregate tonnage of 3,150,000 tons.

20. In all the Australian colonies the **government** is of the same general character with some points of difference in details. The governor, as chief of the executive and representative of the sovereign, is appointed by the Queen and governs in her name. He is assisted by the ministry, who are his constitutional advisers, and the heads of the different departments into which the administration is divided. They must be members of the legislature, to which they are responsible, and whose approval they must secure for their measures. Two separate houses are included in the legislature; the lower, or Assembly, consisting of 86 members, who are elected by manhood suffrage, and paid for their services; and the upper or Council, comprising 42 members, also elected by voters, who, however, must possess a property qualification of a certain value. The Assembly is elected for three years unless dissolved by the governor before the expiration of the full period; and the members of the Council hold office for three years only. Voting by ballot is invariably practised in Victoria as in the rest of Australia. From these remarks it will be evident that

the constitution of this colony is thoroughly democratic, and the administration is in full accordance with those principles. The expenses incurred in carrying on the government are defrayed from the revenue, which is the money raised by authority of the legislature from taxes, sale and lease of land, and the receipts from railways and postage, and from minor sources. About £6,000,000 are obtained by these means annually, and the yearly expenditure for the purposes of government amounts, in round numbers, to the like sum.

21. There is no state **religion** in Victoria, but every sect enjoys full toleration for its opinions and observances, provided the latter do not infringe upon the rights of others. As might be expected in a population of such a mixed character, adherents of many different Christian churches are to be found in Victoria, though the several Protestant denominations and Roman Catholics form the great majority. For example, there are members of the Greek Church, Jews, Christian Israelites, "Friends" or Quakers, and even Mormons and Pagans, the latter being mostly Chinese and aboriginals. In conformity with this neutrality of the state towards various denominations, the established system of **public instruction,** from the primary school to the university, is purely secular. In the schools maintained by the state no charge is made for tuition in common subjects, and attendance thereat is obligatory for children between the ages of six and fourteen years, unless they are efficiently instructed elsewhere, or are kept away from unavoidable causes. It is stated that one person in every six of the population is under instruction in some form. Secondary, or middle-class, education is not aided by the state; but the university is supported at a large expense, and has been attended by large numbers of students. Secondary education is provided in private schools and colleges, which are numerous and efficient. In this respect Victoria takes the lead of all the other Australian colonies, from which pupils are often sent for the sake of the superior instruction believed to be imparted in the leading educational institutions in Melbourne and its vicinity.

22. The **territorial divisions** of Victoria are as numerous as those of New South Wales. There are counties numbering

37, useful in connection with the survey of land; electoral districts, 55 in number, which return members to the Legislative Assembly; provinces, 14 in number, by which members of the Council are elected; shires, within which certain municipal powers may be exercised; and boroughs and towns, which are localities incorporated for municipal purposes. Besides these there is a popular division into districts, of which four are recognized. That on the east and north-east is called **Gipps Land**, after one of the governors of New South Wales. This district, stretching from the crest of the Dividing Chain to the sea, consists of a mountainous region abounding in mineral wealth, but unfit for farming or grazing pursuits; an undulating tract containing rich soil and luxuriant vegetation with valuable timber of various kinds, but requiring a heavy expenditure to prepare it for the plough; and the level country bordering upon the lakes and the ocean, and devoted to agriculture and pasturage. From its fertility it has been termed the garden of Victoria, and it supplies the capital and other large cities with much of the food, animal and vegetable, consumed by the inhabitants. Gipps Land is not less celebrated for the variety and picturesque beauty of its scenery. Between the Dividing Chain and the Murray River lies the **Murray District**. Several rivers drain this portion of the colony, which is mainly pastoral in its character, though it possesses much mineral wealth and several productive gold-fields. Farming is also carried on to some extent, the vine and tobacco being important objects of cultivation. The **Loddon District**, which is named after the Loddon River flowing through it, lies to the west of the Murray District. Though the larger portion is occupied for pastoral purposes, much gold is obtained from the southern part, where some of the most productive "diggings" in the colony formerly existed. The north-west section of the colony constitutes the **Wimmera District**, which, except in its south-east part, where some agriculture is carried on, is exclusively pastoral. The nature of the soil and the climate, together with the scanty supply of moisture, render farming impossible with ordinary appliances; but sheep appear to thrive where the land is not too thickly overgrown with scrub.

23. **Melbourne**, the capital, stands on the banks of the

In a Gipps Land Bush.

Yarra and on the shores of Port Phillip. Besides the city itself there are, adjacent to it, several municipal boroughs which, in size and population, are entitled to rank with any other Australian cities, except those of the first class. Regarding these as portions of the metropolis, it may be stated that Melbourne extends over a large space, but in an irregular shape. It is laid out in broad streets, which cross each other at right angles, and which afford the necessary facility for carrying on the enormous traffic that at all times distinguishes Melbourne. Health and recreation are provided for, however, in the numerous and spacious reserves made in various parts of the city, of which the botanic gardens and the Royal Park are noteworthy examples. The site is, in the highest part, undulating, in many places level, and in a few low and swampy. In a city so large, but having existed for so short a period as fifty years, it might be expected that there would be little uniformity in the character of the buildings. There are, however, many handsome edifices, public and private; and in the better parts of the city the structures are substantial and sometimes massive. The building stone available, locally termed "blue stone," though sombre in appearance, is hard and durable, and gives to edifices constructed of it a characteristic air of strength and solidity. Among the more conspicuous public buildings may be mentioned the Parliament Houses, the Law-courts, the Post-office, the Treasury, the Free Library, and the University. The Town-hall, the Exchange, several banks, and many of the churches, are also worthy of mention for their architectural merits; and some of the mercantile warehouses are remarkable for their size and excellence of construction. Water is abundantly supplied from the Yan Yean reservoir, situated about 20 miles from Melbourne, and the city is well lighted with gas. On the whole it may be said that the drainage, the great difficulty of all Australian cities, is very imperfect. As the seat of government Melbourne derives some of its importance from being the official residence of the governor, the place at which the legislature assembles, and the head-quarters of administration, departmental, judicial, and executive. In some sense it may also be regarded as the centre of intelligence for the country, the inhabitants being distinguished for mental

THE COLONY OF VICTORIA. 135

activity and a spirit of enterprise. Numerous institutions bear witness to the prevalence of a desire for the spread of know-

Houses of Parliament, Melbourne.

ledge, as the noble Free Library, the Art Gallery, the Industrial and Technological Museum, and the Botanic Gardens. Education is provided at the public cost in the state schools and in the flourishing university. Private schools and colleges also supply the means of instruction, chiefly to the children of the middle and upper classes. Although standing high in all these respects, in its industrial aspect Melbourne occupies the first place in Australia. All the ordinary occupations practised in cities of the old world have been introduced, and now give employment to thousands; and manufactures, properly so called, are carried on actively and with success. A still larger number are engaged in matters connected with the enormous commerce of which Melbourne is the centre. The population of the city and its suburbs is estimated at 300,000.

24. As might be expected where the population is confined within comparatively narrow bounds Victoria possesses a larger number of **towns** worthy of the name than any other Australian colony. The existence of so many large towns is, in fact, a special feature of Victorian social and political life. There are also some hundreds of incipient townships which, although possessing at present but a limited number of inhabitants, are situated in somewhat populous districts where productive industries are carried on. This is specially the case with what are locally termed mining townships. In one of these it may happen that but two or three hundred persons inhabit the town itself, while, scattered around, there may be within a few miles some thousands of miners. As, however, the small towns would be too numerous to describe in detail in the following topographical accounts, such only will be included as have a population of 1000 and upwards, except in a few cases of unusual prospective importance.

Beginning with towns on the lines of railway, the first to be mentioned is **Warragul**, on the Eastern line, 61 miles from Melbourne. This town is situated in a rich district, and will become the business centre for the western portion of Gipps Land. The population approximates to 1000.

Sale, in an extensive pastoral and agricultural district, is the chief town of Gipps Land, and the terminus of the eastern railway. The town is well laid out, possesses some handsome buildings, and carries on some manufacturing industries. It is also the head of the navigation of the Gipps Land lakes. The population exceeds 3000.

On the North-eastern line, **Kilmore**, 39½ miles from Melbourne, has a population of 1100. The vicinity is mainly agricultural, the soil being of excellent quality; but there is also some mining for gold as well as local manufactures.

Benalla, 121 miles from Melbourne, is the centre of an agricultural and dairying district, which produces grain, grapes, and other fruits in large quantities. The surrounding country is pastoral in character. The population of the town is 1700.

Distant 145 miles from Melbourne, on the Ovens River, is **Wangaratta**, which has a population of over 1300. Pasturage and agriculture are the great industries of the district, though there are the usual local manufactures. Grain, fruits, and tobacco are the chief products.

Chiltern, 168 miles from Melbourne, has a population of about 1200, who are principally engaged in mining pursuits.

Wodonga, 187 miles from Melbourne, is the terminus of the North-eastern line, and is connected by a bridge across the Murray River with the railway system of New South Wales. The population approaches 1000.

At the terminus of a short branch line from Wangaratta is **Beechworth**, 171 miles from Melbourne. It is the centre of the far-famed Ovens gold-field, from which some millions' worth of gold has been obtained, and which still employs thousands of men in mining. Agriculture and pasturage are also carried on in the district, as well as the industries which are required where quartz-reefing is a regular pursuit. The population numbers about 2500.

Another branch of the North-eastern line terminates at **Wahgunyah**, on the Murray, 173 miles from Melbourne. The district is agricultural and pastoral; and the town, though now possessing but a small population, is likely from its position to increase in size and importance.

Shepparton, 112 miles from Melbourne, on the western extension of the North-eastern line, is the centre of a rich agricultural district in which wheat, barley, and oats are largely grown. The population exceeds 1000.

On the Northern line the first populous town is **Woodend**, which is 48 miles distant from Melbourne, and is inhabited by 1100 persons.

At the distance of 57 miles from Melbourne is **Kyneton**, on the Campaspe River. The district is agricultural, pastoral, and mining, but local manufactures are extensively carried on. The population is 3000.

Malmsbury, 63 miles from Melbourne, is another mining township, gold being obtained both by digging and reefing. The population exceeds 1300.

Taradale, in the same district, 67 miles from Melbourne, is the centre of another rich mining district, quartz reefs being numerous and productive. Farming is also carried on to a large extent. The population of the town and neighbourhood exceeds 1400.

At a distance of 75 miles from Melbourne is **Chewton**, on one of the most productive gold-fields of the colony. Gold-mining is still carried on with success both in alluvial diggings and in quartz reefs. The population numbers 1700.

Castlemaine, 77 miles from Melbourne, is a great railway centre as well as the head-quarters of an extensive gold-mining industry. In addition to this, agriculture and pasturage are also carried on, together with some local manufactures. The town, which is well laid out, has now a population of 6000.

Sandhurst, 100 miles from Melbourne, is one of the most important centres of the gold-mining industry in the colony. Under the name of Bendigo the district was celebrated in the early days of gold-digging for the enormous yields of the precious metal obtained by washing the auriferous soil. Of late years attention has chiefly been given to quartz-reefing, which is now carried on to a large extent and with great success. A large population has consequently gathered in the district, and that of the town alone is 28,000 persons. In addition to mining, farming and vine-culture are prosperous industries, and the local manufactures are numerous and important. The town, or city as it is usually called, has nearly 100 miles of streets, is well supplied with water, and lighted with gas. Many handsome buildings adorn the streets, and there are two reserves for recreation. Altogether, Sandhurst may be regarded as one of the most flourishing of Victorian towns.

From Sandhurst the railway divides into several branches. The most eastern of these terminates at **Echuca**, on the Murray,

Taradale a Mining Township.

156 miles from Melbourne. Situated in an extensive and fertile pastoral and agricultural district, and possessing unusual facilities for trade by rail and river, the town enjoys all the elements of prosperity. Grain is produced in large quantities, the vine is also cultivated; and wool from neighbouring stations as well as from the adjacent colony is a staple commodity of the town, which is the centre of much of the river traffic. A railway bridge spans the Murray at this place. The population exceeds 5000.

Another branch of this line extends to Mitiamo, whence it has been carried to Kerang, and will be further extended to Swan Hill, on the Murray River. The only populous town on this line is **Eagle Hawk**, 106 miles from Melbourne. Like its neighbour Sandhurst, this place derives its prosperity from gold-mining, the country abounding in auriferous quartz reefs. The population exceeds 7000.

From Eagle Hawk a branch line runs in a north-westerly direction, on which is situated **Inglewood**, 130 miles from Melbourne. The district is gold-bearing and agricultural, and mining and farming are consequently the principal industries. The gold is obtained chiefly from quartz. The population is 1400.

Charlton, on the same branch, is 173 miles from Melbourne. The district is agricultural and produces wheat in great abundance. Although the present population is below 1000, the place bids fair to grow in importance. This line terminates at **Wycheproof,** 190 miles from Melbourne, and there is a short branch to **Boort**.

Maldon, on a branch line from Castlemaine, 89 miles from Melbourne, is situated in a pastoral and agricultural district, but possesses in addition auriferous strata, the source of great wealth. The population is 3000.

As the terminus of another branch from the same trunk line, **Daylesford,** 76 miles from Melbourne, is a place of some importance. It is also the centre of a mining district in which the search for gold in quartz rock is carried on in the most improved fashion, and gives employment to a large number of persons. Like most of the mining townships, it is also interested to some extent in agricultural and local manufactures. The population is about 4000.

The North-western railway line may be held to commence at **Geelong**, on the shores of Port Phillip, 45 miles from Melbourne. This town is pleasantly situated, well laid out, and ornamented with many creditable buildings. There are several public reserves for recreation, and the town is well supplied with water and lighted with gas. Corio Bay, the branch of Port Phillip Bay upon which the town is placed, forms an excellent harbour, and ships of large tonnage can be brought alongside the jetties. Its facilities in this respect enable Geelong to take its position as one of the principal ports of the colony. Among the exports wool is an important item. Geelong is also distinguished as a manufacturing town, and in it was established the first woollen factory in Victoria. This industry is still carried on, together with rope-making, tanning, and the usual domestic manufactures. The neighbouring district is agricultural and contains much land adapted for farming. The population is 10,000. Geelong is connected with Melbourne by rail, and is the starting-point of the Western line.

Ballarat (or Ballaarat), the second city of the colony, is on the North-western line, 96 miles from Melbourne. Around it lies an extensive district, which has been without parallel for richness as a gold-producing region. Alluvial digging having been exhausted, the precious metal is now obtained from crushing the auriferous quartz rock; and mining, in the proper sense, is carried on to a large extent and in a scientific manner. In the newer portion the city is well laid out, and, including the two municipalities into which it is divided, contains an area of 13 square miles. It has public recreation reserves, in one of which is a small lake, named Wendouree, much frequented by the citizens for the amusements of sailing and rowing. Trees have been planted in the principal streets, of which there are in all 84 miles; and the number of handsome buildings, public and private, give the city an air of substance and completeness that could hardly have been expected in so young a community. There is a good water supply, and the city is lighted with gas. At present the population is estimated at 38,000. Gold-mining continues to be the great industry of the place, and some of the mines are still very productive. Other occupations, however, are extensively followed, and there are in and near the city itself foundries, woollen mills, flour-mills, breweries, and distilleries, besides other industrial establishments. In the surrounding district, which is undulating and possesses much good soil, agriculture is carried on to a considerable extent, and pastoral pursuits also receive attention, wool of the finest quality being grown on some of the stations.

At Ballarat the railway line divides into two branches. Following the more easterly branch, we reach **Creswick**, 112 miles from Melbourne. This is another mining township, and the work is now carried on in so systematic a manner that it may be regarded as one of the regular industries of the district. The mines were at one period highly productive, and still yield good returns to the owners. Agricultural pursuits occupy many persons in the neighbourhood. The estimated population is 4000.

Clunes, 119 miles from Melbourne, is an important mining centre. The gold is now obtained principally from quartz, and is brought from a great depth below the surface. The population numbers about 6000. The supply of water and lighting with gas are signs of the progress of the community.

At a distance of 130 miles from Melbourne is **Talbot**, also a mining township, but so thoroughly settled as to be provided with water and gas. The population is 2500. The town of **Amherst**, about two miles distant, is, like Talbot, a gold-mining township, with about 800 inhabitants.

Maryborough, 139 miles from Melbourne, is important as a railway centre, and also as the principal town in an extensive gold-producing region. From this town the main line is continued north-westerly to Donald, a branch line running eastward connects with Castlemaine, and a short extension runs westward to Avoca. Quartz-reefing is the principal industry, and the population is estimated at 3500.

Another of the group of mining townships in this district is **Dunolly**, 125 miles from Melbourne, with a population of 1500. The district abounds in auriferous quartz reefs, and some of the largest nuggets ever known were obtained in the neighbourhood.

St. Arnaud, 158 miles from Melbourne, is the centre of a prosperous pastoral, agricultural, and mining district. It has a population estimated at 3000. Much wheat is grown in the district, the soil being of excellent quality.

At the termination of this branch stands **Donald**, 182 miles from Sydney. It is the centre of a splendid agricultural district, but its present population is only about 600.

Avoca, 127 miles from Melbourne, on the branch line from Maryborough, is the centre of another mining district in which also some farming is carried on. The population of the town is about 1000.

Following now the westerly branch line from Ballarat, we reach **Beaufort**, 124 miles from Melbourne, a mining township surrounded by a rich pastoral and agricultural district. It has about 1000 inhabitants.

Ararat, 153 miles from Melbourne, is a town of the same character, the centre of a rich pastoral, agricultural, and mining district. It is also important as a railway centre, being connected with Dimboola in one direction and Portland in another. Its population is about 3000.

Proceeding along the main line, **Stawell** is reached at a distance of 172 miles from Melbourne. This is an important mining town, the neighbourhood abounding in quartz reefs, some of which are worked at great depths. Some agriculture is also carried on in the district. The population numbers 8000.

Passing **Murtoa**, situated in a grain-producing district, **Horsham** is reached at a distance of 225 miles from Melbourne. This town, situated near the edge of the great plain country, is the centre of a rich agricultural district. The soil is admirably suited for the growth of wheat; but the climate is dry, and crops sometimes fail from want of rain. The population is about 1700.

Dimboola, at the termination of this line and 247 miles from Melbourne, is another agricultural centre, with a very small population at present, but with a prospect of future importance.

On the railway line connecting Ararat with Portland, and at a distance of 220 miles from Melbourne, is **Hamilton**, a sort of local capital for the western district. Agriculture is the special industry of this neighbourhood. The population may be estimated at 3000.

From **Branxholme,** a small town on this line, a branch is carried to **Casterton,** on the river Glenelg, 267 miles from Melbourne, a town of about 1000 inhabitants.

Portland, at the termination of the line, 273 miles from Melbourne, stands on the shores of the bay of the same name. It is one of the oldest settlements in the colony, and is the centre of a large pastoral and agricultural district. It is of some consequence as a seaport, having frequent communication with Melbourne by sea. Its exports are wool, tallow, hides, grain, dairy produce, and bark. The population is about 2500.

The Western Line commences at Geelong and runs in a westerly direction. The first populous place on the line is **Colac,** 95 miles from Melbourne. The district is pastoral and agricultural. The population is about 1700.

Camperdown, the present terminus of the line, 123 miles from Melbourne, is the centre of a large pastoral and agricultural district, and is growing in importance. The population is estimated at 1300.

Of towns on the coast, **Queenscliff,** 68 miles from Melbourne, is situated at the entrance of Port Phillip Bay. It is connected with Geelong by railway. It is noted chiefly as a watering-place, and has a population of 1200.

Warnambool, 172 miles westerly from Melbourne, is a seaport on the south-west coast. The district around is pastoral and agricultural, the principal crops being wheat, oats, barley, potatoes, and hops. The population is about 5000. Besides local manufactures, there is a woollen factory. The exports comprise wool, grain, potatoes, and dairy produce.

Farther west is **Belfast,** 180 miles from Melbourne. This port carries on a large trade in wool, grain, and other pastoral and agricultural products, which are drawn from the surrounding districts and shipped to Melbourne. The population is 1800.

In the Gipps Land, **Bairnsdale,** 180 miles from Melbourne, is the outlet for a large pastoral, agricultural, and mineral district, and is likely to increase in importance. The present population is about 1000.

In the same district is **Walhalla,** 120 miles eastwards from Melbourne. This is a mining township, quartz-reefing being extensively carried on in the neighbourhood. The population is about 1700.

Buninyong, 106 miles from Melbourne, is a township on the Ballarat gold-field, and mining is still actively carried on. As the soil in the neighbourhood is productive, some attention is also paid to agriculture. The population numbers about 1600.

On the same gold-field is **Smythesdale,** also a mining township with a population of about 1000, exclusive of the residents in the immediate vicinity.

Heathcote, on the Sandhurst Gold-field, 70 miles from Melbourne, is a town of similar character, with a population of 1200 persons.

In the south-western portion of the colony, between Warnambool and Belfast, is **Koroit,** a township distant 186 miles from Melbourne. The surrounding district, having rich soil, of which much is under cultivation, is highly productive. The population is about 1600.

CHAPTER VII.

THE COLONY OF TASMANIA.

1. Extent and Coast-line. 2. Surface. 3. Drainage—Rivers. 4. Climate. 5. Vegetable and Animal Life. 6. Soil. 7. Population. 8. Roads and Railways. 9. Occupations. 10. Government. 11. Divisions. 12. Towns.

1. Under this designation are included, not only Tasmania itself, but also the numerous islands lying around its coasts. The name is derived from Tasman, the Dutch navigator by whom it was discovered. Tasmania lies between the 40th and 44th parallels of south latitude, and the 144th and 149th meridians of east longitude. It is **bounded** on the north by Bass Strait, and on all other sides by the Great Southern Ocean. In average length from north to south the island measures about 160 miles, and its mean breadth from east to west nearly equals the length. The area is estimated at 26,000 square miles, or more than four-fifths that of Scotland. Roughly speaking, its shape is that of a heart, but the outline is exceedingly irregular, especially on the east and south. On the north side, the principal projections are **Circular Head** and **Cape Portland**, though numerous other less conspicuous headlands mark the coast-line. Several inlets exist on the same coast, such as **Port Sorell** and **Port Dalrymple**, while the largest bays are **Anderson** and **Ringarooma Bays**. On the east, the most remarkable projections are **Freycinet Peninsula** and **Tasman Peninsula**, both of singularly irregular shape, and the latter terminating in Capes Pillar and Raoul. **Oyster Bay** is the most important indentation on this side. The south coast is much broken, being penetrated by numerous bays and estuaries, of which the chief are **Storm Bay** with its branches, and the estuary of the Huon River, though there are others of less note. **Tasman Head, South-east Cape**, and **South-west Cape** are the chief projections on the south; and on the west are **Rocky Point, Point Hibbs**, and **Cape Sorell**, with **Cape Grim** in the extreme north-west. **Port Davey** and **Macquarie Harbour** are the principal inlets on the west. Of the many islands belonging to Tasmania, only the more important can be enumerated. In

Bass Strait are **King's Island,** the **Hunter Islands, Flinders Island** and **Cape Barren Island;** off the eastern coast, **Maria Island;** and on the south the remarkably-shaped island of **Bruni.**

2. So irregular is the **surface** of Tasmania that much difficulty is experienced in describing it accurately and yet concisely. A lofty table-land, rising to the height of 3000 feet, occupies the centre of the island, and presents an abrupt face to the north, declining gradually towards the south. Upon and around this table-land stand ranges of mountains, not connected into any general system, but irregular in direction, length, and height. The surface of the country is consequently more broken and, on the whole, more elevated than that of any of the other Australian colonies. Mountain, table-land, valley, and ravine are intermingled without even the degree of order that usually prevails in mountainous countries; and the scenery of Tasmania derives from this peculiar blending of high and low, level and precipitous, a picturesque character that is uncommon. Two summits, **Ben Lomond** and **Cradle Mountain,** the former on the eastern, the latter on the western edge of the great table-land, somewhat exceed 5000 feet in height; the latter, the culminating point of the island, having an altitude of 5069 feet. Besides these there are at least twenty peaks in various parts of the island that rise to an elevation of more than 4000 feet; and a still greater number exceed 3000 feet. Plains properly so called are wanting in Tasmania, and, generally speaking, the extent of level surface of any kind is very small.

3. In the absence of any great dividing chain the **drainage system** of the island appears to be very confused. The main watershed which divides the rivers flowing northward from those which have a southerly course, begins on the east coast opposite Maria Island, and traverses the country in a sinuous line to West Point on the north-west. Another watershed commences at Eddystone Point on the east coast, and joins the first-mentioned at the source of a stream named the Little Swan Port. A third commences at the intersection of the 42d parallel and the 146th meridian, and runs in a semicircle down to the North Head of Port Davey. There are, therefore, four slopes or drainage areas. Of these the most important is

the southern, which is drained by the **Derwent** and the **Huon**. The former, rising in Lake St. Clair at an elevation of 3500 feet, flows in a south-east direction, and after receiving the waters of numerous streams from each bank in its course of 130 miles, enters the sea by a broad estuary in Storm Bay. Two-thirds of the southern slope and a large proportion of the central plateau are drained by this river and its tributaries. The Huon has its source in the elevated country lying a little to the northward of the 43d parallel, and flows eastward into

The Huon River.

an estuary which is connected with D'Entrecasteaux Channel. The other streams in this slope are small. In the northern slope all the rivers empty into Bass Strait. By far the most important of these is the **Tamar**, which, with its tributaries the Macquarie and the North and South Esk, and their numerous affluents, drains a large portion of the northern quarter of the island. The sources of these streams are widely scattered, some being within a few miles of the east coast, and others to the westward of the main stream. Their courses are, from the mountainous nature of the country through which they flow, extremely circuitous. The Tamar itself is the broad estuary which receives the waters of the rivers before mentioned. Omitting smaller streams, the **Ringarooma**, the **Mersey**, and the **Forth** are worthy of note for their size; they drain considerable areas in the northern slope. Of the rivers on the western slope the principal is the **Gordon**, which rises in a small lake among the ranges that edge the table-land on the west. It flows southward for some distance and then turns to the west and north-west, discharging its waters into Macquarie Harbour. The **King**, the **Pieman**, and the **Arthur** each drains a considerable space of this slope. The narrow eastern slope resembles in many respects the coast district of New South Wales. At no point is the watershed removed to a greater distance from the shore than 40 miles, and in some places it approaches within 5 miles. The **Prosser** is the only river of sufficient importance to need mention. Many of the rivers now described are fed from the surplus waters of the numerous **lakes** which adorn the central table-land. Unlike so many of the Australian lakes, these are filled with fresh water; and though many are but tiny lakelets, some are of considerable extent. **Lake Sorell**, for example, has an area of 26 square miles, and the **Great Lake**, which is the largest, covers 45 square miles. From the foregoing statements it will be seen that Tasmania contrasts very strongly with Australia as regards the number and character of its streams, and that it is abundantly watered in all seasons.

4. Though cooler than the southern parts of Australia, the **climate** of Tasmania is mild and healthy. In the northern portion the temperature is higher than in the south, where also the winter cold is greater. The general character of the climate as regards heat and cold is uniform throughout the island, allowance being made for difference of elevation and the modifying effects of proximity to the sea. The mean annual temperature is usually stated at 54°, but in summer it occasionally rises as high as 110°, falling sometimes to 29° in winter. In the more elevated regions frost and snow are common, though the cold does not endure for any length of time. On the west coast, exposed to the gales from the Great Southern Ocean, rain falls in great abundance, as much as 100 inches having been measured in one year. On the east coast the mean yearly

rainfall is about 20 inches, and on the north 30 inches. This amount of precipitation is, in general, equably spread over the year, and it is estimated that 143 days are wet out of the 365. The prevailing winds blow from the north-west and south-east, and at times the hot northerly winds from the Australian continent are felt, especially on the northern coast. On the whole, the climate may be described as mild, dry, and bright. It possesses great restorative and bracing power, and Tasmania is much frequented by colonists whose energies have been exhausted or overdone by hard work or the more relaxing atmosphere of the northern colonies.

5. The climate is highly favourable to **vegetable life**, and timber of enormous size and excellent quality is found, vieing, in both points, with the best produced in Victoria. Some kinds are valuable as cabinet woods, others for building purposes. Among the latter is the Huon pine, which grows abundantly on the west coast, and is valuable from its durability and from its resisting the attacks of insects. The gum-trees grow here to as great a size as they do in Australia, the blue gum reaching the height of 350 feet, and being employed for ship-building and other purposes. The **animal life** of Tasmania differs but little from that of Australia, except in the possession of two carnivorous marsupials, the Tasmanian "wolf" and the Tasmanian "devil," both of them ferocious and destructive creatures. Salmon and trout have been introduced from Britain into the rivers.

6. Granite, trap, basalt, slate, limestone, and sandstone occur in various localities throughout the island, and the **soils** derived from them are as numerous and as various as these rocks. The alluvium in the river valleys, especially when produced by the decomposition of trap and basalt rocks, is very rich, and this sort of soil is usually devoted to agricultural purposes. Large areas beyond the valleys are covered with a similar soil, black or chocolate in colour, and also highly productive; but it is difficult to bring into proper condition for agriculture, owing to the dense vegetation with which it is covered. On the uplands there is good soil for pasturage, for which purpose it is extensively utilized. Among the mountains and broken ranges, however, there are considerable areas which, for either culti-

vation or pasturage, must be deemed wholly unproductive. With all such drawbacks, however, Tasmania may be correctly described as a fertile island.

7. The **population** of Tasmania is perhaps more completely of British origin or descent than that of any other Australian colony, only one-tenth being derived from other sources. With the exception of a handful of Chinese, this tenth of the population consists of Europeans and Americans. The aboriginal inhabitants, who, it is generally supposed, were a Papuan race, have long been extinct. Exterminating wars were waged against them by the early colonists; and the race is now represented only by half-castes, who were deported to Flinders Island, where they still remain. The whole population of the island is estimated at 135,000.

8. Good **roads** were formed at an early period between the principal settlements, material being abundant and labour cheap. That between Launceston and Hobart was especially noteworthy as being well constructed and kept in good order. **Railway** construction has not made any great advance in Tasmania; for, in addition to the difficulties presented by the nature of the country, capital to the necessary extent was not forthcoming, and the government did not follow the example of the other colonies and make the matter one of state concern. The principal line now in working order is that between Hobart and Launceston, 133 miles in length. The Western line extends from Launceston to Deloraine, with an extension to Formby, at the mouth of the Mersey, a distance of about 70 miles. Other extensions are in contemplation in different parts of the island. Communication by electric telegraph is provided between all the principal settlements. Small coasting vessels are employed to convey goods and produce between the different ports of the island.

9. **Agriculture** occupies a large number of persons, and Tasmanian wheat, barley, tobacco, and hops have an excellent name in all the surrounding colonies. Much attention is also paid to the growth of **fruit-trees**, all the fruits of temperate climates being produced in abundance and of excellent quality. **Pasturage** is less extensively followed, but some breeders devote great energy to the raising of stud sheep, which are

frequently sold in the other colonies at very high prices. Formerly the whaling industry was largely carried on from Hobart, but is now pursued to but a trifling extent. **Mining** for **gold** and for **tin**, both of which are believed to exist in considerable quantities, is still followed with some success. Silver, copper, lead, and iron have also been found; but little enterprise, however, has yet been shown in raising these metals. Bismuth and antimony are also known to abound. Though not plentiful, coal is obtainable in several localities, and has been worked in a few places, but the difficulty of obtaining the mineral and of bringing it to market in so rugged a country has proved a great obstacle to systematic mining. Timber-getting and the collection of wattle-bark (for tanning), for which the island affords unusual facilities, are remunerative employments, and the products of this industry swell the list of exports. Brewing, tanning, and jam-making are the principal manufactures, but all the ordinary handicrafts and domestic manufactures are also practised. **Trade** is carried on with neighbouring colonies by means of steamships which ply between Launceston and Hobart on the one side, and Melbourne and Sydney on the other. Steamships also run from Hobart to London, besides sailing vessels. The principal exports are wool, timber, jam, dairy produce, grain, hops, fruit, hides, ale, and whale oil. The total value of the exports is about £1,500,000. The imports, amounting to £1,700,000, consist of manufactured goods, tea, coffee, sugar, wines, and spirits.

10. The **government** resembles in form those of the other Australian colonies, and includes a legislature consisting of two chambers, both of which are elective. In details of the administrative and judicial arrangements the like similarity is manifest, and no distinctive notice is consequently required. Full toleration of all forms of religion exists. With the exception of a few hundreds professing the Hebrew faith and the Chinese, Christianity is the religion of the people. A state-supported system of primary **education** is in operation throughout the colony; it is unsectarian in its character, and the attendance of children, with the usual conditions, is compulsory. Secondary and higher education is encouraged by means of exhibitions and scholarships, varying in value from £16 to

£200 per annum. The revenue of the colony exceeds the expenditure, the former being for the last few years about £550,000, and the latter, during the same period, about £520,000. Altogether the colony appears to be in a highly prosperous state.

11. The **division** into counties prevailing in the other colonies obtains also in Tasmania. No further use is made of the division into eighteen counties than that connected with the survey of land. Another division is that into thirty-two electorates for members of the Legislative Assembly, and thirteen for members of the Legislative Council. For local purposes municipal districts have been established in many of the more thickly-peopled parts, and these afford facilities for a considerable degree of local self-government.

12. As so large a proportion of the population of Tasmania is engaged in agricultural pursuits, while a considerable number is employed in mining, it will not be expected that many populous **towns** will be found on the island. There are, however, large numbers of villages and hamlets containing one, two, or three hundred inhabitants. These, having no distinctive features, will on that account be omitted from mention in the following remarks upon Tasmanian topography.

Hobart (formerly Hobart Town), the capital and seat of the legislature as well as of the government, is situated in the south on the river Derwent. Having Mount Wellington in the background, the position of the city is highly picturesque. In extent Hobart is nearly two square miles: it is well laid out, with broad streets, lighted with gas, and well supplied with water. The surface is undulating. There is a large public reserve, and some of the buildings are handsome structures. The Derwent forms a safe and commodious harbour, and affords great facilities for carrying on trade. Besides the appliances for building and repairing ships, there are in the city mills, tanneries, and breweries. From the port lines of steamships keep up communication with the mother country and with the Australian colonies, and less frequently with New Zealand. Hobart is also the southern terminus of the main line of railway. On account of its invigorating climate and pleasant surroundings the city is much frequented by visitors from other colonies. The population is about 28,000.

Launceston, on the Tamar, on the north side of the island, is the second town on the island, having a population now estimated at 18,000. Like most of the other towns of Tasmania, Launceston is well laid out with broad streets, and a public reserve for recreation. It is well supplied with water, and is lighted with gas. Some of the public buildings are worthy of note for their style and excellence of construction. Launceston

Mount Wellington.

carries on a large trade, principally with Victoria, and is the northern terminus of the main line of railway. It is also connected by rail with Formby on the Mersey, 70 miles to the westward.

The third place as regards importance is taken by the town of **Beaconsfield**, on the banks of the Tamar, about 33 miles from Launceston. Its importance arises mainly from the fact that the surrounding district is auriferous, and that gold-mining is carried on to a considerable extent in the neighbourhood. The population is estimated at 1600.

Bothwell, on the Clyde, a tributary of the Derwent, is the centre of a pastoral and agricultural district, with a population of about 500.

On the main line of railway, 91 miles from Hobart, is **Campbelltown,** on the Eliza River, a branch of the Macquarie. Pasturage and agriculture, with some fruit-growing, are the chief occupations of the people in the district, in which are several farms devoted to the breeding of high-class merino sheep. The population of the town numbers about 1000.

Deloraine, on the Western Railway, about 45 miles from Launceston, is the centre of a fine agricultural district, the soil of which is highly productive. Pastoral pursuits are also followed to some extent. The population is reputed to be now somewhat under 1000.

Don, at the mouth of a small river of the same name, is a place of some trade and the centre of a rich farming district. The present population amounts to about 400.

Situated on the South Esk River and on the main line of railway is **Evandale,** in a fine agricultural district in which wheat is largely grown. It has about 600 inhabitants.

Glenorchy, about five miles from Hobart, may almost be deemed a suburb of that city. It is surrounded by farms, and produces grain, hops, and fruit. It has a population of 1500.

Near the mouth of the river Mersey, on the north side of the island, is **Latrobe,** a town of about 800 inhabitants. It is connected with Launceston by rail, and is the centre of an agricultural district.

New Norfolk, at the head of the navigation of the Derwent, 20 miles from Hobart, is situated in a fine agricultural district, noted for its production of grain, fruit, and hops. It has a population of 1000.

Oatlands is another agricultural centre, and sheep farming is also carried on in the district. Coal has been obtained in the neighbourhood. It is near the main line of railway, and has a population of about 700.

On the Western Railway, eleven miles from Launceston, is **Perth,** which is an agricultural centre, with a population of about 500.

Richmond, fifteen miles from Hobart, on the Coal River, is surrounded by farms, the soil being of good quality and suitable for the growth of grain crops. The population is estimated at 500.

Ringarooma, at the north-east corner of the island, is the centre of a large agricultural and tin-mining district, and is, with regard to the latter, the most important mining town in the island. Its population is about 400.

At the opposite corner of the island is **Stanley**, also known as Circular Head. This is the centre of a productive agricultural district, and carries on a large trade in wheat, oats, and potatoes, which are exported in considerable quantities to neighbouring colonies. The population of the town itself is supposed to be about 400.

Waratah, or Mount Bischoff, lies about 142 miles westward of Launceston, and is connected by a tramway with Emu Bay, on the north coast. The surrounding district abounds in tin ore, and mining for that metal is carried on extensively. The town population amounts to 900.

Westbury, on the Western Railway, is the centre of an extensive and fertile agricultural district, which produces grain, potatoes, and fruit. The population numbers about 1200.

CHAPTER VIII.

THE COLONY OF SOUTH AUSTRALIA.

1. Boundaries and Extent. 2. Coast-line and Harbours. 3. Surface. 4. Drainage. 5. Rivers. 6. Lakes. 7. Climate. 8. Soil. 9. Internal Communication. 10. Population. 11. Industrial Occupations—pasturage, agriculture, and mining. 12. Manufactures and Commerce. 13. Government. 14. Religion and Education. 15. Territorial Divisions. 16. Adelaide. 17. Other Towns.

1. Although stretching to the northern shore of the continent, South Australia still retains the name bestowed upon it when but a settlement upon the southern coast. Its territory then consisted of about 300,000 square miles, taken from the western portion of New South Wales; but the immense tract known as the Northern Territory has since been added, and the total area now exceeds 900,000 square miles. It is **bounded** on the north by the Arafura Sea; on the south by the Great Southern Ocean; on the west by Western Australia, the dividing line being the 129th meridian of east longitude; and on the east by Victoria, New South Wales, and Queensland, from which it is separated by the 141st meridian and north of the 26th parallel the 138th meridian. In length from north to south it extends over 1850 miles, and in breadth about 650 miles. Lying between the parallels of 12° and 39° S. it stretches over 27° of latitude, more than a third part being within the Torrid Zone.

2. On the south the coast-line is broken—westward by the head of the **Great Australian Bight**, Streaky and other bays, and by numerous projections of no great prominence; and to the eastward by the two large gulfs named **Spencer** and **St. Vincent**, and by the two peninsulas **Eyria** and **Yorke**. In the most easterly part of the coast the estuary of the Murray and Encounter Bay are the principal indentations, and a projection terminating at **Cape Jervis** tends further to diversify the coast-line. In general the coast is high and rocky, though low and swampy in some places, as on the shore of Encounter Bay, where a long and narrow lagoon named the **Coorong** stretches for many miles parallel with the sea, and separated from it by

a narrow strip of land. Besides numerous islands of small size there is one of considerable extent, **Kangaroo Island**, at the entrance to the Gulf of St. Vincent. Many harbours exist at different points on the coast. On the north the coast is in-

dented by the **Gulf of Carpentaria, Van Diemen's Gulf,** and **Cambridge Gulf,** besides numerous bays, and its outline is rendered still more irregular by the Coburg and other peninsulas and by the numerous islands by which it is fringed. **Groote, Melville,** and **Bathurst** Islands are the most important of these. The total length of the South Australian coast-lines is estimated at 2000 miles.

3. Compared with New South Wales and Victoria, this colony presents little diversity of **surface.** Its mountains are not so high and its table-lands are not so extensive, while its plains are more intersected by ranges of hills. It must not be overlooked, however, that large portions of its surface, especially in the Northern Territory, have not been examined, and are known to us only from the reports of two or three ex-

A Mountain Pass.

plorers, whose descriptions are necessarily confined to the tracts through which they passed. So far as is yet known no great mountain system exists in the colony, but low ranges are scattered, in no apparent order, throughout the whole territory. Along the eastern coast of St. Vincent's Gulf, from Cape Jervis to the head of the gulf, one of these ranges runs at a short distance from the sea, and is known as the **Mount Lofty Range,** though it bears other designations in particular parts. Its average elevation is probably less than 2000 feet, and it culminates in **Mount Lofty,** 2334 feet. From latitude 34° S. to 29° S. a series of ranges run in a northern direction, and are termed comprehensively the **Flinders Ranges**. The highest point in them is **Mount Remarkable, 3100 feet;** but there are many others rivalling it in elevation. The average altitude, however, is probably not more than 2000 feet. About the southern tropic, and near the centre of the continent, numerous ranges spread in different directions, the best known being the **M'Donnell Range**. The **Gawler Range** on the north of the Eyria Peninsula is rugged, but of low elevation, not exceeding probably 2000 feet. At the south-east corner of the colony there is a hilly tract containing many extinct volcanoes. Of these the most noteworthy is **Mount Gambier**. While the whole country may be described in general terms as undulating, there are many low-lying and level tracts that may be termed plains. Between the Mount Lofty and Flinders Ranges on one side and the Murray River on the other, for example, the country is very flat. Farther north plains of larger extent are met with, some well adapted for agricultural and pastoral purposes, and others dry, arid, sandy, or stony deserts.

4. Where the elevated land is so irregularly disposed the **watersheds** are confused, and the directions in which the rivers flow are so various as to render any classification as regards drainage areas somewhat difficult. Three slopes may, however, be distinguished—the northern, the southern, and the inland. The first comprehends the belt of territory along the northern coast, drained by the streams which fall into the Gulf of Carpentaria and the Arafura Sea. In the second is comprised the country through which flow the rivers pouring their waters into the Great Southern Ocean. All the remainder of the colony, including probably five-sixths of its area, constitutes an inland basin in which the rivers, when sufficiently filled with water to flow at all, empty themselves into lakes having no outlet or lose themselves in sandy wastes.

5. Few of the **rivers** have any strong claim to be so styled, and these are to be found chiefly on the northern slope. Although little is known of the length of these streams, their lower courses have proved to be navigable for considerable distances, and they will doubtless in the future prove to be of much importance. The principal are the **Roper, Adelaide, Alligator, Liverpool,** and **Victoria**. In the southern slope the

Murray is the river of greatest consequence, but its course in South Australia is short; the others are short coast streams, with a very small volume in each case. Among the rivers of the inland slope the **Barcoo**, from Queensland, takes the first place, and next the **Warburton**, which has the longest part of its course in the same colony. Both these fall into Lake Eyre, which also receives a large number of smaller streams. Other lakes, which will be mentioned immediately, also receive the surplus waters of the rivers which, in a rainy season, are filled to such an extent as to form currents. On the whole South Australia is not a well-watered colony, and compares unfavourably in this respect with both New South Wales and Victoria.

6. **Lakes** are numerous, and some of them are of considerable extent. Nearly all are salt, the exceptions being principally those in the south-east part of the colony, where the **Blue Lake** occupies the crater of an extinct volcano. It has high precipitous banks, and the water, which is very deep, is of a blue colour, from which circumstance its name is derived. The remaining lakes may be divided into two groups. In the first may be placed the large **Lake Amadeus**, near the centre of the continent, and the **Salt Lakes**, which occupy positions in the great Victoria Desert in the western portion of the colony, between the parallels of 27° and 30° S. The second lake region is situated north of Spencer Gulf, and includes **Lakes Eyre, Torrens, Gairdner, Blanche, Frome,** and **Island Lagoon.** Some of these in dry weather become basins filled with mud strongly impregnated with salt. The smaller lakes, scattered about in various localities, require no special mention.

7. Doubtless the extreme dryness of the **climate** accounts for the paucity of rivers, and to some extent for the continued saltness of the lakes. The northern half of the colony has a tropical climate, with only two seasons—the *dry*, lasting from May to September; and the *wet*, from October to April. Except that the rainfall is probably less, there appears to be no essential difference between the climate of tropical Australia and that of other tropical countries. In the southern portion, however, there is the usual distinction of seasons, though the winter can be considered cold only by contrast with the great heat of summer. The maximum temperature in the shade in

summer is about 110°, though occasionally it is much higher, especially in the interior; the minimum temperature of winter seldom falls to the freezing-point, except on the mountains, where frosts sometimes occur. In all but the summer months the temperature is pleasant and the climate highly enjoyable and healthy. To some extent this result is attributable to the absence of moisture; the number of rainy days is small, being about 120 at Adelaide and much less farther north. At Palmerston, on the northern coast, the average yearly rainfall may be estimated at 62 inches; in the central regions at 7 inches; and on the south coast at 30 inches. No mean or average can be stated for the whole colony with any reasonable degree of accuracy. In summer hot winds occasionally prevail, and add to the distressing feeling caused by the intense heat. Notwithstanding this drawback the colony is remarkably healthy, and persons of ordinarily good constitutions do not find the heat insupportable even in summer.

8. Almost every description of **soil** may be found in South Australia, from utterly barren sand to the richest alluvium. The deserts, which take up considerable areas, are in some instances covered with pure sand, shifting with the wind, and in others with stones; in some the sterility is caused by the presence of salt in the soil; others less barren are covered with spinifex grass or a dense growth of scrub. Large tracts are well fitted for pasturage; and there are extensive plains and valleys, which produce large crops of wheat, having a soil admirably suited for farming. Calculations have been made with a view to show that, out of the total area of the colony, one-third is utterly waste desert, rock, and scrub; one-third mountain and forest, that may be utilized for pasture; and the remaining third good pastoral and agricultural land. This probably expresses, in a general way, the proportions of land of these several qualities.

9. It is not to be expected that, in a colony that stretches from one side of the continent to the other, common roads will supply very perfect means of **internal communication**. In the more thickly-peopled districts, however, good roads have been made. But railway construction has been proceeded with so rapidly as to supersede the common roads to a large extent,

and there are now about 1000 miles of rail in operation. The principal lines commence at Adelaide. They are: (1) the North Line from Adelaide to Quorn, with branches to Morgan on the east, and to Moonta on the west; (2) the Great Northern Line from Port Augusta to Farina Town; (3) the Southern Line from Adelaide to Port Victor; (4) Port Pirie and Terowie Line. All the principal lines are the property of the state, but there are two short lines that belong to private companies. Communication by electric telegraph has been established between all the principal towns in the colony, with the telegraphic system of other colonies, including Western Australia, and with the mother country by means of the Overland Line to Port Darwin. The construction of this line was a work of great magnitude, involving a large outlay and requiring much ability to carry out. It has proved to be a great boon to the whole of Australia. No navigable rivers exist in the colony, with the exception of the Murray, the mouth of which is blocked with sandbanks so as to prevent the entrance or exit of vessels of large size. Communication is maintained with the minor ports by means of steamships.

10. Exclusive of aboriginal natives, the **population** may now be estimated at 320,000. In this number, however, are reckoned about 4000 Chinese, who are located principally in the Northern Territory. In the remoter districts the blacks are believed to be comparatively numerous. It is not possible to form even an estimate of their numbers; but in the more civilized parts there are supposed to be about 7000. The great bulk of the population are British subjects and their descendants; but there is a considerable proportion of colonists of German nationality.

11. **Agriculture** is one of the most important occupations of the people. Farming may, indeed, be regarded as the chief industry of the colony, which has long been distinguished for the quantity and quality of its wheat crops, about 2,000,000 acres being at present under tillage. Other plants that have been successfully cultivated are the vine, the hop, the olive, and fruits generally. Pastoral pursuits also give employment to a large number of persons, most attention being paid to the breeding of sheep, 6,500,000 of which were in the colony

in 1885. About one-fourth part of the male population is engaged in agriculture and pasturage. A considerable proportion are occupied in **mining**. Although gold has been found in several localities, the search for it is not vigorously prosecuted at present. **Copper** is the metal most sought for, and the past history of mining for it in South Australia is probably without a parallel in any other country. The mines at Burra Burra and Moonta have become celebrated for their enormous yields, and other localities have also been highly productive. Silver has been worked as well as lead and bismuth, but mining for these metals has been suspended.

12. **Manufacturing industries,** though vigorously carried on for domestic purposes, have not been developed to any large extent for export. The manufacture of flour, wine, and jams is the most important in the latter point of view. The **commerce** of the colony is, considering the population, very great. The value of the exports averages about £6,500,000 yearly. Among the commodities exported wool, wheat, and copper rank in the first class, and after them come flour, bran, and pollard; tallow, hides, and skins; wine, dairy produce, timber, and bark. The imports, valued at £6,000,000, consist of drapery, silks, and woollen goods; hardware and other manufactured articles of metal; sugar, tea, coffee, and tobacco; boots and shoes; timber, coal, spirits, and beer. By far the greater part of these goods comes from the mother country, with which trade is carried on by means of sailing vessels and steamships. Regular communication by steam vessels is also maintained with Melbourne.

13. The **constitution** of South Australia resembles that of the other colonies, and provides a legislature consisting of two bodies, the Council and the Assembly. In the former are twenty-four members elected for three, six, or nine years, one-third of the number retiring every three years. Electors must be at least twenty-one years of age; they must be subjects of her Majesty; and they must have resided for a minimum period of six months in the province for which they vote. A small property qualification is also necessary. In the Assembly there are fifty-two members, elected by voters of full age resident for six months in the electorate. The government includes the

governor, who is the queen's representative, and the ministry, responsible to the parliament, consisting of six members of the Assembly or Council, but usually of the former. As in the other colonies the legislature has full power to make laws upon all subjects that relate only to the colony, those that affect imperial interests being reserved for consideration by the home government. The members of the ministry, as heads of administrative departments, are responsible for the due discharge of the business of the country in all its ramifications. In payment of the cost of this work the revenue raised in the colony slightly exceeds £2,000,000 annually, and the expenditure is about £2,400,000, though the amount, in both cases, varies from year to year.

14. An **educational system** based upon the same principles as those in operation in the other colonies has been established in South Australia, which was the first of the Australian group to pass an educational law. In the primary schools attendance is compulsory with the usual allowances; it is non-sectarian; but parents are required to pay school fees. Little has yet been done towards secondary instruction beyond granting exhibitions and scholarships; but, in the interests of higher education, a university has been established. As to the **religion** of the inhabitants, with the exception of the Chinese, who are Pagans, and the persons of the Hebrew persuasion, the people profess Christianity, about four-fifths being Protestants and the remainder Roman Catholics. The members of the various denominations, of which there are a large number, support their own ministers, no aid for this purpose having ever been granted by the state.

15. The **territorial divisions** of the colony are as numerous as in other parts of Australia. The division into counties is of little use except in relation to the survey and description of land. A more useful division is that into municipalities under "District Councils," which have the power to levy rates for the formation and repair of roads, and are assisted from public funds in proportion to the amounts they expend for such purposes. There are also the four legislative council electorates or districts, Central, Southern, Northern, and North-eastern, and the twenty-six legislative council electorates.

16. **Adelaide**, the capital, is situated upon the river Torrens, by which it is divided into two parts, north and south. The city is distant about 6 miles from the Gulf of St. Vincent, and is connected by road and rail with the port of shipment, Port Adelaide. Including streets and reserves, the total area of the city exceeds 5 square miles, and in form is nearly square. It is well laid out, with 80 miles of broad streets, the principal, King William Street, being 2 chains in width, and has numerous public reserves for recreation purposes. Besides being lighted with gas and well supplied with water, the city is provided with other adjuncts of civilization, such as tramways, markets, and baths. Being built upon a plain, the surface is level. Many of the public buildings are handsome structures, and the streets generally are well built, with banks, insurance offices, and shops that are very ornamental in their appearance. As the seat of government, the legislative, judicial, and administrative business is concentrated in Adelaide, which, moreover, is placed in communication by rail or telegraph with all the more populous places in the colony. Farming is largely carried on in the surrounding district, and pastoral pursuits are also followed to some extent. The usual local industries also flourish. The population, including the suburbs, is estimated at 60,000.

17. **Port Adelaide** is the principal seaport in the colony, and has a large proportion of the foreign trade. It is situated on the Gulf of St. Vincent, about seven miles from the capital, with which it is connected by railway. It is provided with all the usual appliances of a port, and several important industries, such as copper-smelting, brewing, and milling, are carried on in the vicinity. The population numbers about 3000.

The other towns of South Australia are small, very few having as many as 1000 inhabitants. But they are very numerous, and may in time become places of importance. In the following remarks they will be classed as ports, railway-stations, mining townships, and agricultural settlements. Commencing at the western boundary of the colony and following the coast-line, the first seaport worthy of special mention is **Port Lincoln**, on the east side of Eyria Peninsula. Others are **Port Augusta**, at the head of Spencer Gulf, the starting-point of the Great

Northern Railway; **Port Pirie,** on the western coast of Yorke Peninsula; **Wallaroo,** farther south, noted in connection with the smelting and export of copper; **Kingscote,** on Kangaroo Island; **Port Wakefield,** at the head of St. Vincent Gulf; **Glenelg,** south of Port Adelaide, a place of call for the mail steamers; **Port Victor,** near the entrance to the Murray; **Kingston,** on Lacepede Bay; **Robe,** on Guichen Bay; **Beachport,** to the southeast; and **Port Macdonnell,** near Cape Northumberland. Commencing from Adelaide, and following the North Line of railway, the following may be noticed: **Gawler,** 25 miles distant, in a fine agricultural district, and inhabited by about 2000 persons; **Kapunda,** 48 miles distant, a copper-mining locality with 2300 inhabitants; **Morgan,** at the great bend of the Murray River; **Riverton,** in a wheat-growing district; **Saddleworth,** a similar locality; **Kooringa,** supported by the famous Burra Burra copper-mines, which are in the neighbourhood; **Petersburg,** from which a line extends to Port Pirie; and **Eurelia,** farther north. On the Great Northern Line are: **Quorn,** the point of junction with the North Line; **Beltana,** in a pastoral district, and **Farina,** also surrounded by grazing country. On the Moonta Branch Line are: **Kadina,** a copper-mining locality, and **Moonta,** which is at present the richest in copper of all the places in the colony. On the Southern Line are **Nairne,** in a pastoral and agricultural district; **Mount Barker,** a wheat-producing locality; **Strathalbyn,** which produces some wheat, and has gold and copper in the neighbourhood; and **Goolwa,** on the Murray, by means of which it carries on a large trade with Victoria and New South Wales. On the Port Pirie Line the most important places are **Gladstone** and **Jamestown,** both agricultural localities. A short line runs from **Kingston,** on which the principal towns are **Narracoorte** and **Border Town,** in a fine pastoral district. Another short line runs from Beachport, passing **Millicent,** in a pastoral and agricultural district, and terminating at **Mount Gambier** in a district of the same character, but possessing a large area of the richest soil. Among the agricultural settlements may be mentioned **Angaston,** noted for the cultivation of wheat and the vine; **Auburn,** in a wheat-growing district; **Clare,** a town supported by pasturage and agriculture; **Dalkey,** a farming district largely settled by Germans; **Hahndorf**, a similar township, also inhabited by Germans; **Laura**, though mainly agricultural, having some local manufacturing industries; **Penola**, near the Victorian border; and **Tanunda**, also a German settlement. Some of the mining townships have already been referred to in connection with railway-stations, and the only other place of this kind that needs mention is **Blinman**, 348 miles north of Adelaide. In the Northern Territory there is a settlement at Port Darwin, which is the terminus of the transcontinental telegraph line, and the seat of government. The district appears to be in a thriving condition.

CHAPTER IX.

THE COLONY OF WEST AUSTRALIA.

1 Extent and Coast-line. 2. Surface. 3. Drainage. 4. Climate. 5. Soil. 6. Population. 7. Internal Communication. 8. Industrial Occupations. 9. Government. 10. Divisions. 11. Towns.

1. This immense territory occupies nearly one-third of the whole continent, and is the largest of the Australian colonies. In length from north to south it measures about 1500 miles, and in width from east to west nearly 1000 miles. The whole of West Australia is contained between the parallels of 13° and 36° south, and between the meridians of 113° and 129° east. It is **bounded** on the north by the Timor Sea, on the west by the Indian Ocean, on the south by the Great Southern Ocean, and on the east by South Australia, the dividing line being the 129th meridian. It has a coast-line of enormous length, measuring, in all probability, 3000 miles, if all the indentations be taken into account. Considering its extent, the coast-line cannot be considered irregular, none of the indentations penetrating far inland, and few of the projections being very prominent. On the south, the shore of the Great Australian Bight presents few irregularities; but west of the 124th meridian there are numerous bays and capes, not conspicuous for size, and a fringe of small islands may also be observed. **King George's Sound**, in 118° E., is one of the most capacious harbours in the whole continent. **Cape Leeuwin**, at the southern extremity of the peninsula in which Australia terminates to the south-west, and **Cape Naturaliste** on the north side of the same, are two important projections. Others on the west coast are **Steep Point**, the most westerly land on the continent, Cape Cuvier, North-West Cape; and on the north, Capes Leveque and Londonderry. In the same line are such inlets as Geographe Bay, Peel Inlet, Champion Bay, Gantheaume Bay, **Shark Bay**, Exmouth Gulf, **King's Sound**, Admiralty Gulf, and **Cambridge Gulf**. Generally speaking the coast is low and sandy. Many small islands are to be found in different parts of the coast throughout its whole length.

2. No prominent features mark the **surface** of West Australia; the mountains are of low elevation and disposed irregularly in various parts of the colony, so that they form no great connected system; and the table-lands probably do not exceed 1000 feet in height. At the same time, it must be borne in mind that of the vast interior but a very small proportion has been even casually explored, and that consequently many of the views now held on this subject may hereafter be found to need correction. As in the more easterly colonies, a coast range runs nearly parallel with the shore, and distant from 10 to 25 miles from it, from near King George's Sound to the northern extremity of the colony. In average height this range does not exceed 1500 feet, but single peaks attain a higher elevation. In the part named the Stirling Range on the south coast, for example, **Ellen's Peak** is said to rise to the altitude of 3400 feet; and **Mt. William**, in the Darling Range on the west coast, is supposed to be 3000 feet high. Near the northern coast, **Mt. Bruce**, in about 118° east longitude, is estimated at 3600 feet in elevation, and may be considered the culminating point of the whole colony. Eastward of the coast ranges lies a tableland of an undulating character, and having an elevation of about 1000 feet, through which runs in an irregular manner the higher land which forms the division of the waters between the rivers flowing to the sea and those which make their way eastward into the interior. This watershed is probably not more than 300 miles distant from the sea in any part, and from it the land stretches by a gradual slope down to the level of the great central plain of Australia. A large number of isolated mountain peaks dot the surface of the country in every direction, but they are too numerous even for bare mention, especially as but little is known regarding their heights or other claims to notice.

3. From the foregoing description of the surface, it will be inferred that the **drainage system** of the colony is of the same irregular character. There are but two slopes, one towards the coast, the other towards the interior. The rivers draining the former are of considerable size, and include the **Blackwood**, which flows south-westerly into the sea at **Cape Leeuwin**; the **Swan**, which gave its name to the original settlement; the **Murchison**, which

falls into Gantheaume Bay; the **Gascoyne**, rising in the same range as the Murchison, but emptying its waters into Shark Bay; the **Ashburton**, on the north-west, the course of which is not certainly known; and, passing some less important streams, the **Fitzroy**, which has its mouth in King Sound, and the **Ord**, which falls into Cambridge Gulf. Like rivers in the other colonies, these are fed from the uncertain rainfall, and are at one season large and important streams, and at another destitute of water, in their upper courses at least, except in pools occurring at intervals. The rivers flowing towards the interior are short as regards length, and insignificant as regards the volume of water they contain, even at the most favourable time. They terminate either in the numerous lakes which are scattered over the colony, or in the scrubs and sandy wastes. In fact, explorers of this part of the territory have reported in strong terms of the lamentable want of water and the paucity of running streams. South of the tropic **lakes** are abundant, but they are salt and of small extent, the largest being probably Lake Amadeus, which lies partly in South Australian territory. They do not add to the available water supply, and some of them being shallow, become themselves but collections of saline mud.

4. As the colony extends through twenty-three degrees of latitude, there must necessarily be great variation in the **climate** of different portions. In the north the climate is tropical, though free from the excessive moistness that characterizes such climates in general. On the coast in this part of the territory the hurricanes which prevail in the Indian Ocean are sometimes felt. Towards the central part of the colony the heat is often excessive in summer, but the winters are mild. In the south-west, which has been longest settled, and where observations have been regularly made and recorded, the various climatic conditions are better known. The mean temperature of the year may, in this part, be regarded as 64°, the highest as 112°, and the lowest as 34°. During hot winds, which occasionally prevail during the summer months, the temperature is, of course, raised above the usual maximum, and much discomfort is experienced by the colonists, but fortunately such occurrences are rare. In the tropical region rain

falls, as usual, in the wet season only, but the amount is not yet known. In the eastern part of the colony it is small, not exceeding 10 inches in the year, and in the central part of the continent it is probably less. About Perth and the settled district generally the mean annual rainfall is about 31 inches, and the number of rainy days in the year 110. It appears that there is comparatively little variation in the annual rainfall, and that West Australia is exempt from both excessive rain and floods and from prolonged drought. The prevailing winds blow from the sea and moderate the temperature, except in the interior, where westerly winds are the most common as in other portions of the continent. Throughout the whole territory the climate is represented as favourable to health, epidemics being of rare occurrence, and some diseases which in other colonies are rife under certain circumstances being almost unknown. There seems to be no reason to doubt the accuracy of the statement that the death-rate is as low as in any country in the world.

5. In describing the **soils** of West Australia, care must be taken to distinguish between the northern portion and the remainder of the territory. *There,* a large proportion of the land is well fitted for agriculture or for pasturage, and in this district there are extensive tracts adapted for the cultivation of sugar and other tropical products. Of the rest of the colony it may be said in general terms that forests and deserts cover the whole surface in about equal proportions. The forests consist principally of various species of eucalyptus, of which the jarrah is the most worthy of note, though others are also remarkable chiefly on account of their size. Sandal-wood is found in some places and is highly valued. Much of this forest land, when cleared of timber, makes good farms and pasture grounds, though in some localities the latter are infested with plants which, though eaten by cattle and sheep, possess highly poisonous properties. The deserts are tracts of land in which fresh water is either absent altogether or very sparingly supplied. In some parts they are covered with dense scrubs, in others with the dreaded spinifex, and in not a few places with sand and rocks amidst which a few stunted bushes or tufts of coarse grass spring up. One of these barren tracts, known as

the Victoria Desert, lies north of the 31st parallel, and extends from the 125th meridian eastward into South Australia. Others lie to the northward of this, and all are characterized by the presence of salt lakes. At least one-third of the colony is occupied by these barren areas, in which the soil is unproductive and worthless. As if to compensate for the sterility of the country, it is believed to be richly endowed with mineral wealth, and that, as settlement progresses and the underground resources become better known, there will be no cause to complain of the nature of the soil.

6. The **population** of West Australia is now estimated at 36,000. This is a small number to hold so vast a territory, being at the rate of one person for every 27 square miles. It is anticipated, however, that the population will largely and rapidly increase, not only by the formation of new settlements, but also by the influx of persons attracted by the discovery of new gold-fields. To a large extent the population consists of persons of British origin, with a few other Europeans. Many portions of the colony being still in a state of nature, unvisited by the white man, the aborigines are more numerous than in any other part of the continent, and they remain unchanged, for good or evil, by contact with the intruding race. It is, of course, impossible to estimate their numbers. In the settled districts they are gradually disappearing as in other colonies.

7. It is only in the older settled districts that steps have been taken to provide the means of **internal communication.** Coasting steamers now ply between the different ports on the south and west. Roads have also been formed between the different towns. About 120 miles of railway have been completed in two lines, the Eastern and the Northern, and others are in course of construction. The first commences at Fremantle on the west coast, and runs by a circuitous route to Perth and York, and the latter from Geraldton to Northampton. About 2000 miles of electric telegraph are also open. Postal communication is maintained throughout the settled districts.

8. Many valuable **metals** are known, and others are believed to exist in the colony; but, up to the present time, lead and copper only have been worked to any extent. Gold, silver, and

iron are believed to be abundant, and will, doubtless, at no distant period, furnish employment to large numbers of the colonists. Already the Kimberley Gold Field, in the north-west corner of the territory, has attracted a considerable number of miners from other colonies and from New Zealand; but their success seems to have been very moderate. The main dependence of West Australia, however, must, for many years to come, be upon its **pastoral products**, especially wool. At present about a million and a half of sheep are depastured in the colony, besides cattle and horses, and as settlement is extended the numbers of each are likely to be increased. **Timber-getting** is another prominent industry, and, as the forests are practically inexhaustible, one that is likely to be permanent. Besides the jarrah already mentioned, and which is well-nigh imperishable, various gums—red, white, and blue—sandal-wood, acacias, and bark supply valuable material for trade. Farming is also largely carried on, wheat, for which the soil is generally well suited, being the principal crop. English fruits also are cultivated, and the fig, olive, orange, and vine also flourish. Fishing, in the ordinary sense of the word, cannot as yet be regarded as one of the recognized industries of the colony, except as regards the **pearl-fishery**. This branch of industry bids fair to become of considerable importance: the shells themselves, as well as the pearls occasionally found in them, have a commercial value. In time the fish which swarm on the coast, and the bêche-de-mer and dugong, will doubtless be sought after and provide regular occupation for the people. At present the **commerce** of West Australia is not extensive, the imports being valued at little more than half a million annually, and the exports at a sum considerably below that amount. Among the exports, wool takes the first place, the others being sheep, horses, hides, leather, oil, fish, pearl-shell, timber, ore, and guano, the last-mentioned being obtained from the deposits found on the Lacepede Islands. Horses are exported to India. The manufactures of West Australia are all of the kind before spoken of as domestic, and do not require special description.

9. The **government** of West Australia differs from that of other colonies in being less under popular control. The Legis-

lative Council, by which laws are enacted, consists of twenty-four members, of whom only sixteen are elected by the people, the remaining eight being either officials or persons nominated by the governor. A property qualification is required both in the case of electors and members. Besides the governor, who represents the royal authority, the affairs of the colony are administered by four heads of departments, who are also members of the Legislative Council. Aid is granted by the state to the four leading religious denominations, but in all other respects strict religious equality is preserved. The system of primary education supported from public funds is non-sectarian, but aid is also granted to private schools on condition that they be open to inspection on the part of the government, and that secular instruction only be given during four hours on each school-day. Secondary or middle-class schools are also supported by the state.

10. In the south-west corner the colony has been divided into **counties**, which, as usual, have no special organization, but are simply means for the accurate description of lands. A further division of the colony is made into thirteen **electoral districts**, comprising those portions in which settlement has taken place. There are also land districts and magistrates or police districts.

11. **Perth**, the capital, is situated on the banks of the Swan River, about 12 miles from its mouth. As the seat of the legislature and of the government it is a place of some importance, and possesses some handsome buildings. Its population is about 6000. It has communication by road, railway, and river with the town next mentioned.

Fremantle, the principal port of the colony, stands at the mouth of the Swan River. Its harbour is not quite safe at all times, but is likely to be improved. The Eastern Railway commences here, and greatly facilitates trade. The inhabitants number about 4000.

Albany, in the extreme south, on King George's Sound, is the second seaport, and is a place of call for some of the mail steamers from the mother country. The harbour is commodious and safe, but the town is small and possesses but 1000 inhabitants.

Another port is **Bunbury**, on the west coast at the entrance to a small inlet. The surrounding district is mainly agricultural, but timber is also shipped here in some quantity. The population is estimated at 600.

Further north, on Champion Bay, is **Geraldton**, the principal town in the northern portion of the colony. The harbour is said to be safe and commodious. There is regular communication by steamer with Fremantle, and with Northampton by rail. The surrounding district is pastoral and mineral, lead and copper being obtained in abundance. The population is about 1000.

Roeburne, on the Harding River, is another port and the head-quarters of the pearl-fishery. The district is largely pastoral, and exports wool. The inhabitants at present number about 120.

Derby, on King's Sound, and **Wyndham**, on Cambridge Gulf, are two embryo seaport towns, which will speedily rise into importance if the Kimberley gold-field should prove to be fairly rich in the precious metal.

On the Great Australian Bight, 7 miles west of the boundary between this colony and South Australia, is **Eucla**, another township recently established, the meeting-place of the telegraph systems of Western and South Australia.

Although many other settlements exist in the colony, the population gathered into townships is, in each case, but small. The following are the most worthy of note:—**Bussellton**, important for its trade in timber; **Cossack**, 8 miles from Roeburne, a pearl-fishing depot; **Greenough**, an agricultural settlement; **Guildford**, a station on the Eastern Railway; **Newcastle**, a farming locality; **Northampton**, the present terminus of the Northern Line of railway, and the centre of a rich mining district; **York**, the present terminus of the Eastern Railway line, and chief town of a productive farming district.

CHAPTER X.

NEW ZEALAND.—PHYSICAL FEATURES AND NATURAL PRODUCTIONS.

1. Position. 2. Name and Extent. 3. Form and Outline. 4. Indentations of North Island. 5. Indentations of South Island. 6. Surface. *North Island:* 7. Mountains. 8. Drainage. 9. The Hot Lakes. *South Island:* 10. Mountains. 11. Plains. 12. Drainage. 13. Lakes. 14. Climate of New Zealand. 15. Mineral Productions. 16. Vegetable Productions. 17. Indigenous Animals. 18. The Maoris. 19. Stewart Island. 20. The Chatham Islands. 21. The Auckland Islands. 22. Smaller islands and groups.

1. In a part of the Pacific Ocean bounded by the parallels of 34° and 48° S., and the meridians of 166° and 178° E., lie numerous islands which collectively may be called the **New Zealand Group.** Of these the largest and most important are the two islands distinctively known as **New Zealand,** and so named by their discoverer, Tasman, in 1642. The remaining islands are scattered at considerable distances from the central members of the group. **Macquarie** and **Campbell Islands,** for example, lie far away to the south; the **Auckland Islands, Antipodes Islands, Bounty** and **Cornwallis Islands,** are situated to the south and east; and the **Chatham Group** occupies a position at about the same distance due east. To the north-east is the **Kermadec Group,** and to the north-west **Norfolk Island.** Little more can at present be said of some of these than the mere mention of their names. In a geographical point of view, however, they are of some importance, as forming links in the chain of islands which engirdle eastern Australia from north to south at a distance of about a thousand miles. Commencing on the north with New Guinea, this semicircular chain of islands is continued through the Admiralty Group, New Britain and New Ireland, the Solomon Islands, the Louisiade Archipelago, Santa Cruz, the New Hebrides, New Caledonia, the Kermadec Group, New Zealand proper, the Auckland Islands, Campbell and Macquarie Islands. The position of this insular band leads to the belief that in former ages Australia extended eastward far beyond its present limits, and that portion of a great continent once existed where only

a remnant composed of island groups and solitary islets is now to be found.

2. New Zealand proper consists of two large islands known as the **North Island** and the **South** (or Middle) **Island** respectively, and one of smaller dimensions lying at the southern extremity of the South Island, and named **Stewart Island**. It is much to be regretted that some distinctive appellation has not been given to the two larger islands. If, for example, the northern island were named Cooksland, after the great navigator, who spent some time on its coasts, and the middle island were called Greysland, after the governor and legislator who has served the country for so long a period, much trouble would be saved to all interested. The native names, which would otherwise be the most appropriate, are too long and unmanageable. In length the three islands stretch over a space of 1100 miles; the width greatly varies, but nowhere exceeds 150 miles; and the whole surface occupies an area estimated at 100,000 square miles, or about one-sixth less than the British Islands.

3. If a map of New Zealand be inverted a great resemblance may be perceived between the general **form of the country** and the boot shape of the Italian peninsula, with this difference, however, that the toe of the boot, in the two cases, would point in opposite directions, and that the "leg" of one is continuous, while that of the other is cut through in two places. These two places are between the North and the South Island, at Cook's Strait, and between the South Island and Stewart's Island, at Foveaux Strait. Certain important differences in outline may be traced between the two principal islands. The northern island is altogether more irregular in form than the southern, which in its compactness not only contrasts with its northern neighbour, but even reminds one of the comparatively unbroken outline of Australia. In the northern island the chief irregularities of coast-line are on the eastern side and near the northern extremity; in the southern island the more conspicuous indentations occur near the north-east and near the south-west extremity.

4. Besides numerous smaller inlets, of which the Bay of Islands is an example, there are in the North Island two large **indentations** on the north-east coast, the **Hauraki Gulf** and

the **Bay of Plenty**. **Hawke Bay**, on the south-east, is also a prominent feature in the coast-line. On the west side **Kaipara** and **Manukau Harbours** penetrate for considerable distances into the land, the latter approaching to within a few miles of the waters of the Hauraki Gulf. The peninsula formed by these two inlets, and which constitutes the most northern portion of the island, terminates in two prominent capes, that on the east being named **North Cape**, that on the west **Cape Maria van Diemen**. **Cape Egmont**, another projection on the west coast, is formed by the declivities of Mount Egmont, one of the highest mountains in the island. At the southern extremity is **Cape Palliser**; and **East Cape** marks the termination of a large projection forming the north-eastern extremity. The bays on the north-east, spreading their numerous arms into the land, and everywhere studded with islands, present to the spectator's gaze some of the most beautiful scenery in the world, and render this portion of the island more than ordinarily attractive.

5. The South Island, though not possessing such inlets as the Hauraki Gulf, has, in addition to numerous bays, its own characteristic indentations. At the north end are **Golden Bay, Tasman Bay**, and **Cloudy Bay**, with other indentations; on the east, **Pegasus Bay**, bounded on the south by **Banks Peninsula**; less noticeable are, on the south Tewaewae Bay, and on the north-west Karamea Bay. At the south-west extremity the coast is broken by rugged and lofty projections and by arms of the sea cutting deeply into the land. These inlets are locally known as "sounds," but they forcibly remind the voyager of the fiords on the equally broken coast of Norway. No less than thirteen of these sounds occur within a distance of about 100 miles, and penetrate into the land from six to twenty miles. They all resemble each other in their main features. Sailing northward along this part of the coast, the voyager observes nothing on his right hand but lofty and precipitous walls of rock, at the foot of which the rolling waves from the Southern Ocean dash and break in foam. Suddenly the ship's head is turned landwards, and when to all appearance the vessel is in danger of striking against the formidable cliffs, a little cleft appears through which it is safely steered, and a passage not

before observed is found to run into the land, widening out to a breadth of about a mile. When once within the sound, the voyager notes that the smooth still water is inclosed on every side with immense perpendicular walls of rock, backed by yet higher mountains. Islands of various sizes stud the surface, and the whole of the visible land is covered with vegetation, like a mantle of rich and varied green, except where the cliff

Caswell Sound.

is too hard and smooth for even a fern to secure a hold. Over the cliffs waterfalls are tumbling—some derived from melted snow on the mountains dashing down at a leap, and others of smaller size winding like a sparkling thread through the dense green foliage. Such is the general appearance of all the sounds. They differ from each other chiefly in their extent and the heights of the mountains by which they are surrounded. One of them, **Milford Sound**, is hemmed in by mountains that attain an elevation of nearly 7000 feet, and has a "narrow entrance apparently still more contracted by the stupendous cliffs which rise, perpendicular as a wall, from the water's edge to a height of several thousand feet."

6. In its **physical features** New Zealand presents few points of similarity to any Australian country, and the two large islands even differ remarkably from each other in this respect. Generally speaking, the surface in both is greatly diversified. There are no tracts resembling the vast level plains and elevated plateaux of Australia; but mountain and valley, tableland and lowland plain, are mingled in endless variety. This diversity, however, is produced by different causes in the two islands. In the northern island volcanic forces have been and still are in active operation, and the evidences of their presence may be seen in various localities, in beds of scoriæ, boiling and sulphurous springs, and deposits of silica, as well as in the ever-smoking volcano, while even earthquakes are not of unfrequent occurrence. In the southern island, on the other hand, though traces of volcanic action are not absent, they do not point to any recent manifestation of such agencies, the mountains being largely composed of granite and other rocks of the same class. Lakes also are numerous in both islands. In the North Island, however, they are hot, being largely fed from boiling springs; while in the South they are extremely cold, as their waters are chiefly gathered from the melted snow of the mountains and from the ice of the glaciers.

7. Proceeding now to speak of the **surface** in detail, the North Island will be described first. The northern portion of this island is comparatively level, having but few mountain ranges, and these of low elevation, rarely exceeding 1500 feet. Some peaks, however, exceed this height; but they are for the most part isolated, and bear the appearance of extinct volcanoes. Near the centre of the island lies an elevated region from which rise two lofty peaks, **Tongariro** and **Ruapehu**—the former an active, the latter an extinct volcano. Tongariro, 6500 feet in elevation, constantly emits smoke, and occasionally gives more decided symptoms of activity, though it is believed not to have been in a state of eruption for some centuries. Ruapehu is remarkable not only as an extinct volcano, but also as being the highest summit in the island, its elevation being 9195 feet above the sea, and its top being considerably above the line of perpetual snow. From this central knot ranges of mountains branch off in various directions. To the eastward there lie,

with a long narrow valley between them, two parallel chains which stretch in a direction from north-east to south-west, and which form the most extensive highland region in the island. The more westerly of these two chains is about 150 miles in length, with an average height of 4000 feet. Near the middle the range is divided into two parts by a deep gorge through which flows the Manawatu River. The portion lying to the north of this gorge is called the **Ruahine Chain**, the remainder is named **Tararua**. From this chain lateral ranges branch off to the south and west, and terminate at the southern headlands of the island. The more easterly of the parallel chains extends further north, and its southern prolongation is broken up into a number of ranges which give this portion of the country its mountainous character. Besides the two peaks before mentioned there are two others which are noteworthy for their height: **Ikurangi**, in the east, 5535 feet above sea-level; and in the west, Taranaki or **Mount Egmont**, an extinct volcano 8280 feet in elevation.

Lying around the volcanic region is an elevated tract in which are the sources of many of the principal streams. Near the centre of the island and at an elevation of 1250 feet is **Lake Taupo** — a sheet of water about 200 square miles in extent, and remarkable for its great depth. Still further north is the most wonderful and characteristic portion of the island, in which are situated the hot lakes, boiling springs, geysers, and other natural phenomena caused by volcanic agencies. From this central table-land the country declines to the northward, where in places it even becomes low and sandy.

8. The **drainage system** is simple, comprising four main slopes, from the central highlands towards the coast, in the direction of the cardinal points. The principal river, **Waikato**, rises in the slopes of Mt. Ruapehu, flows into Lake Taupo, and then, after running northward for about a hundred miles, turns suddenly to the westward and enters the sea about midway between the 37th and 38th parallels. In the upper part of its course, after passing through Lake Taupo, this river traverses the most remarkable portion of the volcanic region. Its banks on both sides are lined with boiling springs which emit clouds of steam and sometimes throw up volumes of boiling water,

which fall like fountains into natural basins of stone. In this intermittent action they resemble the geysers of Iceland, which also is a volcanic country. A tributary named the Waipa, flowing from the south, joins the Waikato on the left bank, about fifty miles from its mouth; and from this point the stream is navigable. Of rivers flowing northward the **Waiho** or **Thames** and the **Waitoa** are the principal; both have their sources in the central table-land, and debouch into the Hauraki Gulf. Some smaller streams rise in the same district and flow north-east, among which the most considerable is the Whakatane, which falls into the Bay of Plenty. Flowing southward into the South Taranaki Bight is the **Wanganui**, which takes its rise near the centre of the island on the slopes of Mt. Tongariro. Further south is the **Manawatu**, which rises on the east of the Ruahine Range, through which it passes at the Manawatu Gorge and empties itself also into the Taranaki Bight. The remaining rivers are of inconsiderable length and volume, and navigable only for vessels of small tonnage.

9. **Lakes** form an important feature in the drainage system of the North Island. The largest of these, **Taupo**, has already been mentioned. It is remarkable for its great depth and the dark-blue colour of its waters. It is surrounded with evidences of volcanic action, and on its western side is bordered by precipitous cliffs 1000 feet in height. Further north lie numerous lakes which are distinctively known as the "Hot Lakes," as their waters, through the agency of boiling springs, are of a high temperature, and in certain places actually boil. The region in which these lakes are situated is about twenty miles long by twelve in width, and abounds in boiling springs, mud volcanoes, fumaroles, and solfataras—the two latter denoting vents through which issue from the bowels of the earth aqueous, sulphureous, and other vapours. The largest of these lakes are **Tarawera** and **Rotorua**. Another small but most remarkable lake here is **Rotomahana**, which formerly was described as "a rushy mere," about four miles and a half in circumference, mostly supplied with water from the numerous boiling springs surrounding it, and some of which deposited a white flinty substance that coated over the whole margin of the lake. In this way were formed two of the "sights" of this district,

named respectively, from their colours, the White and the Pink Terraces. Both consisted of immense steps or terraces covered with the siliceous crust deposited by the hot water issuing from huge caldrons situated at a considerable height above the lake. Owing to a recent eruption of Mt. Tarawera, a neighbouring volcano, the beauty of these sights has been destroyed —it is feared permanently—and the whole topography of the locality greatly altered, the lake being now a mere pond.

10. In regard to **surface and elevation**, the South Island differs greatly from the North. It is traversed through its whole extent by a chain of lofty and rugged mountains, which towards the northern extremity, and a little to the south of the 42d parallel, divides into several branches. The point of divergence of these ranges is **Mount Franklin**, one of the loftiest summits in the island, being 10,000 feet in altitude, and consequently above the level of perpetual snow; and they terminate in the peninsulas which constitute the northern portion of the island. East and west of Mount Franklin are parallel ranges, which, while of less elevation than the main range, have nevertheless several peaks which in height approach very nearly to the snow-line. Southward from Mount Franklin the dividing chain is continued for more than 200 miles, either as a single range or a series of parallel ranges, and for one-half of this distance there is no pass by which communication can be effected between the two sides of the mountains. Near the centre of this chain, and about midway between the 43d and 44th parallels, the stupendous mass of **Mount Cook** rises to a height of 13,200 feet, and justly deserves the Maori appellation of "Aorangi," the cloud-piercer. This is the culminating point of the chain, and the highest summit in the whole of New Zealand. Throughout the chain the higher peaks rise above the level of perpetual snow, and their ravines and gorges are filled up with glaciers, some of which are of enormous extent. In this respect the mountains of this chain surpass even the Alps, and it may be doubted whether the glaciers of New Zealand are exceeded in extent by those of any country in the southern hemisphere, those of the Antarctic region being excepted. On the western slope the glaciers in some places descend the mountain side to within 750 feet of the sea-level,

while in the Alps they are not known to exist at a lower altitude than 4000 feet above the same level. Everywhere the mountains approach very near to the west coast, to which they present a precipitous and, except in a few spots, impassable acclivity. Transit from one side to the other can be effected in but few places, as the vertical cliffs by which the mountains are faced, often to a height of thousands of feet, interpose an

Mount Cook.

insurmountable barrier. One of the few practicable roads which pierce the mountain change is that through the Otira Gorge, which, at its highest point, is 3000 feet above the sea, and descends rapidly on each side. On the west, the road which is cut out of the solid rock, or carried by embankments across deep ravines, sinks by a series of zigzags to a depth of 1500 feet, the adjacent mountains rising 7000 feet in height, and being clothed with forest up to the snow-line. In the whole chain the scenery is grand in the highest degree, and is reputed to excel in beauty and magnificence that of the Alps.

11. Eastward of Mount Cook lie the **Canterbury Plains** or Downs, an elevated but comparatively level tract of country,

sloping gradually or falling by terraces towards the sea. They are of considerable extent compared with the area of the island, though necessarily much smaller than the Australian uplands. Of plains, in the strictly geographical sense, New Zealand furnishes but few examples, and those of very limited area; but the flat lands at the bottom of river valleys are often thus designated.

12. The **drainage** of the South Island is also simple. Owing to the comparative narrowness of the island, few of the rivers attain any considerable length; and as nearly all have their sources in the main chain, they flow with great rapidity down the steep slopes to the sea. Several small rivers, the Motueka being the principal, rise in Mount Franklin or its spurs, and run northward into Tasman Bay and Golden Bay. On the west the rivers are very short, with the exception of the **Buller** and the **Gray** both of which owe their greater length to the fact that, in the upper part of their courses, they run parallel with the main range. On the east of that chain the principal rivers are the **Waitaki**, which is fed from some of the lakes and flows into the sea at a point on the coast about 45° S.; and the **Clutha**, 150 miles in length, and therefore the longest in the island, which also drains several lakes and debouches into Molyneux Bay. Of all the rivers in the Southern Island, it may be said that while kept constantly flowing by the abundant rains and the discharge from glaciers, they are liable to periodical floodings when the summer heats dissolve the mountain snows. Though at such times they flow with resistless power owing to their volume and rapidity, they do not overspread the country or cause such devastation as is often witnessed in an Australian flood.

13. A conspicuous feature in the aspect of the country, from a picturesque as well as geographical point of view, is supplied by the numerous **lakes** which adorn this island. These, to distinguish them from the hot lakes already described, are usually spoken of as the "cold lakes," being fed from the snows and glaciers of the main range. They are arranged in groups of three. The most northern group, Tekapo, Pukaki, and Ohau, lie about the 44th parallel of south latitude; they are fed from the glaciers of Mount Cook, and drained by the

Waitaki river and its affluents. The next group includes Lake **Wakatipu**, the largest and perhaps the most beautiful of all the lakes; besides Lakes **Wanaka** and **Hawea**, which supply the river Clutha. In the third group, which lie to the south-west, is **Te Anau**, also remarkable for its size and the grandeur of the mountains by which it is surrounded; and also Lakes Manipori and Monowai, all of which are drained by the

Moko Lake.

Waian river. Other smaller lakes are found in the northern portion of the island. The scenery of these lakes, their pellucid waters, the green of the surrounding forests, and the towering mountains white with everlasting snows, render the Cold Lake district no less attractive to travellers than the Hot Lake region, equally wonderful, though in a different fashion, of the North Island.

14. Variety and rapid changes may be said to characterize the **climate** of New Zealand, as that of Australia is distinguished for its lengthened continuance of fine weather, with its accompaniment of desolating droughts, and for its occasional floods. As regards temperature, great differences will naturally be

observed in a country extending over fourteen degrees of latitude, marked by great differences of elevation, and exposed on one side to the gales of the Southern Ocean. In the extreme north, for example, 120° is not an uncommon reading of the thermometer, while in the south the cold in winter is often considerably below the freezing-point even on the coast. Speaking generally, however, the mean annual temperature of the North Island may be estimated at 57°, and that of the South Island at 52°. In this particular the climate resembles that of the south of Europe. It is, however, much moister; and, as compared with Australia, may be considered decidedly wet. Rain falls at frequent intervals, especially on the west coast; but the heavy floods which occur in some parts of Australia are unknown. The rainfall is supposed to be more abundant in the North than in the South Island, excepting the west coast of the latter, where 122 inches have been known to fall in one year. High winds are rather common, particularly on the west coast, while Cook's Strait is peculiarly liable to such bursts of windy weather. Notwithstanding the rapid alternations of heat and cold, caused by changes in the direction of the wind, the average difference between the extremes of daily temperature throughout the year for the whole country does not exceed twenty degrees. Frost is common in the South Island, and snow falls in abundance upon all the higher mountains. On the whole, the climate is salubrious and enjoyable, and favourable alike to animal life and vegetable growth.

15. Although the country has not been thoroughly examined with a view to ascertain the nature and extent of its **mineral deposits**, sufficient is known to justify the assertion that its products of this kind are rich and varied. Notwithstanding the differences between the two islands in point of geological structure, the North being largely volcanic and the South chiefly composed of sedimentary rocks, gold is found in both, and in many different localities, notably in Otago, Westland, and the Thames Valley. Silver also occurs, chiefly as an alloy of other metals. More abundant and varied in composition is iron ore, which is found in several districts, and will doubtless become, in time, a product of great value. Mining for copper has been carried on to some extent, and tin, lead,

mercury, platinum, and manganese are also known to exist. Of other minerals, coal is the most important, and is found of good quality in both islands. Various mineral substances of a valuable kind from a commercial point of view are also produced, as sulphur, alum, asbestos, and plumbago, besides different useful sorts of stone. The soil is in general productive, especially in districts where it has been formed from the decomposition of volcanic rocks. About one-half of the area of the whole country, it is estimated, is fit for agricultural purposes.

16. Probably no country in the world possesses a more peculiar native **vegetation** than New Zealand. While restricted in the number of species it produces, a large proportion of them are found in no other country. Of those which are found elsewhere a great number belong also to Australia; though, on the other hand, none of the specially Australian plants, such as acacias and eucalypti, grow naturally in New Zealand. Ferns, of which about 130 species are indigenous, and mosses, which are even more abundant, form a great proportion of the plants, and everywhere impart a peculiar colouring to the landscape. Some of the ferns attain the dimensions of trees, and reach the height of thirty feet, and even more, while others are equally minute and lowly. Among the plants of this class the edible fern deserves notice, as having formerly furnished a staple article of food to the aboriginal inhabitants, and being still used for the same purpose by the less civilized tribes. One of the plants peculiar to New Zealand is that called the New Zealand Flax, though it really belongs to the lily tribe. Its long sword-shaped leaves contain a strong, tough fibre, which, when properly prepared, makes excellent ropes, and was employed by the natives in weaving mats, cloaks, and baskets. Shrubs are less abundant than might have been expected from the richness of the soil and humidity of the climate, and flowering plants are remarkably scarce. In these points the country contrasts disadvantageously with Australia, which, notwithstanding its generally poorer soil and drier climate, produces flowering shrubs and herbaceous plants in profusion. Perhaps the finest of the New Zealand flowering shrubs is that popularly known as the *glory pea*, which bears

large clusters of flowers of a beautiful crimson colour. A few of the large trees bear flowers of some beauty, but as a rule, however beautiful the foliage, the bloom is inconspicuous. Forest trees are said to number more than a hundred species, comprising two palms and seven pines, the latter furnishing valuable timber. Among these the best known is the *kauri*, which sometimes grows to the height of two hundred feet, and not only supplies most useful timber for building and for ships' spars, but also produces a kind of gum resembling amber, which is employed in making varnishes and for other purposes. Many thousand tons of this gum are exported yearly, and it is procured not only from living trees, but is also dug out of the earth in places where forests formerly existed. The kauri is rapidly disappearing in consequence of the large consumption and reckless destruction of the tree; and as it is confined to a small district north of 37° 10′ south latitude, its total extinction may be looked for at no distant period, unless suitable measures be taken to prevent this unfortunate result. Though in some parts, especially in the South Island, the forests are often largely composed of a species of beech, their general character is that of an intermixture of trees of various kinds, differing in this respect from those of Australia, in which the eucalypti frequently predominate to so large an extent that it would be difficult to discover a tree of any other genus. Of indigenous fruits there is a total absence, and no kind of grain is native to the country. Grassy tracts abound; and the native grasses are said to be possessed of valuable properties for the feeding of sheep.

17. As in other portions of Australasia, none of the larger **mammals,** herbivorous or carnivorous, are indigenous. A dog, a rat, and two species of bats were found, it is said, by the original white settlers, but it is questionable whether the first-mentioned was not introduced by some earlier navigator of whose visit no record has been preserved, or by the present race of aborigines. Moreover, these animals were not numerous, and, with the exception of the bats, are now extinct. It is probable that here, as in other parts of Australasia and in Polynesia, the scarcity of animal food caused by the absence of ruminating quadrupeds, such as the ox and the sheep, was

one of the principal causes of cannibalism. Of mammals that inhabit the seas or haunt the coast—whales, dolphins, and seals—great numbers were formerly found, and of many varieties. These, together with fish, once constituted a large portion of the food of the people residing upon the coast. The inland waters supply eels in large numbers, as well as lampreys and a fish locally known as white-bait. The **reptile** class is but scantily represented in New Zealand. Unlike Australia, where they abound, no snakes inhabit the country, though two species of sea-snakes are found in the coast waters. Twelve species of lizards are met with, but frogs also are scarce, only one species being known, and that confined to a limited tract in the North Island. In respect of the feathered tribes, also, this country contrasts strangely with Australia and the Papuan regions, its **birds** being remarkable neither for their numbers nor for their beautiful plumage. It agrees, however, with other portions of Australasia in the possession of wingless birds. These birds are rapidly disappearing, and the largest, called the Moa, is already extinct. One species of Moa, of which perfect skeletons have been found in a condition that shows that its extinction has taken place in recent times, reached the height of twelve or fifteen feet. It was thus considerably larger than the ostrich. A still existing wingless bird is the apteryx or *kiwi*, of the size of a common fowl. It has a long beak with the nostrils at the end, and is covered with hair-like feathers. Pigeons and parrots form the largest proportion of land birds, and ducks and wading birds are even more abundant. A few birds are remarkable in their appearance, as the parson-bird, which is black, with two tufts of white feathers pendent from the throat; and the *huia* (allied to the starlings), also a black bird, with orange-coloured wattles and a straight bill for the male and much-curved bill for the female. The owl parrot derives its appellation from the owl-like circle of feathers surrounding its eyes. Though usually a vegetable feeder and nocturnal in its habits, in the South Island, to which it is now restricted, it is very destructive to sheep, which it kills by picking holes in their backs to obtain the kidney fat. It is accordingly much detested by flock-masters, who seek to exterminate it as their Australian brethren compass the destruction of the dingo. Some of the insects are peculiar, but their species are not numerous. Moths and butterflies are not numerous, bees are scarce, beetles more abundant. There is a large grasshopper, and a hideous-looking creature called the "weta," which inhabits hollow trees, and is from eight to ten inches in length. But the most remarkable is a caterpillar, from the head of which grows a fungus to the height of three inches, and which has therefore been designated the "vegetating caterpillar."

18. New Zealand is the only portion of Australasia inhabited by a race of **people** which is neither Papuan nor Australian in its origin and relations to other peoples. The "Maori," as the aboriginals designate themselves, are, however, an intruding race which, in times probably not far distant, settled in New Zealand. Six successive waves of immigration are recorded in the traditions of the Maoris, each of which resulted in the establishment of one of the six principal tribes or septs into which they are divided. There is reason to believe that, as is still the case in the Chatham Islands, a weaker and probably Papuan race occupied the land before the immigration of the Maoris, by whom it was either exterminated or absorbed. Occasional traces may yet be seen in the darker skin, crisp black hair, and differently formed nose and lips of individual Maoris, of the Papuan element so incorporated with the invading race. In colour and features the Maoris resemble other Polynesian tribes, being brown, with good features, the nose well formed, and the black hair long and straight, though sometimes wavy or curling. Their language also is Polynesian, closely resembling that of Rarotonga, but having such near affinity to other dialects as to be intelligible to most of the Polynesian islanders. In their manners, customs, and superstitions they exhibit further evidences of their connection with the Polynesian race. The superstitious custom of "tabu" and the horrible practice of cannibalism they shared with other inhabitants of the Pacific islands, but their intertribal wars were conducted with a ferocity peculiarly their own. Apart from these darker traits the Maoris exhibited many of the higher elements of character. They are undoubtedly brave, and their athletic forms and skill in the use of the national

weapons rendered them formidable antagonists even to white men. As their country yielded neither edible grain nor fruits of any consequence, they were compelled to turn their attention to agriculture, and they became skilful cultivators of the sweet-potato, the taro, and the gourd, and they were, moreover, adepts at hunting and fishing. Building houses and fortifications, constructing canoes, weaving cloth and mats from the so-called native flax, and making weapons and other implements, were also pursuits in which they excelled; and, further, all their possessions were ornamented with elaborate carvings, showing some appreciation of art. Tattooing was practised extensively. They had a national religion, which included a belief in a future state; and though they had no written language they were great orators. Their language abounds in vowel sounds, but, notwithstanding its consequent softness, it is forcible and energetic when needed.

19. **STEWART ISLAND.**—This island is sometimes, in the confused nomenclature prevailing, called the South Island of New Zealand, though Stewart Island is now very generally recognized as its proper appellation, being so named in remembrance of the captain of a merchant vessel, by whom it was discovered. It is about forty miles in length, of a triangular, but very irregular shape, and having an area of about 500 square miles. Owing to the numerous indentations its coastline is broken and irregular, from which fact, however, it derives the great advantage of having numerous excellent harbours. The surface is uneven, with no prominent features of any kind, though the culminating point, Mount Anglem, rises to the height of 3200 feet. In its natural productions the island resembles the southern portion of the South Island. Valuable timber abounds in the forests, with which it is largely clothed; its mineral wealth is as yet undiscovered. Fish are plentiful along the coasts, and its oysters are generally held in high estimation. The population is scanty, and consists chiefly of half-castes, with a few Europeans.

20. **THE CHATHAM ISLANDS.**—This group consists of three principal islands, of which the largest, Chatham Island,

is about forty miles long, but irregular in shape; the others, named Pitt and Rangatira Islands, resemble Chatham Island in all important points. The group is situated at a distance of 400 miles to the eastward of Cook's Strait. In the largest island there is one deep indentation called Petre Bay, on the west coast; the others, though numerous, do not break up the coast-line to any considerable extent, and should perhaps be styled Bights rather than Bays. A salt-water lake or lagoon, "Te Wahanga," on the east coast, is separated by sand-banks from the ocean, with which it sometimes communicates, however, by bursting through the intervening barrier. It thus resembles the numerous lagoons to be found on the Australian coasts. As regards surface these islands are low and tolerably even, the culminating point, Mount Patterson, being but 800 feet above sea-level. Rivers are few, the largest being the Mangatu, about twelve miles in length; but lakes are numerous, and, with the exception already mentioned, they contain fresh water. The soil is in general fertile, a large portion of the island being of volcanic origin, but in some parts a peaty formation occupies considerable tracts. With a mild and somewhat humid climate the vegetation of the group, including trees, shrubs, and ferns, is luxuriant, and in its general character bears a strong resemblance to that of New Zealand, though there are some peculiar species, and in particular some fine flowering plants. Phormium, or New Zealand Flax, flourishes in all parts of the group. The animals found in the islands are either identical with or allied to those of New Zealand. When first discovered by Europeans in 1791, the group was peopled with a peculiar race, who are described as possessing many Papuan characteristics, of which mirthfulness and laughter were specially noticeable. They called themselves Morioris, and their numbers were then estimated at 2000. They were, however, nearly exterminated by a horde of Maoris that landed from a European ship in 1831. The present population, numbering about 700, is composed of many and most incongruous elements, the most prominent being Europeans of various nationalities, Maoris, Morioris, and Chinese. These are chiefly employed in agriculture, wheat and potatoes being raised in considerable quantities for the supply of whaling vessels and for export to the Australian colonies. The principal settlement is at Waitangi, on Petre Bay.

21. **THE AUCKLAND ISLANDS.**—The group thus named lies between the parallels of 50° and 51° S. and about 180 miles south of New Zealand. Auckland Island, the largest, is about thirty miles in length; its surface is mountainous, and the highest point is Mount Eden, about 1300 feet high. Basalt and other volcanic rocks compose a large part of the island, and the soil is rich, though often covered with a thick, spongy deposit of peat, which retains the moisture. Vegetation in the valleys, where it is sheltered from the violent gales which prevail around these islands, is luxuriant, and trees attain to a great size and height. On the mountains, however, the trees are stunted, and brushwood covers the ground to a large extent. Flowers are as numerous and brilliant in colour as those of New Zealand are scanty and inconspicuous. The climate is wet and stormy, though mild and healthy. Seals abound on the coast, and among land-birds parrots and pigeons are found in the greatest numbers. The islands are uninhabited.

22. **CAMPBELL ISLAND.**—About 145 miles south-east of the Auckland Islands is Campbell Island, which is about 30 miles in circumference, mountainous, and clothed with vegetation. Like the Auckland Islands, its surface is covered with peat. It is uninhabited.

23. **MACQUARIE ISLAND.**—Still more distant, in the opposite direction, is Macquarie Island, 20 miles long and covered with vegetation, mostly of a grassy description. It is remarkable as being the habitat of a kind of parrot, and is the place most distant from the tropics in which birds of this class are to be found. The island is uninhabited, but is occasionally visited by ships in search of seals, which abound on the coast.

24. **BOUNTY and ANTIPODES ISLANDS.**—Between the Chatham and Auckland groups lie two clusters of islets named respectively the Bounty and Antipodes Islands. They are without interest, except that the latter are nearly at the anti-

podes of Greenwich, through which the first meridian is supposed to pass.

25. **THE KERMADEC ISLANDS.**—This group belongs geographically to New Zealand, from which it is distant about 500 miles. The largest of the group is said to be 12 miles in circumference, mountainous, and wooded. None of the islands are inhabited. Recently these islands have been annexed by the British government, and made dependencies of New Zealand.

CHAPTER XI.

NEW ZEALAND AS A COLONY.

1. Discovery and Settlement. 2. Industrial Occupations. 3. Internal Communication. 4. Constitution and Government. 5. Religion. 6. Education. 7. Political Divisions. 8. *Auckland District:* General Description. 9. Auckland. 10. Other Towns. 11. *Hawke's Bay District:* General Description. 12. Towns. 13. *Taranaki District:* General Description. 14. Towns. 15. *Wellington District:* General Description. 16. Towns. 17. *Nelson District:* General Description. 18. Towns. 19. *Marlborough District:* General Description. 20. Towns. 21. *Canterbury District:* General Description. 22. Towns. 23. *Westland District:* General Description. 24. Towns. 25. *Otago District:* General Description. 26. Towns. 27. *Southland District:* General Description. 28. Towns.

1. Discovered by Tasman in 1642, this country remained unvisited and unknown till Cook explored its coasts in 1770. Some French navigators touched at the islands about the same time, but it is to Cook that we owe what knowledge we possess of the nature of the country and its inhabitants at that period. From this date its bays and harbours were frequently entered by whaling vessels in need of wood, water, and fresh provisions; but although a few runaway seamen landed on its shores, no attempt at colonization was made. Even after the establishment of Christian missions in 1814 the number of European residents was very small, and their presence in the country was suffered only by the permission of the Maori chiefs. In 1840, however, a number of chiefs assembled at Waitangi on the Bay of Islands and concluded a treaty by which the sovereignty of the Queen of Great Britain over the island was acknowledged. As a result of this treaty, agencies were established by merchants at various points on the coast. Systematic efforts for the foundation of colonies were made about the same time, chiefly by the New Zealand Company, which had been formed in England a few years earlier. Through it a settlement was made at Wellington in 1840, and from that time colonization rapidly progressed and other settlements were established at various points in the two larger islands. The most important of these, in the order of their foundation, are Auckland, Wellington, New Plymouth (now called Taranaki), Nelson, Otago, and Canterbury. A constant stream of immigration was kept

up for many years, and the population of European birth or of European descent is now estimated at 550,000. Besides, there may be about 45,000 of the Maori stock; but the race, if not actually dying out, does not increase in numbers. Adding 5000 Chinese, the total population amounts to 600,000.

2. The industrial **occupations** of the colonists are such as might be expected in a country so recently settled and so sparsely populated. To discover the natural resources of the country and to bring them to market must always be the first business of a people who are too few in number and too poorly provided with machinery to be able to compete with older, more densely populated, and more fully organized countries. Of all raw materials gold is generally considered the most valuable; and mining for this metal, though less attractive than a few years ago, still occupies a considerable number of people, principally in the north-east of the North Island, and in the south and west of the South Island. Mining for other metals, although they exist in quantities sufficient to repay the outlay required to obtain them, has not yet been undertaken as a regular industry. Coal and petroleum, however, furnish occupation to a fair proportion of the people, and the number is likely to increase. The collection of sulphur from the volcanoes on the mainland and at White Island in the Bay of Plenty is also a profitable employment. **Agriculture,** for which the country is well fitted by reason of its generally fertile soil and genial climate as well as the regularity of its seasons, is carried on extensively, the principal crops being wheat and other kinds of grain, potatoes, and hay. Fruits of various kinds are also cultivated; in the north the vine, orange, peach, and such others as require a considerable degree of warmth; in the south the fruits of a less genial climate, as the cherry and gooseberry. Pastoral pursuits are also largely followed, especially in the South Island, where sheep-farming ranks as the principal industry. Dairying is also an important branch of industry, and dairy produce forms no inconsiderable item in the list of exports. Fishing for home consumption is successfully pursued on the coasts, which teem with fish. The manufactures in which the colonists engage are such as deal principally with raw materials and the first stages of preparing them for other processes. Such, for

example, are tanning, tallow-making, sawing timber. There are, however, abundant manufactures for what may be termed domestic use—that is, for the supply of the household. **Commerce** occupies a large proportion of the population. The exports may, in general terms, be described as raw produce; the imports, as manufactured goods. Among the former may be enumerated gold, wool, grain and potatoes, tallow and skins, kauri-gum, preserved meats, and phormium, which are sent principally to Great Britain and the Australian colonies. The imports consist chiefly of manufactured goods—apparel, boots and shoes, and drapery, and hardware and ironmongery, besides machinery and groceries. The total value of exports is about £7,000,000, that of imports about £7,500,000.

3. In some parts **internal communication**, so essential for purposes of government and of trade, has been difficult to establish, as owing to the elevation of mountain ranges, the precipitous nature of their slopes, and the absence of natural passes across them, roads have had to be hewn out of the hillsides in some cases, and in others carried over deep ravines by means of raised embankments. In this way, and by taking advantage of every natural facility afforded by the nature of the country, it is now fairly provided with good roads upon which an extensive and effective coaching system has been established. Postal facilities and postal rates are the same as in the Australian colonies. The only exception to the existence of these means of intercommunication is to be found in the "King" country, around Lake Taupo, which is still held by Maoris professing independence of the New Zealand government. These for many years prevented the formation of roads and the erection of telegraph lines, but their opposition has of late greatly diminished. About 4000 miles of inland telegraph line has been brought into operation. Cable communication has been established between the two islands and between Wellington and Sydney, by means of which New Zealand has been brought into direct connection with the whole civilized world. A very large sum of money has been expended in the construction of railroads, of which about 1500 miles have been opened for traffic; and efforts are being made for further extensions, which will result in each island being traversed from

end to end by an unbroken line of rails, besides the numerous branches which diverge from the main trunk. Steamers ply constantly between the various ports, and regular communication is thus kept up between all parts of the colony coastwise.

4. Prior to 1854 New Zealand had been governed as a crown colony by a governor and nominated council; but in that year a responsible legislature was created, the first session of which took place on the 24th May. The form of **government** resembles, in its main features, those of the Australian colonies, full liberty being enjoyed to legislate upon all subjects excepting those in which the prerogative of the sovereign and the interests of the mother country are involved. As in Australia, the legislative body consists of two chambers—a Council or Upper House of 46 members appointed by the crown for life, and an Assembly or Lower House of 88 members elected by the people for three years. Representatives of the Maori race are admitted into both houses, and the members are paid for their services. The franchise is low, and Maoris have the privilege of voting at the election of members of the Assembly if possessing the requisite qualification. The executive authority consists of a governor appointed by and representing the crown, and a ministry selected from and responsible to the Assembly. By this executive all the various departments of the government are carried on, subject, as in other constitutional countries, to the approval of the legislature, and more particularly of the Lower House, by which the necessary funds are voted.

5. There is no established **religion**, all denominations being upon an equal footing in the eye of the law and equally free from state control or interference. Ministers of all denominations, however, must be registered as a condition to the legal celebration by them of the marriage ceremony. The most numerous class of religionists are the members of the Church of England, the Presbyterians ranking second in point of numbers. Some of the settlements were originally founded with the idea of restricting the colonists to one denomination. Canterbury, for instance, was intended to be peopled by members of the Church of England exclusively, and Otago with

Presbyterians. These designs, so utterly opposed to modern ideas of colonization, have, however, long since been abandoned, and members of any church are as free to settle in these districts as in any other portion of the territory. A large proportion of the Maoris profess Christianity in some form, though, on the outbreak of the "Hau Hau" superstition, many relinquished even their nominal adherence to the Christian faith and returned to the heathen practices of their forefathers.

6. **Education**, as in the Australian colonies, is to a large extent controlled by the state. As regards primary schools the whole country is divided into twelve educational districts, each of which is placed under the supervision of a board. The system is free and entirely secular, religious teaching during the ordinary school hours being prohibited, though under certain limitations it may be given at other times. The course of instruction prescribed for these schools is liberal, and includes all the subjects usually taught in the Australian schools. Secondary education is provided for in the numerous high schools, grammar-schools, and so-called colleges which have been established in all the principal towns, and which profess to impart such an education as will prepare a scholar to matriculate at the university or to enter upon the study of professional subjects. The University of New Zealand, with affiliated colleges at Canterbury, Otago, Wellington, Auckland, and Nelson, regulates higher education. It is endowed by the state, and grants from the public lands have been made to colleges and other educational institutions of the higher class. Another university, named from Otago, professes similar aims and seeks for the like recognition by the state. A large number of scholarships have been provided from public funds to enable such as desire it to obtain a high-class education.

7. Formerly the country was divided into provinces, which exercised within themselves considerable legislative and administrative powers. These powers were, however, withdrawn by an act of the parliament of New Zealand in 1876, and the title of **Provincial Districts** was substituted for Provinces. Four of these districts—Auckland, Hawke's Bay, Taranaki, and Wellington—compose the North Island; and five—Canterbury, Marlborough, Nelson, Otago, and Westland—the

South. A further division into counties is also made, 32 being in the North Island, 30 in the South, and 1 in Stewart Island.

8. **Auckland.**—This district occupies the northern portion of the country, extending from North Cape to the 39th parallel, which forms the greater part of the boundary on the south. Its total area is estimated at 36,000 square miles. Owing to its numerous indentations, some of which penetrate deeply into the land, its coast-line is longer in proportion to area than is the case with other districts; and it possesses several excellent harbours. It has also numerous rivers, which, though not remarkable for length, are navigable in the lower portion of their courses, and hence it happens that no locality exists in the whole district which is more than twenty miles distant from navigable waters. The surface is diversified, being broken up by ranges in all directions, some of which, as the Coromandel Range in the peninsula of the same name, are granitic, but a larger number volcanic as may be inferred from their shape. For the most part these ranges do not exceed 3000 feet in height, except near the east coast, where the peak of Ikurangi attains an elevation of 5535 feet. The principal rivers are the Waiho or Thames, and the Rangitaiki, which disembogue upon the east or rather north coast; and the more important Waikato, which discharges its waters upon the west. The lakes and the wonderful phenomena of the lake-district, including the Pink and the White Terraces, have already been noticed. The most northern portion of the district contains a good deal of sterile land covered with fern and scrub, and also much dense forest, together with large tracts of land of good quality. In the central portion, especially in the valleys of the Thames and the Waikato, are extensive areas of the finest agricultural land in the whole colony, and though much of it is still in the possession of the Maoris, settlement upon it is gradually taking place. Gold has been largely obtained, especially in the Thames Valley. Comparatively little is known of the eastern part of the district, the interior being occupied by a fierce and intractable tribe to whom the visits of Europeans are unwelcome. The population is about 130,000.

9. Interesting as the spot first occupied by the Maoris, and as one of the earliest of the European settlements, and long the

capital of New Zealand, the city of **Auckland** continues to be the most populous town in the whole colony. Its position,

The Pink Terraces.

whether regarded from a mercantile or merely picturesque point of view, can hardly be surpassed. Situated on the south side of the Waitemata Harbour, the numerous branches of which extend far inland, the city has practically unlimited facilities

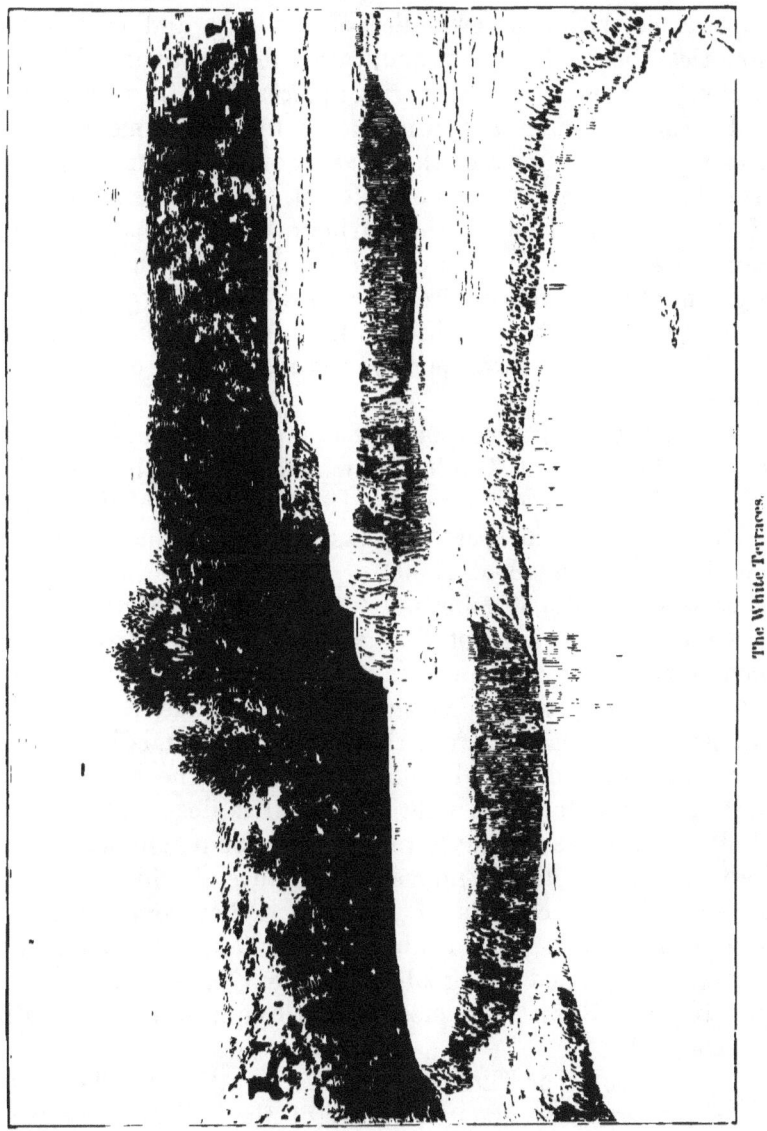

The White Terraces.

for the formation of wharves and other kinds of accommodation for shipping, and the waters are of sufficient depth to allow of the largest vessels entering the port. With these advantages it is natural that the trade of Auckland should be large and increasing. On the west the Manukau Harbour approaches within a few miles of the city, and in time will doubtless be made to communicate with Waitemata Harbour. Railways connect it with various places that lie north, south, and west. Though not remarkable for handsome buildings, either public or private, the beauty of its situation gives to Auckland a large amount of interest. From the higher parts of the city the view of the harbour, with its bays and promontories, and of the island-studded Hauraki Gulf, is exceedingly fine, while the environs present scenes of great beauty. The population with suburbs is over 60,000. Among its suburbs may be mentioned **Devonport** on the north shore of Waitemata Harbour.

10. **Onehunga** is a seaport situated at the head of the Manukau Harbour, about 7 miles from Auckland, with which it is connected by road and railway. It is the centre of the trade of a large agricultural, pastoral, and timber-producing district. The population is about 2500.

Russell, about 130 miles north of Auckland, originally called Kororareka, was the spot first selected as the seat of government when New Zealand became a dependency of the British crown. It is situated on the Bay of Islands, a landlocked indentation so named from the numerous islands by which it is shut in and protected from the gales of the Pacific. The port is accessible in all weathers and has deep water capable of floating vessels of any tonnage. In the neighbourhood are **Kawakawa** and its coal-mines, the produce of which forms one of the principal exports of Russell. Other commodities exported are kauri-gum, timber, wool, flax, and manganese, the last mentioned being obtained from mines situated near the town. Russell is also much frequented by whaling vessels.

Grahamstown or **Thames**, near the mouth of the Thames, is a mining township and the centre of the gold-producing district known as the Thames Gold-field. In and around the town is congregated a population of about 10,000 persons (half in the town), the principal industry being gold-mining. The town is well laid out, and has some good buildings, and is sure to increase.

Hamilton, on the Waikato, 86 miles south of Auckland, with which it is connected by railway, is a rising town in a good agricultural district, with a population of about 1500. Here is the junction of the railway to Grahamstown.

Tauranga is a seaport town, situated on the harbour of the same name, which is an inlet of the Bay of Plenty. It may be considered the capital of the eastern settlements. The district around is agricultural and pastoral. Including Maoris, the population of the town is reported to number about 2500.

Coromandel.—The peninsula which bounds the Hauraki Gulf on the east is named Coromandel, and on its western shore is the town of the same name. This is also a gold-mining district, the precious metal in this case being found in quartz veins.

Whangarei is situated upon a river of the same name which falls into the Pacific on the east coast, about 80 miles to the northward of Auckland. Coal is worked in the neighbourhood, but the district is at present mainly agricultural.

Gisborne, on the shore of Poverty Bay, is remarkable as the spot on which Cook first trod the soil of New Zealand. The surrounding district is pastoral and agricultural, and some trade is carried on in the produce of these industries. Communication by steam-ships with other ports is regularly maintained. This town was the scene of a horrible massacre by the Maoris, who in 1868 surprised the settlement and slaughtered the residents, European and Maori, to the number of seventy. The population is 1800.

11. **Hawke Bay.**—This small district, with an estimated area of only 4440 square miles, occupies a portion of the east coast from 39° S. to the small stream Waimata, and extending westward to the watershed formed by the Ruahine Mountains. It receives its name from the great bight lying between the parallels of 39° and 40°, and which was designated Hawke Bay by Cook, in honour of Sir E. Hawke, a British admiral. The coast-line is irregular, consisting of broken chalk and limestone cliffs, with occasional sandy beaches. Mahia Peninsula is a

remarkable projection on the north side of Hawke Bay. As regards surface the district is much diversified, the west being mountainous, with summits rising as high as 4000 feet, while the eastern portion contains some extensive level plains. Between these two portions the country is hilly, and especially towards the north rugged and broken. The mountains being less than fifty miles from the sea, the numerous rivers which, with one exception, have easterly courses, are short and of insufficient volume to be navigable, though the Wairoa, flowing from the north into Hawke's Bay, does not come under this description. The exceptional river is the Manawatu, which, rising in the Ruahine Mountains, flows southward between that range and another, the Peketoi Range, parallel to it, and then turns westward through the district of Wellington. In the plains and in detached portions the soil is highly productive, but, from the broken nature of much of the country, a considerable extent is better adapted for pasturage, and valuable forests still cover large tracts. As might be inferred from its sheltered position the climate is drier in Hawke Bay than in other parts of the island, but is otherwise favourable to vegetable growth. No minerals of any value have yet been discovered in this district, but limestone occurs in many localities. Timber is one of the most important natural products. Agriculture is successfully carried on in the plains, but sheep-farming is the industry which is at present of the greatest consequence. Vine-culture may in the future be largely carried on. Settlement has not as yet taken place to any great extent, and the towns are few and small. The population is about 25,000.

12. **Napier**, the chief town of the district, is situated on a peninsula near the mouth of the river Tutaekuri. Vessels of light draught can enter the harbour, but those of large burden must lie in the roadstead, where they are exposed to southerly and easterly gales. A railway has been constructed to connect this town with Wellington and Whanganui. Wool and frozen meat are exported. The population is estimated at 7500.

Clive, distant about six miles by train from Napier, is a village that, from its position on the banks of the Ngaruroro River and the resources of the vicinity, promises to become a place of some importance.

Havelock, another village in the same district, is also worthy of note.

Waipawa, Kaikora, and **Wairoa** or **Clyde** are other villages rising into importance.

13. **Taranaki,** formerly called New Plymouth, occupies the western portion of the island, and is bounded on the north by the river Mokau; on the south and west by the sea; and on the east by an artificial boundary line and the river Wanganui. Its area is about 3245 square miles. No indentations worthy of note occur on the coast of this district, but on the north and south of the Taranaki projection are curvatures known as the North and South Taranaki Bights. In general the surface is mountainous, but a level strip of land stretches along the coast, having an average width of about five miles. The projection or peninsula named Taranaki, the point of which is Cape Egmont, is so designated from an extinct volcano which attains an elevation of 8280 feet, and is covered with perpetual snow at the summit. This mountain, also known as Mount Egmont, occupies a base about thirty miles in diameter, from the middle of which the volcanic cone rises with sudden grandeur, and forms a very conspicuous feature in the landscape even at a great distance. The rivers in the Taranaki district, though extremely numerous, are of little importance, the Mokau being the most considerable. Being largely made up of decomposed volcanic rocks the soil is generally good, and when cleared of fern or forest is well adapted for farming purposes; the climate also is favourable to agricultural pursuits. Owing, in a great measure, to troubles with the native tribes some parts of the district have been but slightly explored, and its mineral resources remain unknown, with the exception of the deposits of iron in the sands of the sea-shore near New Plymouth; but it is supposed, from the generally volcanic origin of the country, that it does not abound in mineral wealth. Agriculture and pasturage will therefore constitute the principal industrial pursuits of the people. The population is about 18,000.

14. **New Plymouth,** picturesquely situated on the shore of the North Taranaki Bight, and at the foot of Mount Egmont, is the chief town of the district. The original settlers here

came from Devon and Cornwall, and named the place after Plymouth in England. Some progress has been made towards the connection of this town with the other principal towns of the colony by railway. Its population is estimated at 3800.

Villages are springing up in all directions on the coast plain, but they are too small to need separate description. At the mouth of the river Patea is **Carlyle,** and at the mouth of the river Waitara is **Raleigh. Hawera,** on the south coast, promises to become a place of importance, being the outlet for the agricultural district of Waimato Plains.

15. **Wellington (District).**—The remaining portion of the north island is occupied by the Wellington district, which has an area of about 11,250 square miles. On the east and west the coast is comparatively unbroken, the South Taranaki Bight occupying the greater part of the latter. The south coast is less regular, and is broken into by two considerable indentations, Port Nicholson and Palliser Bay, the latter being much the larger. Mountainous in the north and east, the district comprises large areas of level and undulating land, lying chiefly along the coasts and in the broad valley between the Tararua Mountains and the ranges bounding it on the east. There are numerous rivers in the district, but for the most part their courses are short. The most important is the Wanganui, which rises near Mount Tongariro, flows north into the Auckland district, from which it receives several tributaries, then turns southward, forming the boundary for some distance between Taranaki and Wellington, and finally makes an abrupt bend to the south-east, and empties itself into the Taranaki Bight. The Manawatu, which enters the sea some distance farther south, rises in the Ruahine Range in Hawke Bay district, bursts through the gorge between those mountains and the Tararua, and, swollen by numerous affluents, flows south-westerly to its mouth. Another important stream is the Ruamahanga, which drains the country between the Tararua and the ranges situated to the eastward. It flows southward, and passing through the Wairarapa and Onoke Lakes, the former a considerable sheet of water, falls into Palliser Bay. In the river valleys and in the parts where the country is of a volcanic nature, the soil is excellent and highly productive.

Large portions of the district towards the north are still possessed by the Maoris, and are consequently but little known. As the whole district is occupied by volcanic rocks, it is not expected that mineral wealth will be found in it, but the forests abound in timber of various kinds and of the finest quality. Agriculture and pasturage constitute the chief industries, as export of their products forms the principal portion of commercial effort. Good roads have been formed, and railway extension has been rapidly carried on, the numerous settlements being brought into communication with each other and with the capital. The population is 77,000.

16. **Wellington.**—This city has some claim to priority of foundation, having received its first detachment of settlers in January, 1840, a few days before the proclamation of British sovereignty over the island, and the selection of a site for the present city of Auckland. Situated on the shore of Port Nicholson, an extensive land-locked harbour, easy of access, and with depth of water sufficient for the largest vessels, the city possesses all the requisites for carrying on a vast trade, while the rich territory of which it is the outlet supplies the raw material of commerce in abundance. Since 1865 Wellington has been the legislative and administrative capital of the whole colony. The wharves and other conveniences for shipping are worthy of note, but the public buildings, though extensive, are not remarkable for beauty of design, as the liability to earthquakes, the one drawback of the place, has prevented the erection of stately edifices. The government buildings are a huge wooden structure, said to be the largest timber edifice in the world. As the centre of the railway system of the district, and of the steam maritime service of the whole colony, Wellington enjoys great facilities for intercommunication. The population is about 28,000.

Wanganui, at the mouth of the river bearing the same name, is an important town, as the outlet of a large district possessing great resources. Although, from the shallowness of the river, the navigation is impracticable for large vessels, the town has railway communication with the interior, extending as far even as Napier, and it is contemplated to continue the line to Wellington. The population is said to be about 5000.

Foxton, at the mouth of the Manawatu River, though not pleasantly situated, being surrounded by sands, is a place of some importance as the outlet of a prosperous district. A line of railway commences at this place and is continued to Napier, and steam communication by sea is frequent and regular. The population is about 800.

Palmerston, on the railway line from Foxton to Napier, is a thriving town with about 1000 inhabitants.

Otaki, near the river of the same name, is remarkable as being in the main a settlement of Maoris, of whom about 500 inhabit the place, together with about 150 Europeans.

Greytown, on the Wellington and Masterton railway line, is said to contain 1500 inhabitants.

Masterton, on the same line, has a population of 2000, and is situated in the celebrated Wairarapa Plain.

17. **Nelson (District).**—With the exception of the north-east corner, the Nelson district occupies the northern portion of the south island, and is bounded on the south by the Hurunui River from its mouth to its source; thence by a line to the north side of Lake Brunner, and thence by the rivers Arnould and Grey to the west coast. It is separated from the Marlborough district, once included in it, by a series of lines which do not coincide with any conspicuous natural features. The area of the district is 10,500 square miles. The coast line is but little indented, except on the northern side, where Golden and Tasman Bays, both inlets of considerable size, penetrate to a great distance into the land. As regards surface this district is in general rugged and mountainous, with some valleys lying between the different ranges. For the most part the mountains are branches from Mount Franklin in the main dividing chain, and bear a great variety of names; but there are parallel ranges on the west, the Victoria, Brunner, and Lyell Mountains forming one such range, and the Paparoa a second. Mount Franklin attains an altitude of 10,000 feet, and there are numerous peaks which exceed 7000 feet, and of some of the most prominent the height has not been ascertained. On the west the principal streams are the Grey and the Buller; on the north, the Tekaka and the Motueka and Waimea; and on the east, the Dillon and the Hurunui. Several small

but beautiful lakes are to be found among the mountains. Along the coasts and in the river valleys the soil is fertile; the lower slopes of the mountains afford excellent pasture for cattle, but the higher ridges are of little value for such purposes. Minerals constitute the chief wealth of the district. Gold is found on the west coast and in most of the country bordering on Cook's Strait. Silver, copper, iron, lead, and platinum also exist, and coal is abundant on the west coast and at Golden Bay. Mining is one of the principal industrial pursuits of the colony, large numbers of persons being engaged in gold-digging, coal-mining, and iron and copper smelting. Agriculture also engages considerable attention, and pasturage still more. Little has yet been effected in regard to railway extension, the nature of the country being unfavourable to the construction of such lines, but communication by sea is frequent and regular with all the principal ports of the colony. The population is nearly 30,000.

18. **Nelson**, the provincial capital, is situated near the head of Tasman Bay. It enjoys a delightful climate, and is, from its picturesque and sheltered position, a charming place of abode. It has some manufactures, though offering less scope for business enterprise than the larger towns of New Zealand. The population is about 7000.

Collingwood, at the mouth of the Aorere, on Golden Bay, is a village forming one of the principal seats of the mining industry, gold and coal being found in the vicinity.

Westport, at the mouth of the Buller, which falls into the Karamea Bight on the west coast, has a safe and commodious harbour. It is a place of some trade, the principal export being coal obtained from the Mount Rochfort mines, which are situated at some distance inland. A railway connects the mines and the port. The population is estimated at 2000.

Charleston, situated on the coast to the south of Cape Foulwind, is a mining locality, being surrounded by an extensive gold-field.

19. **Marlborough.**—This district, occupying the north-east corner of the island, was originally a portion of Nelson, from which it is not separated by any natural boundaries. Its area is computed at 4680 square miles. Throughout the surface

of the district is mountainous, and in the more elevated parts rugged. A series of parallel ranges, outliers from the dividing chain, traverse the district from north-east to south-west, having between them valleys of greater or less extent. The more conspicuous of these ranges are the Kaikoura, a double chain culminating in Mount Odin, 9700 feet in height, and having other peaks which exceed 8000 feet in elevation. Among the valleys may be mentioned those of the Wairau, the Awatere, and the Clarence. The rivers, the most important of which are those just named, follow the direction of the mountains. The Clarence, however, after flowing north-easterly for some distance between the two Kaikoura Ranges, turns suddenly to the south-east through a gap in the Seaward Range, sometimes distinguished as Lookers-on Mountains. At the most northerly part of the district the coast is much broken, presenting a series of sounds similar to and little, if at all, inferior, as regards grandeur of scenery, to those at the opposite extremity of the island. The remainder of the coast is less regular than the coast farther south, the largest indentation being Cloudy Bay. In the valleys, which in some places expand into wide plains and upland downs, the soil is generally fertile, but on the mountains is not fitted for agricultural purposes. Gold is produced in the northern part of the district, but generally speaking the mineral resources of the district are little known. Timber of excellent quality is abundant. Mining, timber-getting, agriculture and pasturage, are the chief industrial pursuits. Owing to the nature of the country little has yet been effected as regards railway communication, but the various ports are connected by the regular and frequent visits of steam-ships. The population is about 11,000.

20. **Blenheim**, the provincial capital, is situated in the north-east upon a branch of the Wairau, falling into Cloudy Bay. A railway connects the town with Picton, which may be considered the shipping port. The population is somewhat more than 3000.

Picton, the principal port of the district, is situated at the head of Queen Charlotte Sound. Its harbour is safe, commodious, and easy of access, and steamers run regularly to and from Nelson and Wellington. Coal has been found in the neighbourhood, and copper also is said to exist. The population is over 700.

Havelock, on the Pelorus River and at the head of the sound bearing the same name, is noteworthy for its trade in timber, of which large quantities are exported. Gold is also found in the vicinity.

21. **Canterbury.**—This large district is bounded on the north by Nelson, from which it is separated by the Hurunui River; on the west by the district of Westland, the boundary being the watershed of the great dividing chain (Southern Alps); on the east by the ocean; and on the south by Otago, the limit in this direction being the Waitaki and Ohau Rivers, and a straight line drawn from the outlet of Lake Ohau to Mount Aspiring in the main range. Its area exceeds 13,000 square miles. With some smaller inlets the coast is marked with two considerable indentations, Pegasus Bay and Canterbury Bight. With the exception of the remarkable projection named Banks' Peninsula, which is high and rocky, being formed of extinct volcanoes, the shore is low and sandy. In Pegasus Bay, for example, a sandy and shingly beach extends for forty miles; while on the shore of the Canterbury Bight the Ninety-mile Beach, also low and shingly, extends from Banks' Peninsula to the town of Timaru. From the seashore for about thirty miles inland the country is level, forming the far-famed Canterbury Plains, westward of which lies the undulating tract composed of the spurs from the great dividing chain. This chain occupies the western portion of the district, and is composed of lofty and rugged mountains rising above the level of perpetual snow and interspersed with immense glaciers, which give it a truly alpine character. The slope of the land being toward the east, the rivers run in that direction, and consequently do not attain any great length. Their volume also is inconsiderable, except when rain or melting snow on the mountains converts them into deep and rapid torrents. Of the numerous rivers which water the district the largest is the Waitaki, in the south, which drains several lakes. Other noteworthy streams are the Rangitata, Ashburton, and Rakaia, which fall into the Canterbury Bight, and the Waimakariri, which disembogues into Pegasus Bay. Numerous lakes

are found in this district. They occupy deep depressions in or near the mountains, and it is believed that their beds were hollowed out by glacier action in past ages. Their position among the mountains surrounds them with scenery sometimes highly picturesque, and at others sublimely grand. Among them Lakes Tekapo, Pukaki, and Ohau may be specially mentioned. In point of climate Canterbury is somewhat drier than the other districts, though the general character of the New Zealand climate is retained. On the plains the soil is well fitted for agricultural purposes; on the uplands, less fertile but adapted for pasturage. The mineral resources of this district are as yet not well known, and it appears to be less favoured in this respect than any other. Timber is also less abundant. The great wealth of Canterbury lies in its farms and sheep-walks, which produce grain and wool in abundance and of high quality. Accordingly grain and wool form its chief products and principal articles of export. Good roads have been formed throughout the more level portions of the district, and even in the hilly tracts lying at the foot of the main range. The latter, however, presents a barrier that is crossable in but few places, where practicable roads have, at great expense and difficulty, been formed. Among the passes across these mountains that through Arthur's Pass and the Otira Gorge is the most worthy of notice, the coach road from Christchurch, on the east coast, to Hokitika, on the west, having been carried through it in spite of great obstacles. There are other passes, but they are less frequented. Railway communication has been considerably developed, a line having been constructed to connect Christchurch with the southernmost town in the island, and some progress has been made in its continuation northward. The population numbers some 121,000.

22. **Christchurch.**—Though not remarkable for the beauty of its situation, this provincial capital is a prosperous town and is yearly expanding. It stands on the banks of a small stream called the Avon River, in a plain of large extent, is well laid out, and possesses many fine public buildings, including the government buildings and the museum. It is represented as being "eminently English in its appearance, architecture, and surroundings." It is the business centre for an extensive

agricultural district; and while thriving in this particular, its educational and other public institutions are of a most creditable character. The population of the city and suburbs is about 30,000.

Lyttelton.—Pleasantly situated on the north side of Banks' Peninsula, and possessing a safe and commodious harbour, Lyttelton is not only the port of Christchurch but also the outlet for the produce of the district. It is connected with the capital by a railway, which, though but eight miles in length, was both costly and difficult in construction owing to the necessity of boring a tunnel through a mile and a half of volcanic rock. Its trade, both intercolonial and with the mother country, is very large. The population is estimated at 4500.

Kaiapoi.—This town on Pegasus Bay, at the mouth of the Waimakariri River, is the centre of a fine agricultural district and a place of some trade. Its population is about 1000.

Timaru, at the head of the Canterbury Bight, is an important town, and, as the outlet of a large and fertile district, has the prospect of a flourishing future. The harbour, which is not naturally good, has been improved at great cost. The buildings, constructed of stone obtained in the neighbourhood, are substantial. Education is well cared for. The population is about 3700.

Akaroa.—This town, situated on Banks' Peninsula, possesses one of the finest harbours in the country; its trade, however, is but inconsiderable. The beauty of its position, genial climate, and fertility of the neighbourhood render it a desirable place of residence. The population of the town is estimated at 700.

23. **Westland.**—This small district is bounded on the north by Nelson, and on the east by Canterbury. The boundary lines in these cases have already been described. On the south lies the Otago district, from which Westland is separated by a line drawn from Mount Aspiring to the mouth of the river Awarua on the west coast. The area of the district is estimated at 4500 square miles. The coast-line, which is not marked by any considerable projections or indentations, is generally rugged and precipitous, as the spurs from the main dividing range run down to the shore and terminate abruptly in lofty perpendicular cliffs. In consequence of the near ap-

proach of the mountains to the sea the coast plain is very narrow, and the surface of the remainder of the district is elevated and rugged. Numerous streams water the district, but their courses are short. There are a few small lakes in the province. Except on the lower hills and in the river valleys, where tracts of great fertility exist, the soil is of the character usually observed in mountainous countries. The climate is moist, and gales from the Southern Ocean are of frequent occurrence. Minerals are the most important natural productions of the district, which may, in fact, be described as an extensive gold-field, the precious metal being found even in the sands on the sea-shore. Other metals, as silver, copper, iron, tin, and lead, have been discovered, and coal abounds in the northern end of the district. Timber of first-rate quality is also abundant in the forests, and the climate is most favourable to the growth of the New Zealand flax. Mining, principally for gold and coal, is the most important industrial pursuit, though timber-getting, farming, and grazing also employ many of the inhabitants. The chief exports are gold, coal, and timber. The population is about 16,000.

24. **Hokitika,** the provincial capital and most populous town in the district, is situated at the mouth of the river bearing the same name. Owing to the nature of the coast and the tendency of the river to change its mouth the entrance is difficult of access, a fact which operates greatly to the disadvantage of the district and its trade. A road over the mountains connects it with the railway to Christchurch. It stands in the midst of a productive gold-field, and has a population of 3000.

Greymouth, farther to the north at the mouth of the Grey River, exports coal which is very valuable for the manufacture of gas. Its population is 3000.

25. **Otago.**—This magnificent district occupies the remainder of the island, with the exception of a portion taken from it in 1860 and constituted a province named Southland. Its area is variously estimated at from 20,000 to 23,000 square miles. A striking difference exists in the character of the coast-line on the east and on the west, the latter being deeply indented by numerous inlets, and the former being, in comparison, regular and unbroken. The surface of the district is

mainly hilly or mountainous. Some of the peaks, as Mount Aspiring and Mount Earnslaw, exceed 9000 feet in elevation, and a large number attain the height of 6000 feet. Towards the east coast, however, there are considerable tracts of level country. From the mountains a large number of streams descend to the coast in various directions, draining in their courses the lakes which occupy some of the deeply sunk valleys, or fed by the melting snows from the higher summits.

A Lake View.

The principal of these are the Taieri, the Clutha—which, with its numerous tributaries, drains Lakes Hawea, Wanaka, and Wakatipu—the Toetoe, and the Waiau, which carries off the surplus waters of Lake Manapouri. These lakes are remarkable in some cases for their romantic beauty, and in others for the stern magnificence of their scenery. On the higher ranges the soil is barren and on the lower hills fit only for pasturage, but on the lower lands, especially to the eastward, are tracts of unsurpassed fertility. The climate, owing to the more southern latitude of the district, its exposure to winds from the Antarctic Ocean, and the height of its mountain chains, is much colder than that of more northern parts of the island; and frosts, occasionally severe, are of frequent occurrence in winter. Among minerals gold and coal are found over large areas, and slate and building stone of high quality are also known and worked. Timber is also abundant, especially towards the west. Gold-mining, agriculture, and sheep-farming are the chief occupations of the people; and in these pursuits the inhabitants have shown great energy and enterprise. The trade of the district is already very large and is increasing. A line of railway connects the city of Dunedin with Christchurch in Canterbury and with Invercargill in Southland, besides numerous branches to places of interest or importance. The ordinary roads are good, and communication between the different ports by sea is frequent and regular. The population approaches 150,000.

26. **Dunedin.**—This city, which was so named by the original Scotch settlers from the ancient name of Edinburgh, is the provincial capital of Otago, and is also the second largest and most populous place in New Zealand, the number of its inhabitants, including the suburbs, being about 45,000. The position of the city, on an inlet of the sea, running inwards some 15 miles, is charming, and its public buildings are the finest in the colony, the streets also being paved and lighted with gas. The trade is very extensive. Vessels of moderate size can come up to the city; the large ones unload at Port Chalmers, about 9 miles distant. Besides the railway to the harbour of Port Chalmers there are others connecting the city with the chief towns in Canterbury and Southland, and telegraphic communication is extensive.

Port Chalmers, on the inlet called Otago Harbour, is the port of Dunedin and a place of great trade. It possesses piers, wharves, and jetties for the accommodation of shipping, of which a vast quantity, with an aggregate burden of half a million tons, enters and leaves the port annually.

Oamaru, farther to the north, is splendidly built of a fine white limestone abounding in the neighbourhood, and of such good quality as to form an article of export to neighbouring towns, and even to the Australian colonies. This town, being the centre of a large grain-producing district, carries on an extensive trade in agricultural produce. The harbour works are regarded as fine specimens of engineering skill. The population is 6000.

Waikouaiti is a coast town situated in a fine agricultural district about thirty miles northward of Dunedin. Having a splendid beach it is much resorted to for the purpose of sea-bathing.

Milton, also called Tokomairiro, is situated on the river of this name. Coal and grain are produced in the neighbourhood. The population is estimated at about 1500.

Balclutha, on the Clutha or Molyneux River, is the centre of a fine agricultural district, which also produces "brown" coal. Its population is about 1000.

Queenstown, on the shore of Lake Wakatipu, has gold-workings and good agricultural land in the vicinity. It attracts a good many visitors from its proximity to the magnificent scenery surrounding the lake, which is navigated by steamers and is reached by railway. It has about 800 inhabitants.

Cromwell, at the junction of the Clutha and Kawarau, two of the largest rivers in New Zealand, is the centre of the most important mining region of the district. Besides gold coal is found and mined in the neighbourhood. The town has about 500 inhabitants.

Lawrence, in the first gold region of Otago, has a population estimated at 1000. Here, as in so many other localities in New Zealand, coal and gold are found at no great distance from each other.

27. **Southland.**—The remaining portion of the South Island, together with Stewart's Island, constitutes the district of Southland. Its area is computed at 4300 square miles. Being hemmed in by Otago its coast-line is limited to about eighty miles, but is marked by several large indentations, though the shore itself is generally low. The northern portion of the district consists of elevated land; the southern portion is undulating or level. The river courses have a southerly direction, and the principal stream flowing through the district is the Oreti or New River, which empties itself into the inlet known as Invercargill Harbour. A large proportion of this

small province consists of rich soil, which produces grain and grass in great abundance. The climate, though colder than in the districts farther north, is bracing and healthy. Gold is found in the western portion of the district, and good timber abounds in all parts, but the most important products are wool and grain. A good deal has been accomplished in the way of

In Milford Sound.

railway extension, and excellent roads are common. Mining, farming, and pasturage are the chief industries. The population is nearly 9000.

28. **Invercargill**, built on the shore of the inlet called Invercargill Harbour, is the provincial capital, and has about 5000 inhabitants. The town is well laid out, and already possesses many handsome buildings. Its trade, which is yearly increasing, is very great in proportion to its size. It is connected by railway with Dunedin and with Lake Wakatipu.

Campbelltown, commonly called "The Bluff," from a hill 800 feet high on the promontory which incloses the harbour, is a seaport town, connected with Invercargill by rail. Although the harbour is accessible and commodious the progress of the town has of late years been but slow.

Riverton, at the mouth of the Apurima or Jacob's River, is the centre of the gold-mining region of the district, and also of a large grain-producing tract. Its population is about 1000.

CHAPTER XII.

THE COLONY OF FIJI.

1. Position. 2. Extent and Coast-line. 3. Surface and Drainage. 4. Climate. 5. Natural Productions. 6. Population. 7. Internal Communication. 8. Industrial Occupations. 9. Government. 10. Towns.

1. The archipelago which bears the name of the Fiji Islands consists of about 250 islands and islets lying between 16° and 20° south latitude, and 177° and 182° east longitude, distant about 1200 miles almost due north from New Zealand, and 1600 from the nearest point of Australia. Tasman, the Dutch navigator, who explored so much of the Pacific, discovered this group in 1646; but the islands, beautiful and valuable as they are, remained unnoticed until visited by Cook, more than a hundred years after. Including the island of Rotumah, which forms part of the colony, Fijian territory extends as far north as 12° 48′ s.

2. The area of the group is estimated at about 8000 square miles, of which 7750 belong to inhabited islands. The two principal islands are **Viti Levu** (Great Fiji) and **Vanua Levu** (Great Land), the former 90 miles and the latter 95 miles in length, the breadth of each being, in the widest parts, 60 and 30 miles respectively. Coral-reefs fringe more or less all the islands, and add greatly to the intricacy of the navigation. The coast-line in Vanua Levu is irregular on the east and south, where Nateva and Savu Savu bays are considerable indentations, and numerous small islands lie but a few miles from the shore. Viti Levu is more regular in shape, though its coast also is broken on the eastern side.

3. Nearly all the islands rise steeply from the sea, and evidences of volcanic action are everywhere visible, though no active volcanoes are known to exist. In the larger islands there are mountains that rise to the height of 3000 feet, and some summits even reach more than 1000 feet higher. The **surface** is agreeably diversified with hill and dale, but does not present any remarkable physical features. On the whole it is hilly rather than mountainous, and interspersed with valleys

of no great breadth, in which occur the largest areas of level ground. The drainage is very simple, for as the islands are narrow and the mountain ranges occupy the central portions, the rivers are necessarily short, the longest, which is the Wailevu in Vanua Levu, having a course of about 90 miles, of which 60 are navigable. Others are the Rewa in Viti Levu

A Coast View.

and the Ndreketi in Vanua Levu. Few lakes exist, the most important being one which occupies the crater of an extinct volcano in the island of Taviuni.

4. Although the whole group is situated within the tropics, the **climate** is healthy and agreeable to persons of ordinarily careful habits, and is much less hot than might have been expected in such a latitude. The mean annual temperature is about 80°; in the summer or hot season it has been known to rise above 120°; and in winter it falls to 60°. In reality there are but two seasons: the wet, which lasts from October to May, and the dry, which fills up the remainder of the year. Rain is

everywhere abundant, falling principally, of course, in the wet season. It is most copious on the eastern side, but the average rainfall may be estimated at 100 inches annually, and the number of wet days in the year is probably not less than 140. The prevailing winds are easterly, and, together with the sea-breezes which constantly blow, they serve to moderate the temperature, which might otherwise be much higher. One of the disadvantages arising out of the intertropical position of the group, is its liability to hurricanes, which at intervals devastate the islands, though they do not happen with any great frequency.

5. In **natural productions**, though lacking, in common with the whole of Australasia, some important classes, Fiji is exceedingly rich. Little has yet been done towards ascertaining its mineral resources, but copper, iron, antimony, and plumbago are known to exist. From its rocks of volcanic composition, rich soils are derived which support the most exuberant vegetation. Timber of many kinds abounds in the forests, being furnished by pines, she-oaks, wattles, and other trees, and is useful for house and ship building and for the manufacture of furniture and smaller articles. On the eastern side the vegetation is of the character generally understood by the term "tropical," consisting of gigantic trees bound together with huge interlacing creepers, with a dense shrubby undergrowth beneath. In the more open parts, on the west or leeward side, there are grassy tracts without trees, excepting the screw-pine sparsely scattered over the surface. These districts also produce acacias resembling those of Australia; and of the Australian vegetation, indeed, one is often reminded by the presence of various trees and plants akin to those of the continent. Ferns, including tree-ferns 50 feet high, and orchids also abound. Among the indigenous food-producing plants may be mentioned the banana, bread-fruit, cocoa-nut, sweet-potato, and yam. On the coast, fish of many kinds and excellent quality abound; the pearl-oyster is also found; and trepang or bêche-de-mer is plentiful on the north side of the principal islands. Fish are also found in the rivers, but in smaller quantities. Among reptiles the lizard family is represented by numerous species; there are ten kinds of snakes, all harmless; and several kinds of tree-frogs. Turtle are obtained from

the sea, and the tortoise is found upon the land. Birds are numerous, but they present no special characteristics. None of the larger mammals, either carnivorous or herbivorous, were found in the islands when first discovered by Europeans. It is questionable, indeed, whether there were any truly indigenous quadrupeds; but rats, dogs, pigs, and fowls must have been introduced at a very early period, if they were not natives of the islands. Since settlement began in Fiji the colonists have introduced all the plants in common cultivation, and most of the ordinary domestic animals.

6. Such a country as that before described should be capable of supporting a large **population**. From various causes the progress of settlement by European colonists has been slow, and their number at the present time does not exceed 3500. Immigrants from other parts of Australasia and from India number about 9600, and of native Fijians there are about 115,000. Various estimates have been given by different authorities as to the character of the aboriginal inhabitants of Fiji, and their relations to other races. That view is probably correct which regards them as an offshoot of the Papuan race, modified by intermixture with Tongans and Samoans. In colour they are dark, of a shade variously represented as "olive" and "copper;" tall and robust, with regular and expressive features, and having frizzled hair and beards. They are probably the finest specimens physically of the dark races of the Pacific, and are believed to be equal, if not superior, in intelligence to the most advanced of the Polynesians. Although modest and attentive to personal cleanliness, they were not accustomed in their original state to wear much clothing. They have been charged with cruelty, and the accusation is apparently borne out by the bloody character of many of their heathen customs and by their former cannibalism. Probably, however, these features in their character, which they shared with the Maoris and other Polynesian tribes, should be attributed to their superstitions, rather than to the cruelty of their dispositions. Their religion, though stained with many degrading observances, and defiled with reckless blood-shedding, was of a higher type than that of some of their neighbours, inasmuch as it required priests and temples for the worship of

their gods, and involved belief in a future existence. The Fijians are accustomed to erect good-sized houses and to construct excellent canoes, of which they are expert and fearless navigators. Their weapons, spears, clubs, bows, and arrows are well made, and they practise the arts of pottery and making cloth from the bark of the paper mulberry. By the colonists they have been taxed with laziness, and they are certainly

Natives of Tonga and Fiji.

averse to severe or continuous labour; but it may be urged in excuse that, living in a country where all his wants are supplied by nature at the cost of very little exertion on his own part, the Fijian has little need to labour, and, in common with the Maori and even the white man in the like circumstances, fails to see the utility of engaging himself in hard work.

7. Good **roads** are among the needs and evidences of civilized life; and as so much of the territory is still held by the par-

tially civilized Fijians, it should excite no surprise that roads are practically non-existent. The white settlements are principally on the smaller islands and on the coasts of the larger islands, and communication is maintained between them by means of small steamers and sailing craft. Steamers of large size also ply regularly between Fiji and the Australian colonies and New Zealand.

8. Fijian productive **industries** may be easily described, for with so small a number of European colonists it could not be expected that such industries would be extensively followed. Some tillage is carried on by the native men, who grow, mainly for their own use, bananas, yams, arrow-root, sweet-potatoes, and cocoa-nuts. In the plantations of the white settlers, attempts have been made on a large scale to cultivate sugar-cane, cotton, coffee, and cocoa-nuts; and to a less extent, maize, tobacco, and turmeric. Fruits of various kinds are largely raised, including pine-apples, oranges, lemons, limes, bread-fruit, and tomatoes, and experiments have been made with a view to the introduction of the culture of cinnamon, cinchona, and other tropical products. The great obstacle to success in all these undertakings is the scarcity and costliness of labour; and attempts have been made to get over the difficulty by bringing labourers from other Australasian islands and coolies from India. Mining, under the present form of government, is practically prohibited, as all minerals that may be discovered are claimed by the crown. Pasturage is carried on to a sufficient extent to satisfy the local demand for cattle, but sheep have yet to be imported. Manufactures have been commenced in connection with sugar-making, and the utilization of the waste products from that process. The natives build houses and canoes, and the women manufacture small articles. A considerable amount of **commerce** is carried on for so small a population of whites. Ships now trade regularly with the mother country, and communication is maintained with New South Wales, Victoria, and New Zealand by steamships. On the average of the last few years, it may be calculated that the exports amount in value to between £300,000 and £400,000 per annum, and include chiefly copra (dried cocoa-nut kernels), cotton, sugar, fruit, maize, and molasses. The imports amount

to about the same, the principal articles being drapery, hardware, timber, wine, spirits, and beer; breadstuffs, meats, live stock, boots and shoes, tea, tobacco, stationery, machinery, and other manufactured goods.

9. When Fiji came under British rule it was made a "crown" colony. It has no constitution, but is governed by the Queen's representative, who is responsible to the ministry that may happen to be in power at the time in the mother country. There is a Legislative Council, by which new laws are proposed; it consists of thirteen members, who are either officials or nominated by the governor, and not representatives of the people. A number of native chiefs have been appointed by the British authorities to carry on the government of their respective districts, much in the same way as was done before they came under British rule. The revenue raised for the service of the colony varies from about £80,000 to £100,000, obtained principally from customs and licenses of various kinds; and the expenditure is usually about the same. Religious equality is maintained throughout Fiji. With the exception of the pagan immigrants from other islands and India, all the people are Christians, the Fiji natives having, mainly through the instrumentality of Wesleyan missionaries, renounced heathenism many years ago. Some steps have been taken for the establishment of schools, but not as part of a general scheme under government control.

10. The present seat of government is at **Suva**, situated on the south coast of Viti Levu. It has been established but a few years, but bids fair to become a place of much importance in the future. The island itself is the largest of the group, and has splendid resources awaiting development. At the eastern end is the native town of **Mbau**, which may be considered as the native Fijian capital. On the island of Ovalau is the town and port of **Levuka**, until lately the capital, and still a place of much commercial importance. No other towns have been formed by European settlers, but native villages are to be found in all the islands. In Vanua Levu, the second island in size, is **Methuala**, on the north coast, in the midst of a large native population. **Mbua**, at the western extremity of this island, is also a place of some consequence. On the island

of Taviuni, south-east of Vanua Levu, the town of **Somo Somo** is worthy of notice as the chief place in a very fertile district.

The largest of the southern islands is Kandavu, which furnishes abundance of timber of the Fijian pine. Of the 200 other islands it is necessary only to mention that they are small, and, for the most part, have each but one native village.

CHAPTER XIII.

NEW CALEDONIA AND ITS DEPENDENCIES.

1. Position and Extent. 2. Surface. 3. Productions. 4. Climate. 5. Population. 6. Internal Communication. 7. Industrial Occupations. 8. Government. 9. Noumea. 10. The Loyalty Islands. 11. The New Hebrides.

1. At a distance of about 700 miles in an easterly direction from the Australian coast, and between the meridians of 164° and 167° east longitude, lies an island of considerable size and importance, called **New Caledonia.** Stretching from north-west to south-east, between the parallels of 20° and 23° south, it has a length of about 250 miles; its mean breadth is nearly 40 miles, and its area is estimated at 6000 square miles, or about one-fourth that of Tasmania. A few miles from the shore rises a belt of coral-reefs and sand-banks which encircle nearly the whole island, and which, while heightening the beauty of the scenery, render navigation somewhat dangerous. No considerable indentations break the coast-line, though there are a few secure harbours. Connected with New Caledonia, and lying to the eastward of it, are the Loyalty Islands, of which Uvea, Lifu, and Maré are the most important.

2. Throughout its whole length, and nearer the east than the west coast, a range of mountains traverses the island, rising in some points, it is said, to near the height of 6000 feet. The average elevation may be about 4000 feet—the culminating point is not known. There are no active volcanoes, though there are evidences of the volcanic origin of the island. Towards the north the chain separates into two branches, forming a broad valley between them, and the central portion of the island is occupied by an extensive table-land. Minor ranges branch off from the main chain towards each coast, and give an undulating character to the districts through which they run. With a surface thus diversified, mountain, valley, table-land, and coast-plain being intermingled, the scenery of the island is generally picturesque and pleasing. The streams are from the conformation of the island extremely short, but they are very numerous.

3. Gold is found in the rocks of New Caledonia, and more abundantly nickel, a white metal, hard, malleable, and ductile as iron, susceptible of a high polish, and not easily rusted. Copper also is found and worked, and other metals are believed to exist in various parts of the island, which, however, has not yet been examined with sufficient minuteness to disclose fully its mineral wealth. The valleys are densely wooded and produce many valuable trees, such as the cocoa-nut, bread fruit, mango, and banana, which supply food, and others, which furnish excellent timber. Except towards the north the mountain tops are either bare or covered with scrub and pines. Many of the lower grounds are well grassed. The animal kingdom is but poorly represented. None of the larger mammals are indigenous, and it is doubtful whether even the marsupials inhabit the island. The birds are similar to those of Australia and Polynesia with some peculiar species. Of the reptiles to be found in the islands little is known with certainty.

4. Considering its intertropical position, the **climate** of New Caledonia is cool and dry; yet rain is sufficiently plentiful, and the temperature is high enough to admit of the cultivation of many tropical plants. Occasionally great storms occur, similar in their character and effects to the hurricanes which at irregular periods devastate some of the islands nearer the equator. On the whole the climate is said to be healthy, though fevers are prevalent on the low grounds.

5. To a large extent the island remains in possession of the aboriginal **natives,** who appear to belong to the Papuan race, but with some of the characteristics of that race considerably modified. They are athletic in form, with dark skins, frizzly hair, and marked features. While they use no clothing and are, in some tribes at least, cannibals, they are not wholly destitute of civilized notions, for they build strong, cone-shaped houses, and diligently cultivate the yam, banana, and sugar-cane. They even have recourse to irrigation. The different tribes are almost continually at war among themselves. From this and other causes their numbers are rapidly diminishing. In 1853 the French took possession of New Caledonia, not without strenuous opposition and brave resistance on the part of the natives, who, even now, are disinclined to submit tamely

to the authority of the whites, but still endeavour, in some parts, to maintain their original independence. By the French the country has been used as a place for the deportation of criminals, although some free colonists have been introduced.

Native Hut.

The population of European descent is therefore chiefly of French origin, but there are also some British residents at the ports.

6. The labour of the convicts has been turned to account in the formation of **roads** through the districts occupied by the French either as prison settlements or as farms, and small steamers ply between the capital and the outlying ports. But while so much of the territory remains in the hands of the aboriginal inhabitants the absence of roads is not a matter of great importance.

7. Public works of various kinds employ the majority of the prisoners, and their labour contributes nothing directly to the products of the country. Others are occupied in **agriculture** and pasturage on their own account, or as servants to the free

settlers. Attention is now paid to the rearing of horses, cattle, and sheep, though it cannot be said that remarkable progress has been made in this pursuit. Sugar, coffee, tobacco, and cotton can be grown; but the cultivation of these plants has not yet attained the dimensions of a recognized industry, though sugar culture appears to be flourishing enough to supply the materials to several mills. Some traffic in cattle is carried on with Queensland, and a considerable trade has sprung up between Noumea and Sydney. This trade has been greatly facilitated by the establishment of a line of steamers which runs in connection with the French line from Marseilles.

8. To a large extent the **government** is of a military character. As the majority of the white population are either soldiers or prisoners, no other kind of government seems possible.

9. **Noumea,** or Port de France, the principal settlement, is situated near the south-east extremity of the island. It is the seat of government, and the commercial emporium for all the French possessions in this part of the Pacific. Besides a considerable number of Kanakas, as the aboriginal natives are called, the town has a population of about 5000 whites. Other settlements have been formed in the interior, but they are not of sufficient importance to call for remark. About 30 miles to the south of New Caledonia lies the **Isle of Pines,** which is used as a penal settlement for a class of prisoners whose sentences are of a lighter character.

10. Parallel to New Caledonia, and about 70 miles to the eastward, is the **Loyalty** group. These are of coral origin, and consequently not fertile. Sandalwood is their chief commercial product. In one of the islands, Mare, the English missionaries have been highly successful in civilizing and Christianizing the natives, and to a less degree their labours have produced good results in other members of the group. Since their occupation of the islands, however, the French have done much to thwart the efforts of the missionaries. The native inhabitants are said to resemble the people of the New Hebrides.

11. Contrary to the formal agreement entered into by the respective governments of England and France, the latter has taken military possession of the **New Hebrides,** and seems determined to retain its hold upon the territory thus unjustly

acquired. These islands lie to the north-east of New Caledonia, from which the nearest is distant about 200 miles. Including the Santa Cruz group, they stretch over a space of 700 miles, extending from lat. 21° to 13° south. The whole chain is usually divided into three groups, the Southern New Hebrides, the Northern New Hebrides, which include the Banks' Islands, and the Santa Cruz Islands. With a few exceptions all these are mountainous and volcanic, and several active volcanoes are known to exist, besides the extinct craters to be found throughout the group. Many of the summits are known to be 2500 feet in elevation, and one rises to the height of 5000 feet. In general the soil is fertile, and the vegetation is dense and tropical in its character, with abundance of palms and ferns, besides timber-trees and flowers. Animal life seems to be scarce, the only indigenous mammals known being rats, and even birds are less numerous than in the nearest groups to the north or south. Much difference exists between the natives of the different islands, and there has evidently been a great mixture of races, though nearly all have the frizzled woolly hair of the Papuans. In character they are savage and treacherous, and in many of the islands are still addicted to cannibalism. Wars among themselves are frequent, and this with other causes, but particularly their contact with the whites, is rapidly reducing their numbers, which, upon no very certain data, are estimated at 130,000. Their languages are numerous and diverse, a point in which they resemble the Australian blacks.

The principal islands, commencing from the south, are the following:—**Aneiteum**, a fertile island, with a population of about 2000, who grow cotton, arrow-root, and other crops, and from being savage cannibals, have become Christian and kind-hearted. Sandal-wood is one of the products of the island. **Tanna**, which is of larger size, and has a greater population. The people are still wholly barbarous and cannibal, though they understand the cultivation of taro, yam, arrow-root, sweet-potato, and sugar-cane. There are many natural products which have a commercial value, but owing to the savage character of the people trade is carried on with difficulty. **Erromango** is a fertile island, but has a small population, the people having suffered much from the aggressions of the whites.

Mallicollo is inhabited by a race noted for their ugliness both of form and feature. **Vaté**, or Sandwich, has several excellent harbours, Havannah being the best known. **Espiritu Santo** is the largest of the whole group, though little known on account of the hostility of the natives, who are fierce and untamable savages. **Vanua Lavu**, a small island, is remarkable for its boiling springs. **Vanikoro** is a small mountainous island, surrounded with coral-reefs. The people have a bad reputation for ferocity. **Nitendi**, or Santa Cruz, is inhabited by a powerful but savage and treacherous race, with some marks of civilization, such as the ability to build good houses and to construct large canoes.

CHAPTER XIV.

PAPUA OR NEW GUINEA.

1. Name. 2. Position and Extent. 3. Coast-line. 4. Surface. 5. Drainage. 6. Climate. 7. Natural Productions. 8. Population. 9. Industrial Occupations. 10. Territorial Divisions.

1. This vast island, the largest in the world with the exception of Australia, has been known to Europeans for more than three hundred years; but its physical character is still very imperfectly understood, even as regards the districts near the coast. Its common **name**, New Guinea, was bestowed upon it by a Spanish navigator, because of some resemblance which he fancied the natives bore to the negroes on the west coast of Africa. By a previous visitor, a Portuguese navigator, it had been called Papua, and this is in some respect the preferable name, inasmuch as it is derived from one of the most prominent physical characteristics of the aboriginal inhabitants. The Malay word *papua*, or *papuwah*, signifies "woolly-haired," and men of the true Papuan race are distinguished by the peculiarity of their hair, which is rough and woolly. This name, while possessing the advantage of not suggesting any false relationship, is open to some objections. It is unknown to the natives themselves, who, owing to their division into mutually hostile tribes, have no sense of national unity, and feel no need for a common designation.

2. It lies north of Australia, from which it is distant about 100 miles. At its most northerly point, called the Cape of Good Hope, Papua approaches within half a degree of the equator, and the most southerly point lies in south latitude 10° 40'. Its general direction is from north-west to south-east, and its length is usually stated to be 1490 miles. From east to west it extends over twenty degrees of longitude, from 131° to 151° east; but its greatest width does not exceed 400 miles, and it is in some places narrowed down to 50 miles. Owing to the irregular shape of the island these figures give no accurate notion of its **area**, which has been recently estimated at fully 300,000 square miles. In shape, Papua, like some of the islands to the north,

is extraordinary and even grotesque, for its outline resembles in no slight degree that of some monster of remote ages. It consists of a central mass, with the addition, on the north, of a peninsula almost severed from the main body and otherwise much broken up by the sea, and of another peninsula stretching out like a tail to the south-east. What used to be thought a peninsula projecting from the south-west side is in reality an island, named Frederick Henry, about 100 miles long by 50 in breadth.

3. The **coast-line** is in general high and rocky, except on the south, where it is low and even swampy. Many of the numerous indentations have, as yet, no recognized names. Some of the more important are the following: on the north, Geelvink Bay, Astrolabe Bay, Huon Gulf, and Acland Bay; on the south, the Gulf of Papua; and on the west, M'Cluer Inlet. There are many excellent harbours at various parts of the coast, some of them being protected by the numerous islands which encircle the whole country.

4. Of the **interior** of the country very little is known. Although one-half of it has long been nominally in possession of the Dutch, no attempt was made by systematic exploration to gain a more perfect acquaintance with the country or its inhabitants. Reports of the savage character of the natives and of the frightful diseases which, it was alleged, were certain to attack strangers, long prevented the visits of men who were disposed to undertake explorations on their own account. Such drawbacks, however, have not, in more recent years, deterred scientific inquirers from trusting themselves to the natives for months, and risking the terrors of the climate without protection or help. Their explorations have already added much to our very scanty knowledge. Judging from what is actually known it seems probable that a chain of mountains traverses the island in the direction of its length. Some portions of this chain in the south-east are said to average 7000 feet in height, and Mt. Owen Stanley has an elevation estimated at over 13,000 feet. In the north-west have been seen snow-topped mountains probably 18,000 feet high, which may also belong to this system. South of Astrolabe Bay is a peak reported to be 20,000 feet high. Except as regards the south-eastern peninsula our information is based upon inference and conjec-

ture. Various ranges have been observed running parallel to the coasts, as in New South Wales and Queensland, and it is probable that between these mountains and the main chain there may be a high table-land. An extensive plain occupies the district lying along the southern coast where the island is widest. This plain, which has been visited by several explorers, is described as a vast flat covered with alluvial soil, often so low as to form extensive swamps, and cut up into deltas by the numerous arms of large rivers. The flat is in many parts continued beyond shore, rendering the sea too shallow for navigation except by small boats.

5. Of the **drainage** of the island our actual knowledge is equally limited. If the conjecture as to the general resemblance of Papua to eastern Australia in conformation be well founded, the rivers on the eastern and northern coasts will have short courses; still one recently discovered has been explored for a distance of 400 miles. On the southern coast the rivers are probably longer as a rule, but of them, with one or two exceptions, we hardly know anything. One of them, the Fly, however, has been traced to a distance of 500 miles from its mouth, and its appearance then justified the belief that its source was still 100 miles distant. It has numerous tributaries, and an estuary containing several islands.

6. As in other intertropical regions, the seasons are but two in number, the wet and the dry. In the south the wet season occurs between April and September, whereas on the north coast the period of rainfall is from October to March. Rain is even more abundant than in northern Australia, and its effects are visible in the more luxuriant vegetation of Papua. From the scanty observations taken of the temperature it is inferred that the mean summer heat is 95°, and that of winter 75°. That the **climate** is decidedly unhealthy, especially on low ground, seems to be a well-ascertained fact, the more prevalent disorders being dysentery, fevers, and skin-diseases, from all of which natives as well as strangers suffer. On the higher grounds these complaints are less severe, and probably judicious care of the health would greatly diminish the liability to attack. In this point of view Papua seems to afford but little prospect of suitability as a field for European settlement.

7. Of the **mineral productions** of Papua it is not possible to speak with certainty. Gold has been found, but as yet not in large quantities, though the belief is general that highly auriferous tracts will in time be discovered. Granite has been observed in the north-west, and as this rock is often associated, in other countries, with valuable minerals, there is some probability that such may be the case in Papua. Excellent soil is to be found in every district, as is shown by the luxuriant **vegetation** with which the country is overgrown. In this respect Papua occupies an intermediate position between the Malayan islands and Australia. In its dense forests of gigantic trees lashed together with the supple stems of climbing plants, and in the thick undergrowth of brushwood, it resembles the jungles of some of the islands to the northward and westward, while the abundance of gum-trees and acacias in the south forcibly remind the spectator of Australia. Timber trees of great size and excellent quality have been observed in every direction in which an explorer has penetrated, ironwood and ebony being among the number. At least ten species of palms have been enumerated, one of them stemless; a kind of cinnamon is common; the wild nutmeg furnishes an article of commerce; and there are many species of figs. Among the food-producing plants may be mentioned the cocoa-nut, sago, banana, bread-fruit, and sugar-cane. Of ornamental trees and flowers there are numerous species. In some localities open grassy plains are to be found, but they form a very small proportion of the whole surface. In these many characteristic Australian plants are to be found besides the gum-trees, such as the so-called honeysuckles and bottle-brushes.

In its **animal life** Papua more nearly resembles Australia than the East Indian Islands, not only as regards the species found in it, but also as respects those that are absent. Insects abound, and some orders, as the beetles and the butterflies, are remarkable for their singular forms, their uncommon size, or their resplendent colours. The reptiles, which include crocodiles, are little known. In the mammalian class a marked likeness to Australia is observable. None of the great carnivora of southern Asia and the Malayan islands—lions, tigers, and leopards—are found in Papua; no monkeys, as the orang-outang;

no such animals as the rhinoceros and tapir; and no ruminating animals, as the deer. On the other hand, with the exception of a dog, two bats, a pig, and some mice, all the mammals belong to the marsupial or pouched order and to the same families as those found in Australia. A tree kangaroo is perhaps the most remarkable of the marsupials. Four species of cuscus, a flesh-eating marsupial of small size, and an echidna have also been found.

While the mammals are thus restricted to a few kinds, the birds are numerous and diversified. A large number of species are peculiar to Papua and the neighbouring islands; others are common to it with North Australia; and a third group are identical with birds that inhabit the Malayan islands. Of those which are specially characteristic of Papua it may be said that they are more singular in form, as well as more beautiful in plumage, than the birds of any other island in the world. One of these is the cassowary, which bears a general resemblance to the emu, though stouter and of less height. The largest of the parrot race, the Great Black Cockatoo, and also the smallest of the family, belong to Papua, and some of the remaining species, out of thirty inhabiting the island, are among the most beautiful of their kind. Equally beautiful kingfishers, about forty species of pigeons, some remarkable for size or for beauty of plumage, and various other birds of peculiar form or brilliant colours, render the ornithology of Papua a most interesting study. Exceeding these, however, and, it may be said, all other birds, in elegance and beauty, are the Birds of Paradise, of which many species inhabit Papua and the adjacent islands. No verbal description can convey an adequate notion of the appearance and splendid colouring of these birds.

8. The great mass of the **population** of Papua belongs to a race which is termed the Papuan. On the east coast the race is to some extent mixed, apparently with Polynesians; and on the north a similar mixture has taken place with Malays and people from the neighbouring islands. The purer Papuan stock occupies the remainder of the island. Describing the typical Papuan, Mr. A. R. Wallace, by whom the question was carefully investigated, thus writes: "The colour of the body is a deep sooty-brown or black, sometimes approaching, but never

quite equalling the jet black of some negro races. It varies in tint, however, and is sometimes of a dusky brown. The hair is very peculiar, being harsh, dry, and frizzly, growing in little tufts or curls, which in youth are very short and compact, but afterwards grow out to a considerable length, forming the compact frizzled mop which is the Papuan's pride and glory. The face is adorned with a beard of the same frizzly nature as the

Natives of Papua.

hair of the head. The arms, legs, and breast are also more or less clothed with hair of a similar nature." The same writer considers that in stature the Papuan is equal or even superior to the average of Europeans, though other observers entertain a different opinion. The legs are long and slender as in the Australian aboriginal; "the face is somewhat flattish, the brows very prominent; the nose is large, rather arched and high, the base thick, the nostrils broad, with the aperture hidden, owing to the tip of the nose being elongated; the mouth is large, the lips thick and protuberant." It is difficult to judge of the intellectual character of these people, as they are yet so little known. There is reason to believe, however, that they are not deficient in mental capacity. Although they wear little or no clothing, they pay great attention to personal appearance, especially in regard to the hair. Besides tattooing and painting the skin, they use ornaments for the nose, ears, and neck, and the teeth with some tribes are filed to a point. Their houses, constructed of bamboo, are often raised upon stakes, and even built in lofty trees. Not only the houses, but all their domestic utensils and weapons are decorated with carvings, as is also the case with their "prahus" or canoes, which are hollowed out of the trunks of trees. Their weapons are bows and arrows, spears, knives, and axes, the two latter being formed of stone. With regard to diet they are not nice; they eat the flesh of the wild pig, kangaroo, cuscus, cassowary, lizards, fish, and some kinds of large insects, as well as that of their domesticated animals, the pig, dog, and fowls. They know how to till the soil; and for vegetable food they have sweet-potatoes, yams, bananas, and sugar-cane, to which may be added sago, cocoa-nuts, bread-fruit, mangoes, and other fruits which grow wild. Cannibalism has been attributed to them; but while it is certain that some tribes are addicted to the horrible practice, it has not been proved that the whole race is equally guilty. In point of moral character different reports have been given of the Papuans. Some represent them as fierce, vindictive, and treacherous, and often cruel even to their own children; others give them a very much better character. The practice of hunting men for their heads they share in common with other uncivilized races of the Malay Archipelago. The skulls are kept as trophies and proofs of bravery. Their religious ideas have not been well ascertained, though there are some indications of belief in a supreme Being. Among the coast tribes, where divergences from the purely Papuan type have arisen from the mixture of races, the Papuan traits still predominate, so that even in those districts the inhabitants are all included under the one designation. It is alleged by some writers, however, that in the mountainous interior there is to be found a race whose physical attributes differ widely from those of the Papuans, especially as regards stature, but this assertion cannot yet be definitely accepted as a fact. The total population is conjectured, upon no good grounds, to be about 2,500,000.

9. To a considerable extent the Papuans employ themselves in **occupations** connected with the supply of food, in house and boat building, and in war. Fishing is carried on by the coast tribes, who also cultivate gardens, in which they grow rice, yams, sweet-potatoes, sugar-cane, bananas, and maize, as well as betel and tobacco. Sago is made from the pith of the palm of that name, and bread-fruit is also used as an article of food. The pig and the kangaroo are hunted, and supply animal food. The houses are sometimes built over the water, but in nearly all cases are raised upon stakes. In some instances they are small, so as to accommodate but one family in each; in others they are large enough to contain all the inhabitants of the village. Their prahus or canoes are, some of them, of great size; and they make excellent fishing-nets. Women, among some of the tribes, manufacture pottery and ropes. While from the general fertility of the soil, the heat of the climate, and the variety of its natural products, Papua might become a great exporting country, its trade is at present limited to a few articles such as cinnamon, nutmegs, and birds of paradise, which are bartered with Malays and others who visit the island at certain periods. In the future it may be regarded as certain that among the exports will be numbered timber, sago, copra, bêche-de-mer (trepang or sea-slugs), pearl shell, and other products of tropical lands and seas.

10. Practically there are no colonies, or hardly even settlements, of Europeans in Papua, except where missionaries have established themselves for the purpose of instructing the natives in the truths of Christianity. Their stations are mostly on the west coast of the southern peninsula, where Port Moresby is situated. This is the chief port and centre of trade, as well as a missionary station. West of the 141st meridian of east longitude, Papua is claimed by the Dutch, who, however, have exercised but a nominal authority over the people. An abortive attempt was once made by them to found a settlement, but the project was abandoned after a short trial. The southern and eastern

portion of the remainder was formally taken possession of by the British in 1884, and a protectorate was established over the natives with a view to guard them from the outrages of lawless traders rather than for the furtherance of colonization. More recently the Germans have appropriated the remaining portion, and have established a few stations. The boundary line between the tracts belonging to the two nations is thus described: "Starting from the coast on the 8th parallel of south latitude, it follows that parallel to the point where it is cut by the 147th meridian of east longitude, then runs in a north-westerly direction to the intersection of the 6th parallel and the 144th meridian, and continues in a west-north-westerly direction to the point of intersection of the 5th parallel and the 141st meridian." This line, it is estimated, gives about 70,000 square miles of territory to the German protectorate and 86,000 to the English; and it is believed nearly coincides with the main watershed of the country. The German territory has been named Emperor William's Land. Port Moresby is the seat of government of British New Guinea. It has a population of 800.

CHAPTER XV.

THE SOLOMON ISLANDS, NEW BRITAIN, AND NEW IRELAND.

1. Position and Extent. 2. Surface. 3. Climate. 4. Natural Productions. 5. Population. 6. Settlement.

1. The chain of islands, which extends to the eastward of New Guinea, from the Admiralty Group in the north-west to Rennell Island in the south-east, has a length of about 1300 miles. The northern extremity of the chain would be about the 2d degree of south latitude, and the southern within the 12th. Although constituting geographically but one group, no collective name has been yet devised, and it is therefore necessary to describe the various portions in detail. The **Solomon Islands** form the south-eastern portion of the group. They were discovered and named by the Spanish explorer Mendana, in 1567, but until recently remained unvisited and comparatively unknown, for the natives bore the reputation of being fierce and treacherous. This group includes seven large and many smaller islands, the former being arranged in two parallel lines. In the more easterly line are Malayta, Mahaga (or Ysabel), Choiseul, and Bougainville; and the second line, situated at an average distance of 30 miles to the westward, comprises St. Christoval, Guadalcanar, and New Georgia. The total length of this part of the chain is 700 miles. The chain is continued in **New Ireland, New Hanover,** and the **Admiralty Islands;** while **New Britain** lies at right angles to the axis of the main chain, and from its western extremity stretches a group of smaller islands which approach the shores of New Guinea.

2. All the islands are **mountainous** and apparently of volcanic origin. In Guadalcanar there is an active volcano, another in New Britain, and several on the small islands towards the north. In general the mountains attain the height of 4000 feet, except in the Admiralty Group, where they do not exceed 1600; but the culminating point, a peak in Guadalcanar, has an elevation of 8000 feet. Owing to the hostile disposition of

the natives, explorers have not been able to penetrate into the interior, and our knowledge of the surface is confined to such facts as could be ascertained by observation from the shore. All are known, however, to be well watered, though the rivers

Natives of New Britain.

are short. New Britain is said to be one of the most beautiful countries in the world.

3. The **climate** is tropical. So far as we are yet aware, the temperature is not excessive, being everywhere modified by the sea-breezes. Rain is abundant in the wet season, and the atmosphere as compared with that of the continent is moist. Modified trade-winds prevail throughout the year. As a whole, the climate is reported to be not unhealthy even to Europeans.

4. Little is known as to the mineral **productions** of these islands. In all the vegetation is luxuriant. Magnificent forests

abound; the cocoa-nut and mango are indigenous; and tree-ferns, sandal-wood, ebony, and lignum-vitæ are known to grow to a great size. Both birds and mammals resemble those of New Guinea; and some of the marsupials, as the cuscus and a kangaroo, are representatives of the peculiar animal life of Australia.

5. With some minor differences among themselves, the **inhabitants** must be regarded as offshoots from the Papuan race. All are of a dark colour, some being of a lighter shade than others. Among the northern islands the people are of a moderate height, while in those to the southward the natives are dwarfish in stature. They also vary in features, but the woolly frizzled hair is a common characteristic throughout the whole chain. It is not possible to estimate the number of the inhabitants of this chain; but the different islands appear to be well peopled. The people of New Britain are cannibals, and are not ashamed of the practice, as most cannibals are.

6. Recently a German protectorate has been established over the greater part of this archipelago, and the remainder continues to be unclaimed by any European power. The German portion, including New Britain, New Ireland, New Hanover, and the Admiralty Islands, has received the name of **Bismarck Archipelago**. No colonies proper have been formed on any of the islands and hardly any permanent settlements by Europeans, except such as have been made by missionaries. In a few localities planters have settled and traders have established depots for the purpose of exchanging merchandise for native products, but such stations are liable to be broken up through the violence of the natives. Missionary effort, however, has already accomplished much good in New Britain.

CHAPTER XVI.

THE PAPUAN ISLANDS.

1. Waigiou. 2. Booro. 3. Ceram. 4. Kei and Aroo Islands. 5. Timor Laut. 6. Timor. 7. Flores. 8. Sandalwood Island.

1. These islands lie on the west of Papua, and are so named either on account of their proximity to that island, or because they are inhabited, wholly or in part, by men of Papuan race. Commencing on the extreme north-east, the first of them to be noticed is **Waigiou**. This island consists of elevated land much indented by the sea, so as to be divided into three principal parts. It measures 80 miles in length by 20 in breadth. Dense forests cover the island, which resembles, in most respects, the mainland of Papua, and is the habitat of birds of paradise. The people are of mixed race, but the language is Papuan. In connection with Waigiou may be mentioned Batanta and Salwatty, islands of similar character.

2. **Booro**, which lies some distance farther to the westward, is inhabited in the southern and forest portion by Papuans, and by a mixed race in the north.

3. **Ceram** is a large island of irregular shape, very mountainous and thickly wooded. Very little is known of the interior. As is always the case where sago forms the chief article of food, the people are poor. In the interior savage tribes occupy the country.

4. South of Western Papua are two groups of islands, the **Kei** and the **Aroo Islands**, which are in every sense Papuan. The former are small and thickly wooded, the forests producing timber, which is used in the construction of prahus, the great industry of the group. The Aroo Islands are larger, and are of coral origin. On one of them, at a place called Dobbo, a yearly fair is held, and is attended by traders from great distances. To this place the Papuans bring the products of their labour, and obtain in exchange such commodities as they require. It is estimated that the value of the trade carried on at this mart is about £40,000 annually. The native race in

both groups is the Papuan, but the coast districts are inhabited by people of mixed descent.

5. In the Tenimber group **Timor Laut** is the principal island, of which but little is known. As in most of the islands throughout this region, the interior is inhabited by a black, frizzly-haired race, presumably of Papuan affinities, and the coast by a mixed people somewhat more civilized. The island is said to be fertile.

6. Farther westward is **Timor**, a large island, 300 miles long and 60 broad, and containing an area of 11,000 square miles. It is surrounded by numerous small islands, which may be regarded as belonging to it geographically. Its surface is elevated, mountain ranges traversing the island in the direction of its length. These are said to reach the average height of 6000 feet, though the culminating point is supposed to have an altitude of 11,000 feet. Timor is out of the line of volcanic action which runs through the Malayan islands, but there are traces of volcanic energy in former times. In the interior are table-lands, about 3000 feet in elevation, and adapted by their climate to produce the grain of the warmer portion of the temperate zone. The whole island appears to be less densely wooded than those already mentioned, a result probably of the much drier climate. Except in the wet season, the short rivers have but a small volume of water, and, like those of Australia, sometimes wholly cease to run. Nothing is definitely known as to the mineral resources of Timor, as the country has been little explored. The vegetation resembles, in many respects, that of Australia, and includes some characteristic Australian plants, as the eucalyptus and acacia. Like Australia, also, animal life is scanty, except as regards birds, of which there is a considerable variety. Some of the mammals common in the Malayan islands also inhabit Timor. The most important of these are a monkey, a tiger-cat, and a wild pig. There is also the opossum-like cuscus. The native inhabitants are of the Papuan stock, but not of so unmixed a type as the tribes farther east. Their colour is lighter, and their hair less frizzled than that of the natives of New Guinea, but they have the characteristic Papuan nose. They are more civilized than their eastern brethren, weave cotton cloths, wear clothing, and

rear domestic animals. They also cultivate wheat and potatoes, grow coffee, keep bees, and rear ponies and sheep. They are still pagans, and retain some of the barbarous practices common among the more savage Malay tribes. The two European powers, the Dutch and the Portuguese, that lay claim to Timor, the former to the western and the latter to the eastern half, have done nothing towards developing the resources of the country or civilizing the inhabitants. Some trade, however, is carried on at Coupong, the capital of the west, and at Delli, the chief place in the east. From the former are exported ponies, bees'-wax, and sandal-wood; and from the latter, wheat and potatoes. It is considered that the total population of the island does not exceed 100,000.

7. Passing over Ombay, Wetter, and some smaller islands to the northward of Timor, **Flores** next presents itself. This island, 230 miles in length and about 20 miles broad on the average, is also mountainous and volcanic. It has both active and extinct volcanoes, and some of its peaks are alleged to reach an elevation of 10,000 feet. The interior, however, is almost unknown to Europeans, and most of the statements as to its character and products are conjectural only. Gold, copper, and iron are said to be found here; it is better wooded than Timor; and its forests produce some valuable timbers, including sandal-wood. The aborigines belong to the Papuan stock, are dark and frizzly-haired, and nearly allied to the Timorese.

8. **Sumba,** or **Sandalwood Island,** lies to the south of Flores, and is very little known to Europeans. Like all the neighbouring islands, it is mountainous, and is believed to be volcanic. As the population is apparently large, it is inferred that the soil is fertile, especially as the people grow rice and maize, and possess domesticated animals. Sandal-wood, bees'-wax, edible birds'-nests, and tortoise-shell are exported; but as there are no European settlements the trade is confined to the natives of the neighbouring islands.

> "Messrs. Blackie grudge nothing in the production of a school-book. All that good paper, clear type, and beautiful illustrations can do to help an author, are liberally and wisely done by them.'—*School Board Chronicle.*

CATALOGUE OF EDUCATIONAL WORKS.

INDEX.

	PAGE
Arithmetic,	15, 16, 17, 25
Book-keeping,	16
Books for Teachers,	26
Dictionaries,	26
Drawing:—	
Vere Foster's Drawing Copy-Books,	27
Vere Foster's Drawing Cards,	28
Vere Foster's Water-Color Drawing-Books,	28, 29
Poynter's Drawing for the Standards,	32, and p. 3 of Cover.
Poynter's South Kensington Drawing-Book,	30, 31
Drawing for the Standards,	p. 2 of Cover.
Education, Works on,	26
Elocution:—	
Baynham's Select Readings and Recitations,	12
Miscellaneous Readers,	10, 11, 12
Poetical Reader,	11
Poetry for Repetition,	5
School Classics,	12
English Grammar and Composition,	20
French Grammar,	22
Geography:—	
Geographical Readers,	6, 7
Geographical Text-Books,	19
History and Geography Readers,	9
Maps and Map Drawing,	7
History:—	
Elementary History of England,	9
Historical Readers,	8
Historical Text-Books,	17
History and Geography Readers,	9
London, Past and Present,	11
The Sovereign Reader,	10
Home Lesson Books:—	
For Comprehensive Readers,	5
For Graded Readers,	3
For Geographical Readers,	7
Home Lesson Books—*Continued*.	
For Historical Readers,	8
For History and Geography Readers,	9
Infant Series,	3, 5, 22
Latin,	22
Mathematics,	24, 25
Poetry:—	
Chaucer, Prologue to Canterbury Tales,	12
Poetry for Repetition,	5
Milton's Paradise Lost.—Book I.,	11
Poetical Reader,	11
School Classics,	12
Shakespeare's Plays,	12
Readers:—	
Comprehensive Readers,	4, 5
Graded Readers,	2, 3
Geographical Readers,	6, 7
Historical Readers,	8
Infant Reading Books,	3
Reading Books for the Higher Standards,	10, 11, 12
Science:—	
Science Text-Books,	23, 24
Text-Books for the Specific Subjects,	21, 22
Common Things and Elementary Science,	22
Scripture,	18
Specific Subjects,	21, 22
Teachers' Books,	26
Writing:—	
Vere Foster's Writing Copy-Books.	
Original Series,	13
Palmerston Series,	14
Bold Writing Series,	14
Writing Charts,	15
National Competition in Writing and Drawing,	15

June, 1888.

Adopted by the London and other Principal School Boards.

New Editions, adapted to meet the latest Code requirements.

THE GRADED READERS.

FOR ELEMENTARY SCHOOLS.

In the GRADED READERS effect has been given, as far as possible, to all that writers on the Science of Education, as well as the experience of practical educationists in our own and other countries have suggested for the teaching of Reading.

In the PRIMERS the *matter* of nearly every lesson is first presented to the mind by means of a picture. The child deals with a single difficulty at a time, and in each case proceeds from that which is easier to what is more difficult.

The selection of lessons for the Earlier Readers has been guided by the principle that the association of spoken with written language is, in itself, task sufficient for a child to contend with at first, without his being at the same time embarrassed by difficulties connected with the matter or language of the lessons.

In the Higher Readers the communication of instruction through the reading lesson has been kept more distinctly in view, without sacrificing the needful simplicity and interest. The pieces selected are also such as to attract the pupils to the works of our great English writers.

At the suggestion of many teachers Spelling lists from each lesson for Revisal purposes have been added to Readers I. to IV.

"One of the very best series of Readers now in the market. The freshness of the books is remarkably pleasing. Many of the lessons in prose are from the works of the greatest English writers. The poetical pieces have also been most judiciously selected from the best sources. The illustrations are of the highest order, and the paper and binding are of the best quality."—Schoolmaster.

"They are bright, fresh, and touched with that which is kin to the best spirit of childhood. Great attention is paid to the various devices by which the pupil may be made secure in the art of spelling. There is great variety of subject, and the lessons stretch over a very wide field of human intelligence, literature, culture, thought, and knowledge."—School Board Chronicle.

The Graded Reading Sheets. Illustrated (14 pp. of Primer I. in Facsimile), price 3s. 6d. per set, or mounted on boards, 14s.

The Graded Reading Sheets, Second Series. Profusely Illustrated. 24 Sheets, containing 16 pp., Primer I., size 35 by 27½ inches. Price 6s. per set, or mounted on boards, 21s.

THE GRADED READERS—*Continued.*

Each Book is illustrated in a highly instructive and artistic manner.

Graded Primer, Part I. 32 pp., cloth cover, 2½*d*.; paper cover, 1½*d*.
Graded Primer, Part II. 48 pp., cloth cover, 3*d*.; paper cover, 2*d*.
Graded Primer, Complete. 80 pp., cloth, ... price 4*d*.
First Graded Reader. ... 136 pp., cloth boards, ... price 8*d*.
Second Graded Reader. 136 pp., cloth boards, ... price 8*d*.
Third Graded Reader. ... 200 pp., cloth boards, ... price 1*s*.
Fourth Graded Reader. 232 pp., cloth boards, ... price 1*s*. 3*d*.
Fifth Graded Reader. ... 224 pp., cloth boards, ... price 1*s*. 3*d*.
Sixth Graded Reader. ... 224 pp., cloth boards, ... price 1*s*. 3*d*.

The Original Editions of the Readers can still be had:—FIRST READER, 96 pp., 6*d*.; SECOND READER, 136 pp., 8*d*.; THIRD READER, 200 pp., 1*s*.; FOURTH READER, 288 pp., 1*s*. 6*d*.; FIFTH READER, 320 pp., 2*s*.; SIXTH READER, 384 pp., 2*s*. 6*d*.

HOME LESSON BOOKS.

BASED ON THE "GRADED READERS."

First Reader, 24 pp., price 1*d*. | Third Reader, 40 pp., price 2*d*.
Second Reader, 24 pp., ,, 1*d*. | Fourth Reader, 48 pp., ,, 2*d*.

INFANT READING BOOKS.

By JENNETT HUMPHREYS.

Fully Illustrated with Woodcuts, and one Coloured Plate each. 64 pp., 32mo, cloth. Sixpence each.

TALES EASY AND SMALL for the Youngest of All. In words of not more than three letters.

OLD DICK GREY and Aunt Kate's Way. In words of not more than four letters.

MAUD'S DOLL AND HER WALK. In Picture and Talk. In words of not more than four letters.

IN HOLIDAY TIME: and other Stories. In words of not more than five letters.

"These tales are of a very novel character, and are graded to suit our little treasures' advancement up the ladder of life. The author has shown great ingenuity in producing such nice tales for the very young. We can recommend them with all confidence, as we are sure that they will give satisfaction upon a trial."—*Sch'lmistress.*

ADOPTED BY THE LONDON AND OTHER PRINCIPAL SCHOOL BOARDS.

New Editions, adapted to meet the latest Code requirements.

THE COMPREHENSIVE READERS.

THE COMPREHENSIVE READERS have been compiled by a number of Teachers who have conducted schools of different grades for many years with marked success. They are very carefully graduated and systematically arranged, and are written in language suitable to the minds of children. The subjects selected will be found to foster a love of reading and a high moral tone of feeling and conduct.

Geography, History, and Biography have been introduced into the higher books with a view of imparting useful information, and awakening an intelligent curiosity, which may lead to the further study of these important branches of education.

The series contains an ample selection of the best poetry for repetition, and has throughout been adapted to meet the latest requirements of the Education Department as to *Reading Books*.

At the suggestion of many teachers Spelling lists from each lesson for Revisal purposes have recently been added to Readers I. to IV.

"As specimens of good reading books they cannot be excelled. The exercises are carefully arranged so as to suit the meanest capacity, and at the same time have a tendency to make useful impressions on the minds of young scholars."—**Educational Guide.**

"The printing is remarkably clear and distinct; the paper is much thicker and better than that usually found in reading books; the binding will stand any amount of ordinary wear and tear; and the illustrations are perfect little gems of art."—**Schoolmaster.**

"The graduation is very skilful, both as to matter and substance, and the lessons are well calculated to reach the aim expressed by the author, that of fostering in the youthful mind a love of reading, a high moral tone of feeling and conduct, kindness to animals, and the like. They are good readers."—**School Board Chronicle.**

"Compiled with great care and skill. The subject matter of the lessons has been judiciously chosen, and the language employed is suitable to the capacities of the children in the various standards. The get-up of the books is all that could be desired. There are capital illustrations, and plenty of them."—**School Guardian.**

"We are very pleased with these books, and warmly recommend them to the attention of our readers. The books will take high rank as one of the best series yet compiled for use in schools."—**National Schoolmaster.**

THE COMPREHENSIVE READERS—*Continued.*

Illustrated in a highly instructive and artistic manner.

PRIMER, Part I.   32 pp., paper cover, price 1½d.; cloth, price 2½d.
PRIMER, Part II.   48 pp., paper cover, price 2d.; cloth, price 3d.
PRIMER, Complete.   80 pp., cloth, ...   price 4d.
FIRST READER.   112 pp., cloth boards, ...   price 7d.
SECOND READER.   136 pp., cloth boards, ...   price 8d.
THIRD READER.   200 pp., cloth boards,   ...   price 1s.
FOURTH READER.   232 pp., cloth boards,   ...   price 1s. 3d.
FIFTH READER.   224 pp., cloth boards,   ...   price 1s. 3d.
SIXTH READER.   224 pp., cloth boards, ...   price 1s. 3d.

READING SHEETS to suit Primer I., 2s. 6d. the set;
  Mounted on boards, 10s. 6d. the set.

The ORIGINAL EDITIONS of the FIRST, FOURTH, FIFTH, and SIXTH READERS can still be had.

FIRST READER.   104 pp., price, 6d.
FOURTH READER. 288 pp., price 1s. 6d.
FIFTH READER.   320 pp., price 2s.
SIXTH READER.   384 pp., price 2s. 6d.

HOME LESSON BOOKS.

BASED ON THE COMPREHENSIVE READERS.

First Reader, 24 pp., price 1d. | Third Reader, 40 pp., price 2d.
Second Reader, 24 pp., ,, 1d. | Fourth Reader, 48 pp., ,, 2d.

POETRY FOR REPETITION.

SELECT PIECES, WITH EXPLANATIONS IN SIMPLE WORDS.
Standards I. II., 16 pp., price 1d. | Standard III., 16 pp., price 1d.

"The selection is marked by great judgment, the happy mean between easy and difficult pieces having been hit."—*Schoolmistress.*

[*New Editions, thoroughly revised in accordance with the latest requirements.*

ADOPTED BY THE LONDON AND OTHER PRINCIPAL SCHOOL BOARDS.

BLACKIE'S GEOGRAPHICAL READERS.

By W. G. BAKER, B.A.,
Lecturer at Cheltenham Training College.

The subject-matter of the GEOGRAPHICAL READERS is graduated in accordance with the Education Code, the verbal difficulties being well within the grasp of children of the various Standards.

In the lower Standards the definitions and explanations are simple and concise. The upper Standards contain carefully written descriptive geography, in which ideas and principles, as well as facts are inculcated.

Throughout the series special care has been devoted to the selection of striking and educative pictorial illustrations, and to the introduction of suitable maps.

The summaries have been added by request of many teachers, who have testified to their practical value in schools.

Fully Illustrated by Woodcuts, Maps, and Diagrams.

Standard I.—To explain a plan of the School and Playground. The four Cardinal Points. The meaning and use of a Map. With coloured Map. 112 pp., cloth, 7*d*.

Standard II.—Size and Shape of the World. Geographical Terms explained and illustrated by reference to the Map of England. Physical Geography of hills and rivers. 124 pp., cloth, 8*d*.

Standard III.—Physical and Political Geography of England and Wales. With twelve District Maps. 176 pp., cloth, 1*s*.

Standard IV.—Physical and Political Geography of Scotland and Ireland, British North America, and Australasia. With coloured Map. 224 pp., cloth, 1*s*. 6*d*.

Standard V.—Geography of Europe, Physical and Political. Latitude and Longitude. Day and Night. The Seasons. With coloured Map. 224 pp., cloth, 1*s*. 6*d*.

Standard VI.—ASIA, AFRICA, AMERICA, and especially the BRITISH COLONIES. Interchange of Productions, &c. With four coloured Maps. 288 pp., cloth, 2*s*.

GEOGRAPHICAL READERS—*Continued.*

Standard VII.—The Ocean. Currents and Tides. General arrangement of the Planetary System. The Phases of the Moon. 192 pp., cloth, 1s. 6d.

"This set of Readers is undoubtedly one of the best and most commendable which has come under our notice."—**Athenæum.**

"They are quite the best Geographical Readers we have seen."—**Saturday Review.**

"The books stand in the very first rank for thorough and skilful adaptation to the requirements of the various Standards in elementary schools. Great pains are taken to make the subject interesting to the utmost degree, and to ensure that the intelligence of the child is exercised and encouraged."—**School Board Chronicle.**

"These are models of what Geographical Readers should be. It would be difficult to give them praise which should exaggerate their merits."—**Practical Teacher.**

BLACKIE'S HISTORY AND GEOGRAPHY READERS, for the Scotch Code. See under Historical Readers, page 9.

AUSTRALASIA; A Descriptive and Pictorial Account of the Australian and New Zealand Colonies, Tasmania, and the adjacent lands. By W. WILKINS, Late Under-Secretary for Public Instruction in New South Wales. Fully illustrated with Woodcuts and Maps. Crown 8vo, cloth, 2s. 6d.

HOME LESSON EXERCISES
ON THE GEOGRAPHICAL READERS.

Standard II., 16 pp., 1d. **Standards III. IV. V. VI. and VII.**, 32 pp., 2d. each.

MAPS
TO ACCOMPANY THE GEOGRAPHICAL READERS.

AN ATLAS of 17 Coloured Maps. Small 4to, paper cover, 4d.

MAP DRAWING.
COPIES FOR SCHOOL AND HOME LESSONS.

A Series of Maps adapted for the special requirement of Map-drawing in the Government examinations. In Three Sections, paper covers, price 3d. each. Also in one vol., limp cloth, 1s. 3d.

Sect. I. for Standards III. & IV.—England & Wales.—British Islands.—Scotland.—Ireland.—Australia.—New Zealand.—British N. America.

Sect. II. for Standard V.—France.—Spain.—Italy.—North Sea.—River Danube.—Rhine.—Volga.—Mediterranean Sea.—Baltic Sea.

Sect. III. for Standards VI. and VII.—India.—Africa.—South America.—Nile Basin.—United States.—Mississippi.—Atlantic Ocean.—Pacific Ocean.—Ocean Currents.

ADOPTED BY THE LONDON AND OTHER PRINCIPAL SCHOOL BOARDS.

BLACKIE'S HISTORICAL READERS.

By GEORGE GIRLING, Head Master of Burghley Road Board School, London

The First and Second Books are suited for the Third and Fourth Standards, and treat the whole course of English History. Reader No. II. is arranged as a class-book for schools in which the pupils in Standards IV. to VI. are united in one class for reading, and deals with the History of England from the Tudor Period to our own time.

Readers Nos. III. and IV. form together a complete history treated more in detail than in the earlier books, and in a style of diction suited to the higher Standards. Explanatory notes are given, and questions are appended to each chapter.

The series is profusely illustrated with maps diagrams, and portraits.

"Mr. Girling has the happy knack of saying the right thing in a few words, and of infusing spirit and life into his narrative. A calm, judicial view of past events, free from all prejudice or bias."—Educ. Times.

"The matter is bright, intelligent, and original; and the narrative is admirably sustained. The printing, binding, and illustrations are worthy of the highest praise."—Schoolmistress.

With Interesting Illustrations of great educational value.

No. I. for Standard III.—STORIES FROM ENGLISH HISTORY, in simple language; from Earliest Times to end of the Plantagenet Period. 160 pp., cloth, 1s.

No. II. for Standard IV.—ENGLISH HISTORY, from the beginning of the Tudor Period to Latest Times. 192 pp., cloth, 1s. 3d.

No. III. for Standard V.—OUTLINES OF THE HISTORY OF ENGLAND, Part I., from Early Times to the end of the Tudor Period. 248 pp., cloth, 1s. 6d.

No. IV. for Standard VI.—OUTLINES OF THE HISTORY OF ENGLAND, Part II., from James I. to the Present Time. 222 pp., cloth, 1s. 6d.

Nos. III. and IV. complete in one volume. 454 pp., cloth, red edges, 2s. 6d.

HOME LESSON BOOKS
For the HISTORICAL READERS, 2d. each.

ADVANCED HISTORICAL READER, for the Higher Standards. Consisting chiefly of choice extracts from MACAULAY, FROUDE, SCOTT, CARLYLE, &c.

> Part I.—From the Earliest Times to the Death of Richard III. 224 pp., cloth, 1s. 6d.
>
> Part II.—From the Accession of Henry VII. to the Battle of Waterloo. 224 pp., cloth, 1s. 6d.

ELEMENTARY HISTORY OF ENGLAND. By GEORGE GIRLING. Illustrated. Cloth limp.

> Standard IV. To the Norman Conquest, 5d.
> Standard V. From Norman Conquest to Accession of Henry VII., 8d.
> Standard VI. From Henry VII. to Death of George III., 10d.

BLACKIE'S HISTORY AND GEOGRAPHY READERS, for the Scotch Code.

This Series of Historical and Geographical Readers has been prepared to meet the requirements of the new Scottish Education Code. The essential facts are given within a moderate compass, and with sufficient but not too great detail. While care has been taken to give a clear presentation of historical and geographical ideas, simplicity of diction has been aimed at. Pictures and maps have been freely interspersed with the descriptions.

The summaries, lists, and tables appended to each book will be found specially useful for the purposes of revisal.

> Standard III.—HISTORY—Bruce and Mary. GEOGRAPHY—Definitions of Terms, Scotland. 160 pp., cloth, 10d.
>
> Standard IV.—HISTORY—Union of the Crowns to Death of Queen Anne. GEOGRAPHY—The British Isles. 224 pp., cloth, 1s. 3d.
>
> Standard V.—HISTORY—George I. to Death of George III. GEOGRAPHY—Europe, with British North America and Australasia. 256 pp., cloth, 1s. 4d.
>
> Standard VI.—HISTORY—From Death of George III. to Present Day. GEOGRAPHY—The World, specially British Colonies and Dependencies. With Five Coloured Maps. 256 pp., cloth, 1s. 6d.

HOME LESSON BOOKS

To Accompany the HISTORY AND GEOGRAPHY READERS, Standards III., IV., and V., 2d. each. Standard VI., with five coloured maps, 3d.

ADDITIONAL READING BOOKS.
FOR UPPER CLASSES.

BLACKIE'S SHAKESPEARE READER. EXTRACTS FROM SHAKESPEARE. With Introductory Paragraphs and Notes, Grammatical, Historical, and Explanatory. 160 pp., cloth, 1s.

"The extracts are admirably suitable as aids to the study of English History. . . .

The book is all that could be desired."—**Aberdeen Free Press.**

SHAKESPEARE'S PLAYS. A Series of the most suitable plays to be used as Reading books. Carefully edited, with simple and useful Notes.

"Annotated with unusual fulness and discrimination."—**Educational News.**
"All the introductory and auxiliary matter is plain and easy for young students, and is marked by culture and breadth of view."—**School Board Chronicle.**

KING RICHARD II. Complete with Notes. 96 pp., cloth, 8d.
JULIUS CÆSAR. Complete with Notes. 96 pp., cloth, 8d.
HENRY THE EIGHTH. Complete with Notes. 100 pp., cloth, 8d.
KING JOHN. Complete with Notes. 96 pp., cloth, 8d.
THE MERCHANT OF VENICE. Together with the Prose Narrative of the Play, from Lamb's Tales from Shakespeare. 104 pp., cloth, 8d.
THE TEMPEST. Complete with Notes. 96 pp., cloth, 8d.
AS YOU LIKE IT. Complete with Notes. 96 pp., cloth, 8d.

Others in Preparation.

GOLDSMITH'S COMEDIES. Edited by HAROLD LITTLEDALE, B.A., Vice-principal of the High School, Baroda.

THE GOOD-NATURED MAN. With Life of Goldsmith, and Notes. 96 pp., cloth, 1s.
SHE STOOPS TO CONQUER; OR, THE MISTAKES OF A NIGHT. With Notes. 100 pp., cloth, 1s.

"We have seldom seen so satisfactory an edition for school purposes of an English classic. The work ought to become a great favourite."—**Schoolmaster.**

THE SOVEREIGN READER: Scenes from the Life and Reign of Queen Victoria. By G. A. HENTY, Author of "Facing Death," &c. Illustrated. 256 pp., f'cap 8vo, cloth, 1s. 6d.

"Mr. G. A. Henty has succeeded in producing a really admirable volume, describing with some completeness the eventful reign of Queen Victoria with its stirring events and wonderful progress, right down to the present year."—**Teacher's Aid.**

READINGS FROM THE SPECTATOR: being a selection of papers contributed by Addison. With Notes. 192 pp., f'cap 8vo, cloth, 1s. 3d.

"We have pleasure in recommending this book to the notice of all teachers desiring an interesting and instructive reading book."—**Practical Teacher.**

READING BOOKS—*Continued.*

READINGS FROM SIR WALTER SCOTT. THE TALISMAN, IVANHOE, ANNE OF GEIERSTEIN, and MARMION. With Notes, &c. 192 pp., f'cap 8vo, cloth, 1s. 3d.

"We welcome these books as among the best of their kind."—**Journal of Education.**

"The incidents related are of such a romantic and fascinating character as to delight and instruct at the same time. The book is a model as to binding, typography, and materials."—**Aberdeen Free Press.**

MARY QUEEN OF SCOTS: being Readings from THE ABBOT by Sir Walter Scott. With Notes. 192 pp., f'cap 8vo, cloth, 1s. 3d.

"One of the most suitable reading-books for the upper Standards with which we are acquainted. It will be sure to charm the children."—**Teacher's Aid.**

READINGS FROM ROBINSON CRUSOE. With Copious Notes, and 23 Illustrations by GORDON BROWNE. 192 pp., cloth, 1s. 3d.

"There is not likely to be any complaint of overpressure in the class that reads this masterpiece: it will be the means of communicating to many a scholar the first impulse to read books as a pleasure instead of a task."—**North British Mail.**

MILTON'S PARADISE LOST.—BOOK I. With Life of Milton, and Explanatory Notes, by E. F. WILLOUGHBY, M.D. Cloth, 10d.

"The annotations are a valuable, learned, and far-reaching, body of notes."—**School Board Chronicle.**

POETICAL READER, SELECTIONS FROM STANDARD AUTHORS. For the use of Elementary Schools. 224 pp., cloth, 1s. 6d.

"This book will give a good idea of the poetic beauties which abound among poets on both sides of the Atlantic. The selections are well made, and the book as a whole is a successful piece of compilation."—**Schoolmaster.**

THE BRITISH BIOGRAPHICAL READER. SKETCHES OF PROMINENT MEN by Macaulay, Alison, Brougham, Emerson, Scott, &c. With numerous Portraits. 288 pp., f'cap 8vo, cloth, 2s.

"As a reading book for advanced classes this volume cannot be surpassed either for interest of subject or as a means of forming literary taste."—**Aberdeen Free Press.**

THE NEWSPAPER READER. SELECTIONS FROM LEADING JOURNALS OF THE NINETEENTH CENTURY ON PROMINENT EVENTS. By H. F. BUSSEY and T. W. REID. 288 pp., f'cap 8vo, cloth, 2s.

"The idea of the book is admirable, and its execution is excellent."—**Scotsman.**

"Can hardly fail to delight as well as inform the young."—**Glasgow Herald.**

LONDON, PAST AND PRESENT. Being Notices Historical and Descriptive of Ancient and Modern London, and of the counties on which it stands. With Illustrations. 288 pp., f'cap 8vo, cloth, 2s.

"Will form a tempting variation upon the customary reading books, and will stir up interest in the young class readers, not in London alone."—**Sch. Board Chron.**

READING BOOKS—*Continued.*

THE PROLOGUE TO THE CANTERBURY TALES OF GEOFFREY CHAUCER. With Life of the Author, Explanatory Notes, and Index to Difficult Words. By E. F. WILLOUGHBY. Cloth, 1s. 6d.

"By far the most satisfactory edition of this fragment of Chaucer's work for the use of schools yet issued. The text is carefully and freely annotated. The work is one which we can heartily recommend."—**Athenæum.**

BAYNHAM'S SELECT READINGS AND RECITATIONS; with Rules and Exercises on Correct Pronunciation, Gesture, Tone, and Emphasis. By GEO. W. BAYNHAM, Certified Master to Glasgow University, &c. 384 pp., crown 8vo, cloth, 2s. 6d.

"A work which will be welcomed by the heads of many colleges and schools. The selections given of dramatic scenes will afford excellent material for private acting amongst the scholars."—**Governess.**

MYTHS AND LEGENDS OF ANCIENT GREECE AND ROME. A HAND-BOOK OF MYTHOLOGY, for Schools and private Students. By E. M. BERENS. Illustrated from Antique Sculptures. 330 pp., cloth, 3s.

"It is worthy of the highest commendation. Lucid, comprehensive, and finely illustrated, it is all that is necessary for advanced schools."—**Daily Review.**

SCHOOL CLASSICS.

Selections from Standard Authors, with Biographical Sketches and Explanatory Notes. Each 32 pp., paper, 2d.; cloth, 3d.

For STANDARDS IV, V, VI, and VII.

The Merchant of Venice, Acts I. III. and IV., ...Shakespeare.
Selections from Henry Eighth and Julius Cæsar,...........Shakespeare.
Selections from Richard II. and Henry IV., Part II., ...Shakespeare.
Essays (selections from),...Bacon.
L'Allegro & Il Penseroso,...Milton.
The Deserted Village,......Goldsmith.
The Traveller, ...Goldsmith.
Cotter's Saturday Night, &c., Burns.
Prophecy of Dante, Cantos I. II., Byron.
The Prisoner of Chillon,....Byron.
Fire Worshippers, Parts I. II., Moore.
The Ancient Mariner,.......Coleridge.
The Lady of the Lake, Canto I., The Chase,..................Scott.
The Lady of the Lake, Canto V., The Combat,..................Scott.
Marmion, Canto VI.,........Scott.
Lay of the Last Minstrel, Canto I., Scott.
The Village,................Crabbe.
The Pleasures of Hope, Pt. I., Campbell.
The Queen's Wake, ...Hogg.
The Elegy—Ode on Eton College—The Bard,.................Gray.
The Lay of Horatius, ...Macaulay.
The Armada, &c.,..........Macaulay.
Essay on Bunyan,..........Macaulay.

Evangeline (64 pp., paper, 3d.; cloth, 4d.),..Longfellow.

With ADDITIONAL ETYMOLOGIES. 40 pp., paper cover, 3d. each.

The Prisoner of Chillon.   Lay of the Last Minstrel.   Marmion.

"Thoroughly adapted for schools in which English literature forms a branch of study, or where a portion of some English classic is selected for examination."—**Schoolmaster.**

Adopted by the London and other principal School Boards, and by the National Board of Education in Ireland.

VERE FOSTER'S WRITING COPY-BOOKS.
ORIGINAL SERIES.

The special features which preferentially distinguish Mr. VERE FOSTER'S WRITING COPY-BOOKS are as follows:—

(1) The more faithful imitation of natural writing.

(2) The combination in the greatest possible degree of legibility with rapidity of execution. The formation of all the letters, and notably of the letters *a, d, g, q,* is adapted to this end.

(3) The writing of each word continuously from end to end, with the sole exception of the letter *x*.

(4) The tailed letters of moderate length.

(5) The systematically progressive arrangement and variety of headlines—two lines on each page.

(6) Traced lines under each copy, to be written over (in Book 1).

(7) Guide lines to regulate the length of tailed letters (in Books 1½ to 6).

(8) The same clear style of writing for both sexes—*there being no reason why girls should be taught a cramped illegible hand.*

*** In the regulation recently issued to H.M. Inspectors from the Education Office it is stated that "in Standard IV. and those above it writing should be running, free, and symmetrical, as well as legible and clear." No better terms could be found to describe the writing secured by the use of these Copy-books.

Superior Edition, 2*d.* each number.   Popular Edition, 1*d.* each number.

Contents of the Numbers.

1. Strokes, Letters, Short Words.	10.* Plain and Ornamental Lettering.
1½, 2. Long Letters, Short Words, Figures.	11. Exercise Book.—Wide Ruling.
	11½. Exercise Book.—8vo size. Price 1*d.*
2½. Words of Four, Five, or Six Letters.	12. Exercise Book.—Ruled in Squares.
3. Capitals, Short Words, Figures.	12½. Exercise Book.—8vo size. Price 1*d.*
3½, 4. Sentences of Short Words.	13.* Exercise Book.—For Book-keeping.
4½. Quotations from Shakespeare.	14.* Essay Book.—Ruled for Composition.
5, 6. Sentences.—Maxims, Morals, &c.	15.* Exercise Book for Beginners.—Ruled for Small Text.
5½.* Sentences, in Writing of Three Sizes.	16.* Civil Service or Official Style. Medium Hand.
6½.* Sentences, in Writing of Two Sizes.	17.* Civil Service or Official Style. Small Hand.
7. Sentences and Christian Names.	
8.* Sentences.—One Line on each Page.	X. Copy-Book Protector and Blotter.
9.* Sentences.—Two Lines on each Page.	Keeping the Books clean. Price 1*d.*

* Not in Popular Edition.

"More progress is made by Vere Foster's than by any other method which has come under my notice."—Mr. M'CALLUM, H.M. INSPECTOR.

"I know no series by means of which children can be so quickly taught to write with freedom and legibility."—Mr. NEWELL, H.M. INSPECTOR.

VERE FOSTER'S WRITING COPY-BOOKS.
BOLD WRITING SERIES.
UPRIGHT, BOLD, AND LEGIBLE.

This Series has been prepared by Mr. VERE FOSTER in conformity with the Code, and is specially adapted to meet the views of those Inspectors and Teachers who prefer Large and Text Hand, and a more bold, round, and upright style than that of the Original Series.

The principle adopted in the construction of the letters is precisely the same as in Vere Foster's Original Series. The writing is continuous; each word being written from end to end without lifting the pen; but the loops are still shorter than in the Original Series. By means of this series a legible and rapid style of handwriting is certain to be formed.

NOW READY, PRICE TWOPENCE EACH NUMBER.

1. **Large Hand** (3/8 inch ruling). Strokes, Short Letters, Easy Words.
2. **Half Text Hand** (1/4 inch ruling). Easy Words of Short and Long Letters. Figures.
3. **Half Text Hand** (1/4 inch ruling). Short Words of Five or Six Letters. Figures.
4. **Large and Half Text Hand.** Sentences of Short Words. (*For Inspection, Standards I. and II.*)
5. **Half Text Hand.** Proper Nouns with Capitals. Figures.
6. **Half Text Hand.** Sentences of Short Words. Figures.
7. **Large Round Hand.** Sentences with several Capitals. Figures.
8. **Medium Round Hand.** Sentences with one Capital.
9. **Small Round Hand.** Sentences with several Capitals.
10. **Small Round Hand.** Sentences with one Capital.
11. **Large, Half Text, & Small Hand.** Capitals, Figures, Sentences. (*For Inspection, Standard III.*)
12. **Small Hand.** Select Quotations from Shakespeare. Figures.
13. **Small Hand.** Topographical—Important Towns in the United Kingdom.
14. **Small Hand.** Historical—Events in the History of the United Kingdom.
15. **Small Hand.** Biographical—Eminent Natives of the United Kingdom.
16 and 17. **Small Hand.** (Two Sizes.) Civil Service Writing.

PALMERSTON SERIES.
In Eleven Numbers. Price Threepence Each.

These books resemble the Original Series, but are printed on Superior Paper, and neatly ruled with Red and Blue lines. They were designed by Mr. VERE FOSTER, to carry out the principles of clear and legible handwriting, as laid down by the late LORD PALMERSTON FOR THE CIVIL SERVICE. The writing is such as will impart a simple, rapid, and elegant style for general correspondence.

Contents of the Series.

1. Strokes, Easy Letters, Short Words.
2. Short and Long Letters, Easy Words, Figures.
3. Capitals, Short Words, Figures.
4, 5. Sentences of Short Words (Proverbs, Maxims, Precepts).
6, 7, 8, 9, 10. Sentences (Wise Sayings, Quotations, Aphorisms).
11. Plain and Ornamental Lettering. The most perfect collection yet published—comprising Thirty-three different Alphabets.

VERE FOSTER'S WRITING CHARTS FOR CLASS TEACHING.

Two sheets showing the Shapes and Proportions of Letters as adopted in Vere Foster's Series of Writing Copy-Books. *Size 25 × 20 inches.*
Price in Sheets, 1s. per pair; Mounted on Millboard, 1s. 6d.

VERE FOSTER'S IMPROVED HAT INK-WELLS.

The "HAT" INK-WELL (stoneware) is suitable for either School Desk or Private Table. It will fit into various sized holes *in* School Desks without falling through. It will stand steadily *on* desk or table. It will economize ink. It can be easily stopped with an ordinary cork. It is neat in appearance, very strong, and very cheap. Price 1s. per dozen.

NATIONAL COMPETITION IN WRITING AND DRAWING.

MR. VERE FOSTER has awarded prizes for Writing and Drawing for many years. 4874 Prizes, in sums of from 5s. to £5, have been already distributed, amounting to over £2200. List of prize-takers for present year and scheme for the Eighteenth Annual Competition, 1888, will be sent post free on application to Mr. VERE FOSTER, Belfast, or to the Publishers.

ARITHMETIC, &c.

THE COMPREHENSIVE STANDARD ARITHMETICS.

These arithmetics are the work of one of Her Majesty's Inspector's Assistants, who has a practical knowledge of the prevalent causes of failure in this subject.

They are quite up to date. The book for Standard V. *begins* with easy lessons in Fractions; the "unity method" is taught in that book, and is used throughout the higher rules where possible.

They are graded in separate sets to meet the requirements of the English and Scotch Codes.

>   Standard I.— 32 pp., paper, 1½d.; cloth, 2½d.
>   Standard II.— 32 pp., ,,   1½d.; ,,   2½d.
>   Standard III.— 32 pp., ,,   1½d.; ,,   2½d.
>   Standard IV.— 48 pp., ,,   2d.; ,,   3d.
>   Standard V.— 64 pp., ,,   3d.; ,,   4d.
>   Standard VI.— 64 pp., ,,   3d.; ,,   4d.
>   Standard VII.— 64 pp., ,,   3d.; ,,   4d.

Standards VI.–VII. together: reduced to the exact requirements of the Code.—64 pp., paper, 3d.; cloth, 4d.

ANSWERS to each part, 3d.; or complete ANSWERS, cloth, 1s. 6d.

CLARKSON'S TEST-CARDS. A series of Arithmetical Test-cards. By A. J. CLARKSON. For Standards II. to VII. Each 1s. per packet in cloth case.

"A thoroughly good set of Test-cards. Excellent results *must* accrue from an intelligent use of the set."—**Schoolmaster.**

ARITHMETIC—*Continued.*

BLACKIE'S ARITHMETICAL TEST QUESTIONS. Standards II. to VII. Each 16 pp., crown 8vo, stitched, 1*d.* Answers, 3*d.*

These Test Questions consist of Clarkson's Test Cards printed in book form.

THE STANHOPE ARITHMETICAL TEST-CARDS. For boys and girls. Code 1886. For Standards III. to VII. Each 1*s.* per packet in cloth case.

Each card contains *two* tests, one on each side, varying in style and difficulty, and printed in distinct colours. On one side is a fair average test for *Girls;* on the reverse a more difficult one for *Boys.*

THE WHITEHALL ARITHMETICAL TEST-CARDS. For Standards III. IV. V. VI. and VII. Each 1*s.* per packet in cloth case.

A COMPLETE ARITHMETIC. For the Higher Standards and Pupil-teachers. With Answers, 234 pages, 1*s.* 6*d.* Exercises only, 192 pages, 1*s.* Answers only, in limp cloth, 6*d.*

"Prepared by one who has the science of Arithmetic well in hand. The explanations are brief but to the point, and are given in such a familiar chatty style that what has often been 'dry bones' becomes full of life and attractions."—**Schoolmaster.**

MENTAL ARITHMETIC; Consisting mainly of Problems designed specially to give the power of ready solution. Cloth, 6*d.*

"The exercises are original, carefully graduated, and will be of great use to pupil-teachers and others preparing for government examinations."—**Teacher.**

THE PUPIL'S MENTAL ARITHMETIC. (Addition—Interest.) Stitched, 2*d.*; cloth, 3*d.* Answers, 3*d.*

"The exercises are many and well prepared. We can heartily commend this book for use in class."—**Schoolmaster.**

THE YOUNG CALCULATOR; A series of Arithmetical Tablets for the First Standard. By Henry J. Thomas, C.M. Packet, 1*s.*

A PRACTICAL ARITHMETIC on an entirely new method, for Schools, Colleges, and Candidates preparing for Matriculation, Civil Service, Excise, University, Local, and other Examinations. By John Jackson. Second Edition, 416 pp., foolscap 8vo, cloth, 4*s.*

"This excellent manual eminently merits its title of *practical.* We say with confidence that the work is well adapted for boys preparing for a mercantile career."—**The Academy.**

A PRACTICAL TREATISE ON BOOK-KEEPING BY DOUBLE-ENTRY, for the use of Schools and for Self-instruction. With concise methods for Commercial Calculations. By David Tolmie, Accountant. 64 pp., crown 8vo, cloth, 1*s.* Key, 2*s.* 6*d.*

"A sensible practical work. Every important principle of book-keeping is elucidated."—**Teacher's Aid.**

ARITHMETIC—*Continued.*

EXAMINATION ARITHMETIC; Containing 1200 Arithmetical Problems and Exercises (with Answers), selected from Oxford and Cambridge Local Examination Papers, &c. Classified by T. S. HARVEY, F.S.Sc.Lond. Cloth, 2s.

"We have no hesitation in saying that of all the examination arithmetics which have come under our notice this is by far the best. It reveals on almost every page the hand of the practised craftsman."—**Practical Teacher.**

KEY TO ABOVE. The Problems fully worked out. Cloth, 4s. 6d.

HISTORY.

OUTLINES OF THE WORLD'S HISTORY, ANCIENT, MEDIÆVAL, and MODERN, with special relation to the History of Civilization and the Progress of Mankind. By EDGAR SANDERSON, M.A., late Scholar of Clare College, Cambridge. With many Illustrations and Eight Coloured Maps. 664 pp., crown 8vo, cloth, red edges, 6s. 6d.

"Surpasses most of its predecessors in usefulness, because it lays more stress on the contributions made by the chief peoples of the world to the common stock of civilization, than on the deeds of kings, and queens, and statesmen."—**Westminster Review.**

A HISTORY OF THE BRITISH EMPIRE. With Pictorial Illustrations, Genealogical Tables, Maps, and Plans. By EDGAR SANDERSON, M.A. 444 pp., cloth, 2s. 6d.; or in Two Parts, 1s. 6d. each.

"It is not a mere collection of dry facts, but is a spirited outline, well designed and faithfully executed. . . . It is a thoroughly good book."—**Schoolmaster.**

HISTORY TEXT-BOOKS. SCOTCH CODE.

 Standard III.—48 pages. 2d. paper cover; 3d. cloth limp.
  History and Geography combined. Cloth limp, 6d.
 Standard IV.—64 pages. 3d. paper cover; 4d. cloth limp.
  History and Geography combined. Cloth limp, 7d.
 Standard V.—80 pages. 4d. paper cover; 5d. cloth limp.
  History and Geography combined. Cloth boards, 9d.
 Standard VI.—80 pages. 4d. paper cover; 5d. cloth limp.
  History and Geography combined. Cloth boards, 9d.

HISTORICAL READERS. See page 8.

HISTORY AND GEOGRAPHY READERS, for the Scotch Code. See page 9.

OUTLINES OF THE HISTORY OF ENGLAND from Early Times to the Present Day. By GEORGE GIRLING. PROFUSELY ILLUSTRATED. 454 pp., cloth, red edges, 2s. 6d.

"For the upper Standards of schools and junior pupil-teachers this book appears to us to be unrivalled."—**Schoolmistress.**

HISTORY—*Continued.*

OUTLINES OF BRITISH HISTORY from the Accession of James I. to the Death of George III. 96 pp., cloth limp, 7*d.*

HISTORY OF SCOTLAND to the Union of the Crowns. By ALEXANDER WHAMOND, F.E.I.S. With Map, cloth, 1*s.*

SHORT HISTORY OF SCOTLAND. For Junior Classes, with Illustrative Readings from Standard Authors. 128 pp., cloth limp, 9*d.*

A SYNOPSIS OF ENGLISH HISTORY: OR, HISTORICAL NOTE BOOK. For the use of Pupil-Teachers, Students, &c. Compiled by HERBERT WILLS. 144 pp., crown 8vo, cloth, 2*s.*

"An excellent abstract of the memory work of history: well designed and ably executed. We can recommend it with the greatest confidence."—**Schoolmaster.**

A SYNOPSIS OF SCOTTISH HISTORY: OR, HISTORICAL NOTE BOOK. For the use of Students and Teachers. Compiled by HERBERT WILLS. 154 pp., crown 8vo, cloth, 2*s.*

"The arrangement of the book is admirable, and the amount of information amazing. The student will find it an invaluable companion."—**Glasgow Herald.**

AN EPITOME OF HISTORY, ANCIENT, MEDIÆVAL, AND MODERN. For Higher Schools, Colleges, and Private Study. By CARL PLOETZ. Translated by W. H. TILLINGHAST. 630 pp., post 8vo, cloth, 7*s.* 6*d.*

"In the excellence of its arrangement, as well as the fulness and general accuracy of its details, the work is almost unique."—**The Times.**

"We can imagine nothing better. We recommend it in the strongest terms to all our colleges and middle-class schools."—**Liverpool Mercury.**

SCRIPTURE.

SCRIPTURE BIOGRAPHY AND ITS TEACHINGS. For the use of Sunday-school Teachers and other Religious Instructors. By JOSEPH HASSELL, A.K.C. Lond. Crown 8vo, cloth, 2*s.* 6*d.*

"Will be pronounced by teachers and parents best able to judge the best book of the kind that has yet come into their hands."—**Christian Leader.**

COMMENTARIES FOR BIBLE-CLASSES. By Professor T. M. LINDSAY, D.D., Free Church College, Glasgow. With Maps and Notes. Each, paper cover, 4*d.*; cloth boards, 7*d.*

  The Gospel according to St. Mark.
  The Acts of the Apostles. CHAP. I. to XII.
  The Acts of the Apostles. CHAP. XIII. to XXVIII.
  The Gospel according to St. Luke. CHAP. I. to XII.
  The Gospel according to St. Luke. CHAP. XIII. to XXIV.

GEOGRAPHY.

GEOGRAPHICAL READERS. See page 6.

HISTORY AND GEOGRAPHY READERS. SCOTCH CODE. See page 9.

INTRODUCTORY GEOGRAPHY. By W. G. BAKER, B.A. With 70 Illustrations, and a Coloured Map. 128 pp., f'cap 8vo, cloth, 1s.

ELEMENTARY GEOGRAPHY. By W. G. BAKER, B.A.
    Part I. Elementary Notions of Geography.   Paper, 2d.; cloth, 3d.
    Part II. England and Wales. Two Coloured Maps.   „ 4d.; „ 5d.
    Part III. Scotland, Ireland, and the Colonies.   „ 6d.; „ 8d.

PHYSICAL GEOGRAPHY. An Elementary Treatise, for use in Public Schools. Illustrated. Cloth limp, 4d.

A PRONOUNCING VOCABULARY OF MODERN GEOGRAPHICAL NAMES, nearly ten thousand in number; with Notes on Spelling and Pronunciation, and explanatory Lists of Foreign Words. By GEORGE G. CHISHOLM, M.A., B.Sc. F'cap 8vo, cloth, 1s. 6d.

GEOGRAPHICAL TEXT-BOOKS. SCOTCH CODE. By W. G. BAKER, B.A.

    No. I. Standard III.—Geographical Terms, with Geography of Scotland. With Illustrations and Coloured Map. 48 pages. 2½d. paper cover; 3½d. cloth limp.
    No. II. Standard IV.—The British Isles, with Illustrations and Coloured Map. 64 pages. 3d. paper cover; 4d. cloth limp.
    No. III. Standard V.—Europe: with British North America and Australasia. With Coloured Map. 64 pages. 3d. paper cover; 4d. cloth limp.
    No. IV. Standard VI.—The World, specially British Colonies and Dependencies. Productions, &c. Coloured Map. 64 pages. 3d. paper cover; 4d. cloth limp.

    For History and Geography combined see page 17.

AUSTRALASIA; a Descriptive and Pictorial Account of the Australian and New Zealand Colonies, Tasmania and the adjacent lands. By W. WILKINS, late Under-secretary for Public Instruction in New South Wales. Fully illustrated with Woodcuts and Maps. Crown 8vo, cloth, 2s. 6d.

THE REALISTIC TEACHING OF GEOGRAPHY: Its Principles, especially in regard to Initiatory Notions; the correction of prevalent errors; and examples of simple demonstrative and dramatic methods. By WILLIAM JOLLY, F.R.S.E., F.G.S. Crown 8vo, cloth, 1s.

GRAMMAR.

ELEMENTARY ENGLISH GRAMMAR.

One of the distinctive features of this Grammar is that the pupil is trained from the first to place his work out by Analysis, before beginning to parse, and thus many difficulties in parsing are at once cleared away. Apt exercises follow every lesson, while at the end of each book further exercises are provided. In Standards V. and VI.-VII. Composition and Derivation are thoroughly dealt with.

    STANDARDS II. and III. in paper covers, each 1*d*.; cloth, 2*d*.
    STANDARDS IV. and V. in paper, each, 2*d*.; cloth, 3*d*.
    STANDARD VI.-VII. paper, 3*d*.; cloth, 4*d*.

Also in Two Divisions.

    DIVISION I. comprising Standards II. III. IV., limp cloth, 6*d*.
    DIVISION II.   ,,   ,,   V., VI.-VII., ,, 6*d*.

"Admirably conceived, and well carried out. Grammar has never been dealt with more intelligently than in these little books." —**School Board Chronicle.**

"The type is clear, the exercises are very numerous, and the supplementary lessons on the derivation of words unusually good." —**School Guardian.**

COMPLETE ENGLISH GRAMMAR AND ANALYSIS. 180 pp., cloth boards, 1*s*.

ELEMENTARY MANUAL OF ENGLISH ETYMOLOGY. Paper cover, 2*d*.; cloth, 3*d*.

TEST-CARDS IN GRAMMAR AND ANALYSIS. Based on the Complete English Grammar for Standards II. to VI. Each packet, 9*d*.

COMPENDIOUS ENGLISH GRAMMAR. For Intermediate and Higher Schools and Pupil-teachers. 192 pp., cloth, 1*s*. 6*d*.

"A clear, simple, sensible elementary grammar, adapted for the use of the higher forms in middle-class schools."—**Journal of Education.**

THE ENGLISH LANGUAGE AND LITERATURE: An outline for Schools, Pupil-teachers, and Students. By DAVID CAMPBELL. 72 pp., f'cap 8vo, cloth limp, 6*d*.; cloth boards, 9*d*.

"For a beginner this is a capital little book."—**Teachers' Aid.**

HAND-BOOK OF ENGLISH COMPOSITION EXERCISES. Comprising Short Stories, Subjects and Hints for Essays, Rules and Models for Letters, &c. Foolscap, cloth, 1*s*.

"This book is a decided boon; and teachers will find that while lightening their work, it improves the results."—**Educational News.**

STORIES AND ESSAYS: A Series of Exercises in English Composition. Carefully arranged and graduated Stories for Exercises, and a number of classified Examples for Essays. F'cap, cloth, 1*s*.

TEXT-BOOKS for the SPECIFIC SUBJECTS.

Adapted to meet the Code requirements.

ANIMAL PHYSIOLOGY. By VINCENT T. MURCHÉ.

    The author of these books has kept simplicity always before him, and as far as possible no difficult terms or lengthy sentences have been employed. At the same time nothing is omitted which could help the student to a satisfactory result. Instead of reference letters, the diagrams have the names printed in red on the actual parts. These diagrams and the coloured plates are found to be of such assistance in teaching, that often where *Huxley* or *Carpenter* is used as a Text-book the teachers supplement them with these little manuals.

    Book   I.—First Year's Course. Paper, 4*d.*; cloth, 5*d.*
    Book II.—Second Year's Course. Paper, 5*d.*; cloth, 6*d.*
    Book III.—Third Year's Course. Paper, 5*d.*; cloth, 6*d.*

    Also in one volume, 144 pp., cloth boards, 1*s.* 6*d.*

"The get-up of this book leaves nothing to be desired; it is certainly one of the best on the subject, and shows the hand of a practical teacher. The diagrams are simply perfect, both as to simplicity and execution."—**Schoolmaster.**

PRINCIPLES OF AGRICULTURE.

    Book   I.—First Year. Paper, 3*d.*; cloth, 4*d.*
    Book II.—Second Year. Paper, 3*d.*; cloth, 4*d.*
    Book III.—Third Year. Paper, 3*d.*; cloth, 4*d.*

    Also in one volume, 144 pp., cloth boards, 1*s.*

"An admirably prepared little book. The information is full without being superabundant; it is accurate without being too technical; it is practical as well as theoretical. The illustrations are remarkably well executed."—**Educational News.**

BOTANY. By VINCENT T. MURCHÉ.

    Book   I.—First Year. Paper, 3*d.*; cloth, 4*d.*
    Book II.—Second Year. Paper, 3*d.*; cloth, 4*d.*
    Book III.—Third Year. Paper, 3*d.*; cloth, 4*d.*

    Also in one volume, 144 pp., cloth boards, 1*s.*

"We cordially recommend this little work, which hits the requirements of the Code better than any we have yet seen. The illustrations are all that could be wished, and, best of all, technicalities are reduced *almost* to a minimum."—**Schoolmaster.**

MAGNETISM AND ELECTRICITY. By W. G. BAKER, B.A.

    Part   I.—Magnetism. Paper, 3*d.*; cloth, 4*d.*
    Part II.—Frictional Electricity. Paper, 3*d.*; cloth, 4*d.*
    Part III.—Voltaic Electricity. Paper, 3*d.*; cloth, 4*d.*

    Also in one volume. 144 pp., cloth boards, 1*s.*

"The writer is evidently a practical electrician. The experiments are carefully chosen, carefully described, and best of all carefully gradated."—**Prac. Teacher.**

TEXT-BOOKS, &c.—*Continued.*

ALGEBRA.
    Book   I.—Notation to Division. Paper, 3*d.*; cloth, 4*d.*
    Book II.—Simple Equations, &c. Paper, 3*d.*; cloth, 4*d.*
    Book III.—Easy Quadratic Equations, &c. Paper, 3*d.*; cloth, 4*d.*
                 ANSWERS TO EACH PART, 3*d.*

Also in one volume, with ANSWERS. 240 pp., cloth boards, 2*s.*

DOMESTIC ECONOMY. By E. RICE, Late Lecturer on Domestic Economy at Cheltenham Training College for Mistresses.
    Part   I.—Food. Clothing, &c. Paper, 3*d.*; cloth, 4*d.*
    Part II.—Food. The Dwelling. Paper, 3*d.*; cloth, 4*d.*
    Part III.—Food. Rules for Health. Paper, 3*d.*; cloth, 4*d.*

Also in one volume, with SUPPLEMENT for Pupil-teachers, Students, &c. 232 pp., cloth boards, 1*s.* 6*d.*

"A book whose only fault is that it is too good. No abler or better guide can be found than this work."—**Educ. News.**
"This is one of the best *practical* books on Domestic Economy that we have seen. Nothing could be clearer or more sensible than her descriptions of the work of a household."—**Practical Teacher.**

PRACTICAL FRENCH GRAMMAR. By C. O. SONNTAG.
    Part   I.—First Year's Course. Paper, 4*d.*; cloth, 5*d.*
    Part II.—Second Year's Course. Paper, 4*d.*; cloth, 5*d.*
    Part III.—Third Year's Course. Paper, 4*d.*; cloth, 5*d.*

"Practical, well arranged, and thoroughly reliable. It seems to us just the thing for elementary school work."—**Schoolmaster.**

OBJECT LESSONS.

COMMON THINGS AND ELEMENTARY SCIENCE, in the form of Object Lessons. By JOSEPH HASSELL, F.S.Sc.Lond. With 200 Illustrations. Sixth Edition. 384 pp., crown 8vo, cloth, 3*s.* 6*d.*

"A most complete hand-book of object lessons: well arranged, fully illustrated, and accompanied by valuable hints as to method. Every page impresses the reader with the very thorough treatment the various topics have received."—**Prac. Teacher.**

LATIN.

DR. BURNS'S PRAXIS PRIMARIA. Progressive Exercises in Writing Latin, with Notes on Syntax, on Idiomatic Differences, and on Latin Style. Seventh Edition. F'cap 8vo, cloth, 2*s.* KEY, 3*s.* 6*d.*

BLACKIE'S SCIENCE TEXT-BOOKS.

EARTH-KNOWLEDGE: A Text-Book of Elementary Physiography. By W. JEROME HARRISON, F.G.S., Author of "The Geology of the Counties of England and Wales;" and H. ROWLAND WAKEFIELD, Science Demonstrators for the Birmingham School Board. Adapted to the Syllabus of the South Kensington Science Department, Elementary Stage. F'cap 8vo, cloth, 1s. 6d. Part II., 2s.

"The style is clear and concise, and the matter up to date. The hand of the practical teacher is seen throughout. It will prove an invaluable aid to science classes, and be especially useful to private students."—**Teachers' Aid.**

AN ELEMENTARY TEXT-BOOK OF DYNAMICS AND HYDROSTATICS. By R. H. PINKERTON, B.A., Assistant Lecturer on Mathematics at the University College of South Wales and Monmouthshire. Adapted to the requirements of the Science and Art Examinations in Theoretical Mechanics. F'cap 8vo, cloth, 3s. 6d.

"The fundamental units are thoroughly well explained, and, which is saying a great deal, they are used consistently throughout. From a mathematical point of view, the book leaves nothing to be desired."—**Nature.**

AN ELEMENTARY TEXT-BOOK OF PHYSIOLOGY. By J. M'GREGOR-ROBERTSON, M.A., M.B., Author of "The Elements of Physiological Physics;" Senior Assistant in the Physiological Department, Glasgow University, &c. Adapted to the Syllabus of the South Kensington Science Department. Illustrated with Engravings in the text and a large Anatomical Plate. F'cap 8vo, cloth, 4s.

"A good system of arrangement and clear expressive exposition distinguish this book. The definitions of terms are remarkably lucid and exact, a matter of the highest importance in a work of this kind. The woodcuts and explanatory diagrams are numerous and good."—**Saturday Review.**

ANIMAL PHYSIOLOGY. By VINCENT T. MURCHÉ, Head-master of Boundary Lane School, Camberwell, London. With Text Engravings and Coloured Illustrations. 144 pp., f'cap 8vo, cloth, 1s. 6d.

"The get-up of this book leaves nothing to be desired; it is certainly one of the best on the subject, and shows the hand of a practical teacher. The diagrams are simply perfect, both as to simplicity and execution."—**Schoolmaster.**

MAGNETISM AND ELECTRICITY. By W. G. BAKER, B.A., Lecturer at Cheltenham Training College. 144 pp., f'cap 8vo, 1s.

"The writer is evidently a practical electrician. The experiments are carefully chosen, carefully described, and carefully gradated."—**Practical Teacher.**

SCIENCE TEXT-BOOKS—*Continued.*

DESCHANEL'S NATURAL PHILOSOPHY. An ELEMENTARY TREATISE. By Professor A. PRIVAT DESCHANEL, of Paris. Translated and Edited by Professor J. D. EVERETT, D.C.L., F.R.S. 9th Edition, revised throughout, and brought up to the present time. Illustrated by 783 Engravings on wood, and 3 Coloured Plates. Medium 8vo, cloth, 18s.; also in Parts, limp cloth, 4s. 6d. each.

    Part I.—Mechanics Hydrostatics, &c.
    Part II.—Heat.
    Part III.—Electricity and Magnetism.
    Part IV.—Sound and Light.

"Systematically arranged, clearly written, and admirably illustrated, 'Deschanel' forms a model work for a class in experimental physics."—**Saturday Review.**

OUTLINES OF NATURAL PHILOSOPHY FOR SCHOOLS. By J. D. EVERETT, D.C.L., F.R.S., Professor of Natural Philosophy in Queen's College, Belfast. With 216 Woodcuts. F'cap 8vo, cloth, 4s.

"A book of great merit; it possesses all the systematic arrangement and lucidity of the author's former publications."—**Athenæum.**

ELEMENTARY TEXT-BOOK OF PHYSICS. By Prof. EVERETT, D.C.L., F.R.S. Illustrated by many Woodcuts. Fourth Edition. Foolscap 8vo, cloth, 3s. 6d.

"After a careful examination we must pronounce this work unexceptionable, both in the matter and the manner of its teachings."—**Journal of Science.**

MATHEMATICS.

EUCLID'S ELEMENTS OF GEOMETRY; with Notes, Examples, and Exercises. Arranged by A. E. LAYNG, M.A., Headmaster of Stafford Grammar School; formerly Scholar of Sidney Sussex College, Cambridge. BOOK I. Crown 8vo, cloth, 1s.

BOOK II., 6d. BOOK III., 1s. *The other Books to follow.*

In this edition of Euclid a system of arrangement has been adopted whereby the enunciation, figure, and proof of each proposition are all in view together, while the Notes and Exercises are directly appended to the propositions to which they refer.

"A thoroughly workmanlike little text-book, which has our heartiest commendation."—**Teachers' Aid.**

ALGEBRA, UP TO AND INCLUDING PROGRESSIONS AND SCALES OF NOTATION. For Schools, Science Classes, Pupil-Teachers, Students, &c. By J. G. KERR, M.A. F'cap 8vo, cloth, 2s. 6d.

"A well-arranged, clear, and useful little book."—**Athenæum.**

Blackie & Son's Educational List.

MATHEMATICS—*Continued.*

ELEMENTARY TEXT-BOOK OF TRIGONOMETRY. By R. H. PINKERTON, B.A. Foolscap 8vo, cloth, 1s. 6d.

"An excellent elementary text-book. The exposition and demonstration of principles are remarkable for clearness and fulness. . . . A prominent and valuable feature of the book is the abundance of practical examples."—**Athenæum.**

ELEMENTARY TEXT-BOOK OF DYNAMICS AND HYDROSTATICS. Adapted to the requirements of the Science and Art Examinations in Theoretical Mechanics. By R. H. PINKERTON, B.A. F'cap 8vo, cloth, 3s. 6d.

BLACKIE'S ELEMENTARY ALGEBRA. From Notation to Easy Quadratic Equations. Cloth, 1s. 6d. With Answers, cloth, 2s.

"A very good book indeed: the examples are numerous and the explanations clear."—**Schoolmaster.**

ALGEBRAIC FACTORS. HOW TO FIND THEM AND HOW TO USE THEM. By Dr. W. T. KNIGHT, F.S.Sc.Lond. Cloth, 1s. 6d.

"This book will prove invaluable to young students."—**School Guardian.**

MATHEMATICAL WRINKLES for Matriculation and other Exams. Consisting of Six Sets of London Matriculation Papers in Mathematics, with full Solutions. By Dr. W. T. KNIGHT, F.S.Sc.Lond. F'cap 8vo, cloth, 2s. 6d.

"The work is thoroughly done, and the result is a book likely to be very serviceable to students."—**Academy.**

AN INTRODUCTION TO THE DIFFERENTIAL AND INTEGRAL CALCULUS. With examples of applications to Mechanical Problems. By W. J. MILLAR, C.E. Cloth, 1s. 6d.

"It is clearly written and the examples are well chosen."—**Nature.**

ELEMENTARY MENSURATION, LINES, SURFACES, AND SOLIDS. With numerous Exercises. By J. MARTIN. F'cap 8vo, cloth, 10d.

"A valuable manual of Mensuration. The rules are plain, the illustrations simple, and the exercises numerous and varied."—**Educational News.**

A PRACTICAL ARITHMETIC on an entirely new method, for Schools, Colleges, and Candidates preparing for Examinations. By JOHN JACKSON. Second Edition. F'cap 8vo, cloth, 4s.

"We say with confidence that the work is well adapted for boys preparing for a mercantile career."—**The Academy.**

EXAMINATION ARITHMETIC; Containing 1200 Arithmetical Problems and Exercises (with Answers), selected from Oxford and Cambridge Local Examination Papers, &c. Classified by T. S. HARVEY, F.S.Sc.Lond. Cloth, 2s. Key, 4s. 6d.

"We have no hesitation in saying that of all the examination arithmetics which have come under our notice this is by far the best."—**Practical Teacher.**

BOOKS FOR TEACHERS.

THE COMPREHENSIVE EXAMINER: A Hand-book for Teachers and Students. Being a full set of Questions on the principal subjects prescribed in the Code. By DAVID CLARK. 320 pp., cr. 8vo, cloth, 3s.

"To teachers desirous of testing their classes by an independent and reliable standard, while saving their time and labour, this useful work will prove highly acceptable."—Schoolmaster.

WHAT AND HOW: A Guide to Successful Oral Teaching. By JOSEPH HASSELL, F.S.Sc.Lond. F'cap 8vo, cloth, 1s.

"Should find a place in every teacher's library."—Educational News.

THE PRINCIPLES AND PRACTICE OF TEACHING. A Manual of Method for Assistant Masters and Mistresses and Pupil-Teachers. By A. PARK, F.R.G.S. Interleaved with ruled paper. Fifth Edition. F'cap 8vo, cloth, 3s.

CONTRIBUTIONS TO THE SCIENCE OF EDUCATION. By WILLIAM H. PAYNE, A.M. Crown 8vo, cloth, 6s.

MANUAL TRAINING. The Solution of Social and Industrial Problems. By CHARLES H. HAM. Illustrated. Crown 8vo, cloth, 6s.

"We commend Mr. Ham's book to every teacher, and especially to young teachers."—Teacher's Aid.

DICTIONARIES.

ANNANDALE'S CONCISE ENGLISH DICTIONARY. A Concise Dictionary of the English Language, Literary, Scientific, Etymological, and Pronouncing. Based on Ogilvie's Imperial Dictionary. By CHARLES ANNANDALE, M.A., LL.D. 832 pp., foolscap 4to, cloth, 10s. 6d.; half-morocco, 15s.

"The *Concise Dictionary* stands first—and by a long interval—among all the one-volume English Dictionaries hitherto published."—The Academy.
"We do not hesitate a moment to bestow upon the *Concise Dictionary* our very highest praise. It forms in truth a priceless treasury of valuable information. Every teacher should possess a copy."—Practical Teacher.

THE STUDENT'S ENGLISH DICTIONARY, ETYMOLOGICAL, PRONOUNCING, and EXPLANATORY. By JOHN OGILVIE, LL.D. For the use of Colleges and Advanced Schools. Illustrated by 300 Engravings on wood. Imp. 16mo, Roxburgh, 7s. 6d.; half-calf, 10s. 6d.

"This is the best Etymological Dictionary we have yet seen at all within moderate compass."—Spectator.

DR. OGILVIE'S SMALLER ENGLISH DICTIONARY, for the Use of Schools. Abridged by the Author from the "Student's Dictionary." Imp. 16mo, cloth, red edges, 2s. 6d.; Roxburgh, 3s. 6d.

"We know no Dictionary so suited for school use as this."—Brit. Quarterly Review.

Approved by the Science and Art department, South Kensington.

VERE FOSTER'S DRAWING COPY-BOOKS.

With Instructions and paper to draw on. SUPERIOR EDITION, in Numbers at 2*d*. POPULAR EDITION (a selection), at 1*d*. COMPLETE EDITION, in Twelve Parts, at 9*d*. (Each part complete in itself.)

Nos. **Part I.—ELEMENTARY.**
A 1 Initiatory Lessons.
A 2 Letters and Numerals.
B 1 Familiar Objects (Straight Lines).
B 2 Domestic Objects (Simple).

Part II.—OBJECTS.
C 1 Domestic Objects (Flat).
C 2 Domestic Objects (Perspective).
D 1 Leaves (Flat).
D 2 Leaves (Natural).

Part III.—PLANTS.
E 1 Plants (Simple Forms).
E 2 Plants (More Complex Forms).
G 1 Flowers (Simple Forms).
G 2 Flowers (More Complex Forms).

Part IV.—ORNAMENT.
I 1 Elementary Forms.
I 2 Simple Forms (Fretwork, Ironwork, &c.).
I 3 Advanced (Carving, Sculpture, &c.).
I 4 Ornament (Classic, Renaissance, &c.).

Part V.—TREES.
J 1 Oak, Fir, &c., with "touch" for each tree.
J 2 Beech, Elm, &c. do. do.
J 3 Oak, Chestnut, Birch, &c., do. do.
J 4 Larch, Poplar, Lime, Willow, &c., do

Part VI.—LANDSCAPE.
K 1 Rustic Landscape in Outline.
K 2 Shaded Objects and Landscape.
K 3 Shaded Landscape and Rustic Scenes.
K 4 Advanced Landscape and Rural Scenes.

Nos. **Part VII.—MARINE.**
M 1 Boats, Foregrounds, and Nautical Bits.
M 2 Fishing Craft, Coasters, and Traders.
M 3 Yachts and Vessels of every Rig and Sail.
M 4 Coast Scenes, Waves, &c.

Parts VIII. and IX.—ANIMALS.
O 1 Birds and Quadrupeds.
O 2 Poultry, various breeds.
O 3 British Small Birds.
O 4 British Wild Animals.
O 5 Horses (Arab, Hunter, Dray, &c.).
O 6 Horses (Racer, Trotter, Pony, Mule, &c.).
O 7 Dogs (Seventeen Species).
O 8 Cattle, Sheep, Pigs, Goats, &c.
O 9 Cattle, Sheep, Lambs, Ass and Foal, &c.
O 10 Foreign Wild Animals and Birds.

Part X.—HUMAN FIGURE.
Q 1 Features (from the Antique and from the Life).
Q 2 Heads, Hands, &c. (from Cast and Life).
Q 3 Rustic Figures, by Duncan.
Q 4 Figure, from the Antique (Outline).

Part XI.—PRACTICAL GEOMETRY.
R 1 Definitions and Simple Problems.
R 2 Practical Geometry (Circle, Polygon, Ellipse).
R 3 Applied Geometry *for Practical Mechanics, &c.*

Part XII.—MECHANICAL DRAWING.
T 1 Initiatory and Simple Subjects.
T 2 Details of Tools and Working Parts, &c.
T 3 Models for Working Drawings, &c.
T 4 Details of Machines and Engines.
Z Blank Exercise Book.

Popular Edition. A selection of the above numbers printed on thin paper, price 1*d*. each number. The following are in print:—A, B, C, I3, I4, J2, R2, R3, T1, T5, T6, T7, T8, Z.

"If any parent who reads these lines has a boy or girl who wishes to learn how to be an artist, let us boldly recommend Vere Foster's Drawing-Book. It is not only the cheapest but by far the best that we have seen."—**Graphic.**

"It would be difficult to over-rate the value of this work—a work that is not to be estimated by its cost: one is great, the other very small."—**Art Journal.**

Approved by the Science and Art Department, South Kensington, and Adopted by the London and other principal School Boards.

VERE FOSTER'S DRAWING-CARDS.

BEAUTIFULLY PRINTED ON FINE CARDS AND DONE UP IN NEAT PACKETS.

First Grade, Set I.—Familiar Objects, 24 cards, price 1s.
First Grade, Set II.—Leaf Form, geometrically treated, 24 cards, price 1s.
First Grade, Set III.—Elementary Ornament, 24 cards, price 1s.
Second Grade.—Ornament, by F. E. HULME, 18 large cards, price 2s.
Advanced Series.—Animals, by HARRISON WEIR, 24 cards, price 1s. 6d.

BLOCKS SPECIALLY PREPARED FOR SKETCHING FROM NATURE.
No. 1 (6½" × 4½"), Threepence. No. 2 (9" × 6½"), Sixpence.

VERE FOSTER'S
WATER-COLOR DRAWING-BOOKS.

"We can strongly recommend the series to young students."—The Times.

PAINTING FOR BEGINNERS. First Stage. Teaching the use of one color. Ten Facsimiles of Original Studies in Sepia by J. CALLOW, and numerous Illustrations in pencil. With full Instructions in easy language. Three Parts 4to, 6d. each; or one vol., cloth elegant, 2s. 6d.

"Sound little books, teaching the elements of 'washing' with much clearness by means of plain directions and well-executed plates."—Academy.

PAINTING FOR BEGINNERS. Second Stage. Teaching the use of seven colors. Twenty Facsimiles of Original Drawings by J. CALLOW, and many Illustrations in pencil. With full Instructions. In Six Parts 4to, 6d. each; or one volume, cloth elegant, 4s.

"The rules are so clear and simple that they cannot fail to be understood even by those persons who have no previous knowledge of the art of drawing. The letterpress of the book is as good as the illustrations are beautiful."—Birmingham Gazette.

SIMPLE LESSONS IN FLOWER PAINTING. Eight Facsimiles of Original Water-Color Drawings, and numerous Outline Drawings of Flowers, after various artists. With full Instructions for drawing and painting. Four Parts 4to, 6d. each; or one vol., cloth eleg., 3s.

"Everything necessary for acquiring the art of flower painting is here: the *facsimiles* of water-color drawings are very beautiful."—Graphic.

SIMPLE LESSONS IN MARINE PAINTING. Twelve Facsimiles of Original Water-Color Sketches. By E. DUNCAN. With numerous Illustrations in Pencil, and Lessons by an experienced Master. In Four Parts 4to, 6d. each; or one vol., cloth elegant, 3s.

"The book must prove of great value to students. Nothing could be prettier or more charming than the marine sketches here presented."—Graphic.

VERE FOSTER'S DRAWING-BOOKS—*Continued.*

SIMPLE LESSONS IN LANDSCAPE PAINTING. Eight Facsimiles of Original Water-Color Drawings, and Thirty Vignettes, after various artists. With full instructions by an experienced Master. In Four Parts 4to, 6*d.* each; or one volume, cloth elegant, 3*s.*

"As a work of art in the book line we have seldom seen its equal."—**St. James's Gazette.**

STUDIES OF TREES. In Pencil and in Water-Colors, by J. NEEDHAM. A Series of Eighteen Examples in Colors, and Thirty-three Drawings in Pencil. With descriptions of the Trees, and full instructions for Drawing and Painting. In Eight Parts 4to, 1*s.* each; or First Series, cloth elegant, 5*s.*; Second Series, cloth elegant, 5*s.*

"We commend them most heartily to all persons of taste who may be wanting to cultivate the great accomplishment of Water-color Drawing, or who want a gift-book for a lad or girl taking up the study."—**Schoolmaster.**

ADVANCED STUDIES IN FLOWER PAINTING. By ADA HANBURY. A series of Twelve beautifully finished Examples in Colors, and numerous Outlines in Pencil. With full instructions for painting, and a description of each plant by BLANCHE HANBURY. In Six Parts 4to, 1*s.* each; or one volume, cloth elegant, 7*s.* 6*d.*

"Apart from its educational value in art training this is a lovely book: we have seen nothing to equal the coloured plates."—**Sheffield Independent.**

"The handsomest and most instructive volume of the series yet produced."—**Daily Chronicle.**

"Coloured sketches of flowers which it is literally no exaggeration to term exquisite."—**Knowledge.**

EASY STUDIES IN WATER-COLOR PAINTING. By R. P. LEITCH and J. CALLOW. A series of Nine Pictures executed in Neutral Tints. With full instructions for drawing each subject, and for sketching from Nature. In Three Parts 4to, 1*s.* 6*d.* each; or one volume, cloth elegant, 6*s.*

SKETCHES IN WATER-COLORS. By T. M. RICHARDSON, R. P. LEITCH, J. A. HOUSTON, T. L. ROWBOTHAM, E. DUNCAN, and J. NEEDHAM. A series of Nine Pictures executed in Colors. With full instructions for drawing each subject, by an experienced Teacher. In Four Parts 4to, 1*s.* each; or one volume, cloth elegant, 5*s.*

"To those who wish to become proficient in the art of water-color painting no better instructor could be recommended than these two series."—**Newcastle Chronicle.**

ILLUMINATING. Nine examples in Colors and Gold of ancient Illuminating of the best periods, with numerous Illustrations in Outline, Historical and other Notes, and full descriptions and Instructions by the Rev. W. J. LOFTIE, B.A., F.S.A. In Four Parts 4to, 1*s.* each; or one volume, cloth elegant, 6*s.*

"The illuminations are admirably reproduced in color. Mr. Loftie's practical instructions enhance the value of an excellent handbook."—**Saturday Review.**

Sanctioned by the Committee of Council on Education.

POYNTER'S
SOUTH KENSINGTON DRAWING-BOOK.

NEW EDITION.
With Instructions and Diagrams to the Examples.

This new series of Drawing-Books has been issued under the direct superintendence of E. J. POYNTER, R.A., who has selected the examples for the most part from objects in the South Kensington Museum. The original Drawings have been made under Mr. Poynter's supervision by Pupils of the National Art Training School.

Each Book has Fine Cartridge Paper to draw on.

Freehand First Grade. Simple Objects, Ornament (Flat and Perspective). Six Books, 4*d*. each.

Freehand Elementary Design. Simple Forms, Leaves, and Flowers. Two Books, 4*d*. each.

Freehand First Grade—Plants. Six Books, 4*d*. each.

Freehand Second Grade. Ornament (Greek, Renaissance, &c.). Four Books, 1*s*. each.

Adopted by the London and other principal School Boards.

THE SAME SUBJECTS ON CARDS.

Freehand Elementary Design Cards,	Four Packets,	Price	9*d*.	each.
Freehand First Grade Cards,	Six	,,	1*s*. 0*d*.	,,
Freehand First Grade—Plants, Cards,	Six	,,	1*s*. 0*d*.	,,
Freehand Second Grade Cards,	Four	,,	1*s*. 6*d*.	,,

"The choice of subjects is admirable; there is not an ugly drawing in the book. Parents and teachers who have been looking in vain for drawing-books that should really train the eye in the study of beautiful forms, as well as the hand in the representation of what the eye sees, will be very grateful to the Science and Art Department for these cheap and most satisfactory productions."—*Pall Mall Gazette*.

"Mr. Poynter's is probably the best series of the kind yet published."—*The Academy*.

"The *Plants* are a valuable addition to the series. They will be appreciated and welcomed generally by all teachers. In execution, accuracy, and beauty, these copies have few rivals, and these they easily and entirely excel."—*Journal of Education*.

SOUTH KENSINGTON DRAWING-BOOK—*Continued.*

ELEMENTARY HUMAN FIGURE. Four Books, 6d. each.

    Book I.—MICHELANGELO'S "DAVID"—Features (Eye, Nose, etc.).
    Book II.—MASKS, from Antique Sculpture.
    Books III. and IV.—HANDS AND FEET, from Sculpture.

"Will be simply invaluable to beginners in drawing whether working alone or assisted by masters."—Graphic.

"The examples are beautifully drawn and are admirably calculated not merely to teach a good knowledge of form, but also to create and foster, dignity, simplicity, and breadth of style."—St. James's Gazette.

"It is impossible to overrate the value of such aids to high study and culture in drawing as are presented in this series."—School Board Chronicle.

HUMAN FIGURE, ADVANCED. Three Books, imp. 4to, 2s. each.

    Book I.—HEAD OF THE VENUS OF MELOS.
    Book II.—HEAD OF THE YOUTHFUL BACCHUS.
    Book III.—HEAD OF DAVID BY MICHELANGELO.

"Admirably adapted for use in the upper Standards of elementary schools, and also in those secondary schools where drawing is made a special feature."—Schoolmaster.

"Foremost in importance amongst the art educational books of the day are the recent additions to Mr. Poynter's South Kensington Drawing-Books. The outlines are perfect and the descriptive letterpress and explanations all that can be desired."—Graphic.

FIGURES FROM THE CARTOONS OF RAPHAEL: Twelve Studies of Draped Figures. Drawn direct from the Originals in the South Kensington Museum. With Descriptive Text, and Paper for Copying. Four Books, imperial 4to, 2s. each.

"The hints on drapery are very clear and good; the examples are in all cases taken direct from design or cast, never from photographs or engravings."—The Portfolio.

"We can imagine no aid more welcome to students than these drawings."—Pall Mall Gazette.

"The educational value of Raphael's Cartoons is immense, and Mr. Poynter has done wisely in furnishing this set."—Magazine of Art.

ELEMENTARY PERSPECTIVE DRAWING. By S. J. CARTLIDGE, F.R.Hist.S., Lecturer in the National Art Training School, South Kensington. Four Books, 1s. each; or one volume, cloth, 5s.

    Book I. } For Second Grade Examination of the Department.
    Book II. }
    Book III.—ACCIDENTAL VANISHING POINTS.
    Book IV.—HIGHER PERSPECTIVE.

"Invaluable to the conscientious student of scientific drawing. It states clearly what is indispensable to the correct knowledge of the principles which form the basis of pictorial art."—Graphic.

"As far as perspective-drawing can possibly be made interesting it has been done in this book. A student who does not master the art after studying this book had better turn to something else, for his case may safely be pronounced hopeless."—Pall Mall Gazette.

www.ingramcontent.com/pod-product-compliance
Lightning Source LLC
Chambersburg PA
CBHW032103220426
43664CB00008B/1113